Cicero
and the Roman Republic

John Murrell

CAMBRIDGE
UNIVERSITY PRESS

CAMBRIDGE UNIVERSITY PRESS

Cambridge, New York, Melbourne, Madrid, Cape Town, Singapore, São Paulo, Delhi

Cambridge University Press
The Edinburgh Building, Cambridge CB2 8RU, UK

www.cambridge.org
Information on this title: www.cambridge.org/9780521691161

First published 2008

Printed in the United Kingdom at the University Press, Cambridge

A catalogue record for this publication is available from the British Library

ISBN 978-0-521-69116-1 paperback

ACKNOWLEDGEMENTS
We are grateful for permission to reproduce copyright photographs:

akg-images: p.34; © Wolfgang Kaehler/Alamy: p.30; G. Garvey/Ancient Art & Architecture
Collection Ltd: p.45; copyright Prisma/Ancient Art & Architecture Collection Ltd: p.64;
The Art Archive/Archaeological Museum, Rabat/Gianni Dagli Orti: p.131; The Art
Archive/Museo Nazionale Taranto/Gianni Dagli Orti: p.157; © Natalia Blomeier: p.99;
Formia, Lazio, Italy/Alinari/The Bridgeman Art Library: p.174; Louvre, Paris, France/
Lauros/Giraudon/The Bridgeman Art Library: p.44; copyright © The British Library, all
rights reserved (Manuscript Facs 72(73) Volume 2): p.118; © Mimmo Jodice/Corbis: p.35;
© Sandro Vannini/Corbis: p.73; Peter Ferenczi Photography, photographersdirect.com:
p.85; reproduction by permission of the Syndics of the Fitzwilliam Museum, Cambridge:
p.153; James Morwood: pp.1, 41, 125; © NTPL/Paul Mulcahy: p.154; © 1990 Photo Scala,
Florence: p.63; © 1990 Photo Scala, Florence – courtesy of the Ministero Beni e Att.
Culturali: pp.4, 23, 26; © 2003 Photo Scala, Florence – courtesy of the Ministero Beni e
Att. Culturali: p.152; Guido Alberto Rossi/Tips Images: p.39; Werner Forman Archive: p.8;
copyright 2007 by The Regents of the University of California – all rights reserved: p.120.

Cover picture
Cicero in the Senate Accusing Catiline of Conspiracy on 21st October 63 BC, 1889, by
Maccari, Cesare (1840–1919)/Palazzo Madama, Rome, Italy/copyright Prisma/Ancient Art
& Architecture Collection Ltd.

Picture research by Sandie Huskinson-Rolfe of PHOTOSEEKERS

Contents

Preface

More of Cicero's works survive than those of any other Roman author. We know more about the late Roman Republic than almost any other period of Roman history, and much of that knowledge derives from Cicero himself. His varied and prolific writing enables us to learn about many aspects of Roman life (politics, religion, oratory and philosophy). Although Cicero is best known as the greatest Roman orator, he also wrote poetry, and works on oratory and philosophy. Then there are his letters, some nine hundred of them (see the note on p. 9), which provide a unique insight into his life and into the times and society in which he lived. No other figure from antiquity can be known so well.

Cicero was an important politician in republican Rome, where there was no division between those who shaped events and those who wrote about them. The major political figures (for example Caesar and Cicero) could also be major authors. They have, for this reason, to be read with a critical eye. It is possible to do this in the case of Cicero because we can compare what he said in the senate with what he said on the same subject before a meeting of the people, or we can compare a public speech with his private correspondence. These letters also allow us a first-hand look at other figures of the late Republic (Caesar, Crassus, Pompeius, Cato, Marcus Antonius, Brutus and Cassius, and Octavianus).

The late Republic was a crucial period in Roman history that saw the transition from a republican system of government (the Senate and the Roman People, which had been in place for centuries) to the Principate (the emperor, Augustus, ruling over a notionally restored republic). It was to the Roman Republic that the Founding Fathers looked when they wrote the American constitution and set in place a system of checks and balances, while it was on Augustan imperialism that Il Duce, Benito Mussolini, modelled his regime in Italy in the 1920s. This contrast, perhaps, helps us to understand the radical change that was taking place during Cicero's lifetime and why he felt so strongly about the *respublica*, to the extent of paying for his convictions with his life.

The chapters in this book follow a chronological outline. The extracts shed light on Cicero's family and education and his political and social life, while at the same time seeking to show the strains and pressures on the Republic which eventually led to the rule of one man. The book concludes with notes on ancient authors other than Cicero and a glossary explaining the terms used in the book.

That I was able to study and then for some three decades to teach Roman history is due to the good fortune of enjoying a traditional English classical education. Thereafter I learned much from the many colleagues with whom I worked in the

Joint Association of Classical Teachers, especially when I was a member and then chairman of the Ancient History Committee. It was there that I first met Professor Michael Crawford, whose work on Roman republican coinage and Roman statutes has made a lasting contribution to the subject. I have benefited from his vast knowledge of Roman history and his generous friendship. The General Editors have been generous with their time and help. James Morwood originally persuaded me to undertake the book. He has kept a close eye on its progress and reined in my follies. I am grateful too for the efficient and professional help of Fiona Kelly at Cambridge University Press.

Introduction

The period of Cicero's life (106–43 BC) witnessed the struggle of the Roman nobility to maintain their political supremacy against leaders of the people and warlords who opposed them. To understand the life and career of Cicero, a knowledge of the political institutions and the politics of the Roman Republic is essential. This introduction aims to provide some of that knowledge.

The Senate and Roman People

To describe *who* governed Rome in the late Republic is relatively easy; but to describe *how* Rome was governed is a much more complex task. The letters SPQR (Senatus Populusque Romanus – the Senate and Roman People) provide the simplest introduction and are still visible on every drain cover and bus in modern Rome. The Roman people, the total body of Roman citizens, were the ultimate source of power. They elected magistrates, they enacted laws and they acted as a lawcourt.

A modern Roman drain cover.

A Roman might be a citizen by birth, by manumission – the procedure by which a slave was freed by his master and became a 'freedman', and his children freeborn citizens – or by grant of citizenship (as was the case after the Social War with all freeborn persons in Italy south of the river Po; see Chapter 2). A Roman citizen possessed certain rights and responsibilities: for example, he had the right to marry a freeborn Roman woman and to make contracts enforceable by law. He was required to do military service but did not pay any direct tax.

A citizen had the right of appeal against a magistrate. He was protected by law from flogging and summary execution and could prosecute a magistrate who violated his rights. Of course in practice it might be difficult to ensure protection away from Rome or overseas and it is highly unlikely that this right of appeal had much value for the urban poor; they would experience summary 'justice' from the three commissioners responsible for prisons and executions – a fate not unknown in some poorer parts of the world today. All Roman citizens enjoyed liberty, but dignity – their standing in society – depended on birth, wealth and achievement; in the late Republic the Romans had no notion of equal opportunities or rights for all. Freeborn Roman women did not qualify for citizenship, which was a male preserve.

There were, however, restrictions upon this power of the people. They could meet in assembly to transact business only when summoned by a competent magistrate, and then only to decide on what that magistrate proposed – in Rome there was no 'Who wants to speak?' so characteristic of the assembly of democratic Athens. Magistrates, who were drawn only from the wealthy elite, always retained the initiative in politics. There were two main assemblies of the Roman people and each Roman citizen belonged to one of the 35 tribes in the tribal assembly and to one of the 193 centuries in the centuriate assembly. A citizen was allocated to a specific century (determined by his wealth) and to a tribe (determined by the family to which he belonged, or where he lived).

The centuriate assembly was organized in such a way that the richest had a disproportionately greater influence, since the centuries that they belonged to tended to consist of fewer individuals and got to vote first, thus often influencing the voting habits of other centuries. While the individual citizen possessed his (not her) vote – and in the first century BC it was a secret vote – it was the vote of the century or tribe as a whole that counted, not that of the individual (in a similar way to the US presidential election system, where if a presidential candidate wins even just 50.1 per cent of votes in a particular state, all the electoral votes of that state go to that candidate).

Most legislation and regular business was carried out in the tribal assembly, which was less subject to the influence of the rich; the centuriate assembly elected the chief annual magistrates and decided questions of war and peace. Originally the Roman people under arms, it met outside the walls in the Campus Martius because citizens were not supposed to carry arms within the city. The Roman people might have power, but Rome was not a democracy.

The senate was the great advisory body of the *respublica*; there were 300 members who were senators for life; membership was regulated by two censors, who filled vacancies when senators died and replaced members who had fallen below the necessary property qualification or who were ejected for gross misbehaviour.

The senate could only meet on the summons of a competent magistrate, who would call upon members to speak in order of rank; it was here that there could be some genuine debate, and once speaking a senator could discuss affairs in general and even attempt to filibuster by talking until nightfall and thereby preventing a vote. It was above all the ex-magistrates, consuls and praetors who spoke in debates; the members of lower rank, *pedarii* ('foot-senators'), would move close to the speaker whose view they supported. Members were expected to be present at meetings unless away on state business or for some other good reason.

The main regular magistracies of the *respublica* were, in order of importance: two consuls, six praetors, four aediles, and a number of quaestors – originally two but regularly increasing as Rome's overseas commitments grew so that there were eventually 20. Consuls and praetors possessed *imperium* – the power to issue orders – as did provincial governors; a sign of this power was the *fasces* – the bundle of rods around an axe signifying their powers of punishment. Mussolini used this emblem – hence the word 'fascist', now loosely used as a term of political abuse, including a recent hybrid, 'Muslim fascist'.

Every five years two censors were elected. Their tasks included a review of the senate and the *equites* (originally, the cavalry) and a census of Roman citizens to record their property and other wealth, and to assign them to their appropriate class, century and tribe. The censors were the only officials whose period of office lasted for more than one year, since their tasks required more time. All other magistrates were elected for one year and had colleagues in office with them; a magistrate of equal or greater power than another could obstruct or veto any proposal or action that seemed not in the interest of the state, whether in his own view or that of the senate. There was thus a check on the use and abuse of power. Consuls, praetors, censors and two aediles held curule magistracies, so called because of their right to use the folding ivory chair without back or arms, the curule chair. Those who had held office in Rome as consuls or praetors were often then sent out to govern Rome's overseas provinces as proconsuls and propraetors.

There was one other office, extraordinary in character and of great significance: the office of tribune of the plebs. Each year the plebeians (the poor majority of the Roman people) elected ten tribunes of the plebs and two plebeian aediles. In the period of the late Republic tribunes summoned and presided at the assembly of the plebs, called either the *concilium plebis* or the tribal assembly of the plebs; its decisions were binding on all Roman citizens. Tribunes possessed the right to summon the senate, to be present at its meetings and to veto any proposals they claimed were contrary to the interests of the plebs. Their bench was strategically placed in front of the entrance to the senate house. They could also use their veto against proposals in the assemblies. They possessed the 'right of help' within the city of Rome, which enabled them to help any citizen making an appeal to them against arbitrary actions of magistrates. The office of the tribune had been created as the result of sustained political pressure by the plebs in the fifth century BC during a period of revolution known as the 'conflict of the orders', and its revolutionary character was never forgotten; however, over a period of time the tribunate came to be seen as a regular magistracy and to become an arm of the senate through which that body blocked proposals and actions of which it did not approve. It was in the late second and first centuries BC that certain tribunes actively revived its original character.

A political career could only be contemplated by a citizen whose family had wealth – and that meant land; he must be known or noble (noble is derived from

the verb 'know') because he had forebears known to have held office, or because he himself was known for his achievements on the field of battle and/or in the courts; and he must normally come from a senatorial or, at least, an equestrian family. If he aspired to reach the consulship, the top of the ladder of offices, then he must have consular forebears: many nobles regarded that post as defiled if held by a 'new man', one in whose family there had been no consular ancestor, and who in extreme cases might be the first member of his family to enter the senate, as was the case with Cicero. Entry to the senate and junior magistracies was not so exclusive and there were many first-time senators, the *pedarii*.

This fine bust of a thoughtful Cicero dates from the first century BC.

Roman politics

The Romans did not have political parties such as exist in Britain or the United States today with an organization, a membership, a programme and manifesto and discipline, and this must be kept firmly in mind when dealing with the language of Roman politics. The language of politics and morality merged: one's political allies were *boni*, 'good men', one's opponents 'wicked', 'dishonest', 'scoundrels' and the like. A 'fault line' may be discerned between those who supported and believed in the authority and direction of political business by the senate, the *optimates* (the 'best men'); and those individuals who supported the power of the Roman people and who argued that in the last resort the will of the people was supreme, the *populares*. Though Cicero might claim on occasion to be a *popularis*, his political stance and his letters show clearly that he was an unequivocal optimate; in the period covered by this book there were two outstanding, though very different, *populares* – Gnaeus Pompeius Magnus and Gaius Iulius Caesar.

The last generation of the Roman Republic saw the emergence of leaders – Sulla, Pompeius and Caesar – whose power was based on their armies. Their soldiers, who saw their primary allegiance to be to their commander, came to represent a fundamental threat to the state; while politicians faced difficult choices about whom to support and what line to follow – choices that could have fatal consequences.

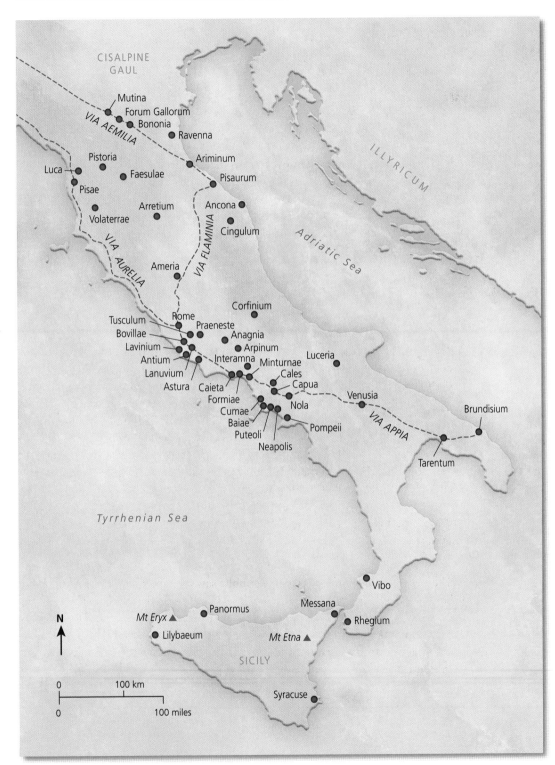

Italy and Sicily at the time of Cicero.

1 Arpinum and Rome

Marcus Tullius Cicero was born on 3 January 106 BC at the family home just outside Arpinum, a Volscian hill town some 70 miles south-east of Rome. The citizens of that *municipium* had received Roman citizenship in 188. Cicero's family belonged to the local nobility and had connections with leading political figures in Rome. His municipal origin would define and haunt Cicero's life and career and differentiate him from, for example, his life-long friend and confidant, Titus Pomponius Atticus, who was a Roman born and bred. This becomes clear from a number of incidents in Cicero's life and in a dialogue, *On the Laws*, which he composed in the late 50s, and in which he portrays himself walking with Atticus around his country estate. Cicero will have received his earliest education (alphabet, reading, writing and elementary mathematics) at home – his father was a devoted student of literature and keenly interested in his sons' education – and possibly at a local school in Arpinum.

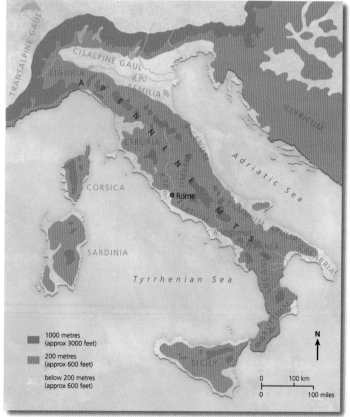

Italy: physical features and regions.

Arpinum

3   MARCUS   Now, when it is possible for me to get away for more days, especially at this time of year, I make for the beauty and the healthy climate of this place, though it is seldom possible. But there is in fact another reason that gives me pleasure, which does not apply to you, Titus.

ATTICUS   And what is that?   5

MARCUS   This is, to tell the truth, my own and my brother's real fatherland. Here are the most ancient roots from which we are descended; here are our family shrines, here our family, here the many traces of our ancestors. Furthermore this house, as you now see it, was enlarged through the efforts of my father; because he was of weak health he 10 passed almost all his time here in literary studies. But in this very place, while my grandfather was alive and the house was small in the ancient fashion, like that house of **Curius** among the Sabines, I tell you I was born. And so something exists and lies hidden in my mind and consciousness, which, perhaps, makes this place give me more 15 pleasure …

5   ATTICUS   I am quite delighted to have made its acquaintance too. But that remark that you made a moment ago that this place – for I assume you were speaking about Arpinum – is your real fatherland: what did you mean? Do you have two fatherlands, or is there one that we 20 share? Was the fatherland of wise old **Cato**, perhaps, not Rome but Tusculum?

In this family shrine from the house of the Vettii at Pompeii, the father is in the centre, making an offering to the household gods, who stand on either side of him holding drinking horns. Underneath, the sacred serpent is about to consume an offering laid out for it.

Curius   Manius Curius Dentatus, early Roman hero, four times consul, noted general, who conquered the Sabines and was renowned for his rectitude and frugality; he was much admired by the elder Cato.

Cato   the elder Cato, Marcus Porcius Cato, 'Cato the Censor' (234–149 BC), a dominant and influential figure in the political and cultural life of his age.

MARCUS   I really think that both Cato and all those who come from the *municipia* have **two fatherlands**, the one by birth, another through citizenship: in the same way that Cato, although he was born at 25 Tusculum, was admitted into the citizenship of the Roman people, so that, though he was by birth a Tusculan and by citizenship a Roman, he had one fatherland through birth and another through law … But it is necessary that the land whose name, *respublica*, embraces the whole citizen body should take precedence in our affection; for 30 it we ought to die and to it we should give ourselves completely; and in it we ought to place and, as it were, to consecrate everything we have. But the land that gave us birth is almost as sweet as the one that admitted us. Thus I will never deny that this is my fatherland, though that other one is the greater and this one is contained within it. 35

Cicero, *On the Laws* 2.3–5

---

1   Cicero was born in a country town, which was a disadvantage in his pursuit of a political career in the city of Rome. Does the place of one's birth have any such advantage or disadvantage today?

2   Do you feel any particular devotion to the place of your birth? If so, why?

3   Can you imagine any circumstances in which your loyalty to your locality (e.g. home, town, province, county, state) could come into conflict with your duty to your country?

---

two fatherlands perhaps 'homelands' would be better. Cicero states explicitly that a Roman citizen may possess only one citizenship, that is, Roman citizenship: 'under our civil law no Roman citizen is able to be a citizen of two states' (Cicero, *Balbus* 28). However, as Cicero makes clear, citizens of municipal and Italian background might nonetheless retain strong ties with the place of their birth; in a letter of early 46 Cicero declares: 'while it is my habit to look after my fellow townsmen, I have a particular concern and responsibility towards them this year. It is my wish that my son, my nephew, and a very close friend of mine, Marcus Caesius, should be appointed aediles to set the affairs of the *municipium* in order' (Cicero, *Friends* 13.11.3 (*278*)). (There are four collections of Cicero's letters: to *Atticus*, to his *Friends*, to his brother *Quintus*, and to *M. Brutus*. In every case the traditional reference is followed in brackets by the number in the various editions and translations by D. R. Shackleton Bailey, the most convenient and complete of which is the Loeb Classical Library edition, 1999–2000.) Three aediles were the chief magistrates at Arpinum. The enfranchisement of all Italy, following the Social War of 90–89 BC, gradually loosened these ties, though even in the first century AD men such as Pliny the Younger could use their wealth to benefit their municipal birthplace – in his case with a library and welfare for children of the poor.

Education in Rome

By the late 90s BC, when Cicero was in his teens, his father had taken him and his brother, Quintus Tullius Cicero, some three or four years his junior, to Rome so that they could receive a suitable education to enable them to enter public life. Here the brothers continued their studies of Greek and Latin language and literature and began to study rhetoric, law and philosophy. Their father had ambitions and aspirations for his sons; his connections put them in the household of the great orator, **Lucius Licinius Crassus**. They received further education from Crassus and from **Marcus Antonius**, another noted orator.

1   When we were boys, **my dear Quintus**, there was a widespread opinion, if you recall, that L. Crassus had attained no more learning than he had been able to get from the elementary instruction of a boy of his time, while M. Antonius had been wholly ignorant and without education. There were many people who did not think such was the case but made such statements about those orators as I have stated, 5 so that they might more easily deter us from being taught when we were fired with enthusiasm for oratory. If men without education had achieved the highest level of proficiency and unbelievable eloquence, then all our hard work might appear pointless and the attention of our father, an excellent and most sensible man, to

2   our education might seem stupid. As boys we used to prove such people wrong 10 using witnesses from our own homes – our father, our relative Gaius Aculeo, and our uncle Lucius Cicero: our father and Aculeo – he was married to our mother's sister and Crassus held him in the very highest regard – and our uncle, who had gone abroad with Antonius to Cilicia and returned home from service with him, often told us many things about Crassus, his application to study and his learning. 15 In the company of our cousins, the sons of Aculeo and our aunt, we were not only studying such subjects as Lucius Crassus considered suitable but were also being instructed **by those teachers who were in his circle**; being in his house we often realized – even as boys we were able to appreciate it – that he spoke Greek

Lucius Licinius Crassus   Crassus (140–91 BC), outstanding and influential orator, teacher of the young and ambitious. He was consul in 95 with Mucius Scaevola *pontifex* (the priest). In politics he seems to have been in favour of reform, supporting the proposal to enfranchise the Italians.

Marcus Antonius   grandfather of the triumvir Marcus Antonius, he was consul in 99 BC, a distinguished orator who opposed Greek influence. He did not write down his speeches but composed an unfinished work on public speaking; Cicero listened to him and made him one of the principal speakers in his work *On the Orator*. He was killed in Rome in 87.

my dear Quintus   Cicero's younger brother is the addressee of the dialogue, *On the Orator*.

by those teachers who were in his circle   one of these teachers, the poet Licinius Archias, was apparently a great influence upon the young Cicero; some thirty years later Cicero defended him in court when he was charged with falsely assuming Roman citizenship.

in such a way that he seemed to know no other language; and that when he put 20
topics by way of enquiry to our teachers, and in every discussion where he himself
dealt with topics, there seemed nothing novel to him, nothing he had not heard
of. We had often heard from our uncle, a man of great culture, how Antonius
had devoted himself to conversations with the most learned men in Athens or
at Rhodes. As a young lad I myself often put questions on many subjects to him, 25
so far as the modesty of one entering upon manhood allowed. What I write will
certainly be no news to you, for you often heard it from me at that time: as a result
of many varied conversations I considered him neither untaught nor ignorant of
any topic among subjects on which I could have any opinion.

Cicero, On the Orator 2.1–3

3

---

1 What, if any, are the requirements today for a political career? How
   important is the ability to speak well?

2 What did the Romans see as the purpose of education? Are there any modern
   parallels?

3 In Rome the government appeared to play little or no part in education. Why
   do you think this wasn't considered part of the state's duty towards its young
   citizens? Why do modern governments play a part in the educational system?

Education in the law

A young man aspiring to a career in politics needed training and education in
public speaking and in the law. Cicero describes his legal education.

1 Now, having assumed the *toga virilis*, I had been introduced by my father to
Scaevola the augur on the understanding that, so far as I was permitted and he
would allow it, I should never leave the old man's side. And so I used to commit
to memory many of his clever arguments and many of his brief and fitting
comments and I was keen to become more learned from his wisdom. After his 5
death I took myself to **Scaevola** the *pontifex*, who I venture to declare was for
ability and integrity the outstanding man in our state …

---

toga virilis the toga of manhood, which a young man assumed on reaching the age of
16; in 90 BC this event perhaps occurred on 17 March, the traditional day for this family
ceremony.

Scaevola Quintus Mucius Scaevola, the augur, born c.170 BC, learned in law, consul 117.
He was now an old man and died after 88. He appears in several of Cicero's dialogues,
including that *On Friendship*, the topic which 'was on the lips of many people'.

Scaevola the *pontifex* Quintus Mucius Scaevola the *pontifex* (priest), born about 140
BC, nephew of the augur. He became a priest following the death of his father in 115
and head of the priestly college in 89. He was a noted specialist in law and a teacher,
and was consul with Crassus in 95, when they enacted a law removing illegal immigrants
from Rome, an immediate cause of the Social War. He was murdered on the orders of the
consul, Marius the younger, in 82.

2 I have many frequent recollections of the augur but one in particular: when he was sitting at home on a semicircular bench, I and just a few of his close friends were with him; he entered upon a topic of discussion which about that time was 10 on the lips of many people.

Cicero, On Friendship 1–2

> • Do you have any vivid recollections of a learning experience such as that described by Cicero at the end of the passage?

Cicero in the household of Scaevola

An anecdote records how Cicero met and listened to the women within the household: 'I often heard **Laelia**, the daughter of **Gaius**, speak; I saw that her speech was coloured by the good taste of her father and that of her daughters, the **Muciae**, with both of whom I had conversation' (Cicero, *Brutus* 211).

• Roman women as a rule had no formal education beyond the elementary stage. Why do you think this was?

• How do you imagine the women in the household of Scaevola became such engaging conversational partners?

The timely death of Licinius Crassus

Cicero, a devoted pupil, wrote an obituary of his revered teacher and believed that his death was a benefit for Crassus in that he avoided the dreadful times that followed, which the teenage Cicero experienced.

His death brought grief to his own family, distress to his native land, pain to all *boni*. Such, however, have been the disasters befalling the *respublica* that I think it was not life the immortal gods snatched from L. Crassus but death that they gave him as a present. He did not live to see Italy ablaze with war, the senate

---

Laelia   daughter of Laelius, wife of Quintus Mucius Scaevola the augur; her style of speech and that of her daughters attracted the young Cicero when he met them in the house of Scaevola.

Gaius   Gaius Laelius, influential political and cultural figure of the second century BC, nicknamed 'the wise'. He was a noted orator, consul in 140, and died after 129.

Muciae   the two daughters of Q. Mucius Scaevola and Laelia, the elder of whom married L. Crassus, the revered teacher of Cicero; Crassus elsewhere remarks that she retained an old-style pronunciation, a consequence of the fact that women did not converse with a large number of people, and that her speech was neat, even and smooth (see Cicero, *On the Orator* 3.45).

aflame with malice, the leaders of the state on trial for a wicked crime, his 5
daughter's grief, his son-in-law's exile, **C. Marius'** dreadful flight, the savage and
indiscriminate massacre on his return; lastly, he did not see the state, in which at
its most flourishing stage he had stood much the most distinguished citizen, now
disfigured in every aspect.

Cicero, On the Orator 3.8

Cicero, for whatever reason, records little detail of these years. It is hard to
appreciate what it must have been like for the young Cicero, but imagine
being a teenager in Berlin in 1944–5 or in Beirut in 2006 or Gaza in 2007.

The Social War, 91–89 BC

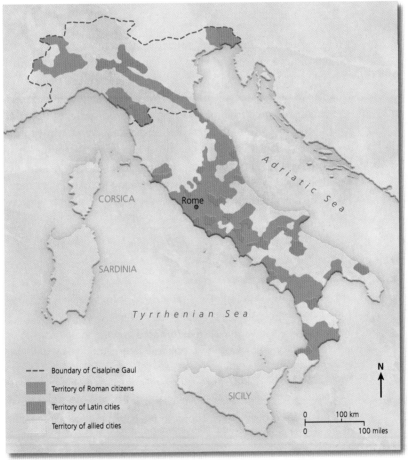

Romans, Latins and Italian allies before the Social War of 91–89 BC.

C. Marius   seven times consul, the greatest general of his age, having most recently
annihilated a German invasion (102–101 BC); now in his late sixties, he wished to be the
commander of Roman forces against Mithradates.

The tribune **Drusus** had proposed in 91 BC to give the Italian allies Roman citizenship, which they had sought for three decades. They desired equality with Roman citizens and to share the benefits of the empire which they had helped to build by their service in the armies. The Romans, elite and plebs alike, opposed this aspiration of their allies, and Drusus' proposal was not put to the vote. He was assassinated, whereupon the Italians rose in revolt. Bitter and bloody fighting followed. Cicero was obliged to do **military service** and served in 89 in the armies of **Sulla** in the south and then with the consul **Pompeius Strabo** in the north.

For a short time he did military service under Sulla in the war against the **Marsi**.

Plutarch, Cicero 3.2

I remember meetings with the bitterest enemies and with citizens in the most violent disagreement. Cn. Pompeius, son of Sextus, the consul, held a parley with P. Vettius Scato, the leader of the Marsi, between the two camps in my presence, when I was a new recruit in his army. I recall that Sextus Pompeius, the brother of the consul and a man of learning and good sense, came from Rome especially 5 for the meeting. Scato greeted him and asked, 'What am I to call you?' The latter replied, 'I wish it were a friend, but it has to be an enemy.' It was a fair-minded meeting, no fear, no suspicion lurking beneath the surface; even the animosity was restrained; for the allies were not seeking to take our citizenship away from us but to be admitted into it. 10

Cicero, Philippic 12.27

Drusus   M. Livius Drusus, noble, tribune in 91, introduced a raft of proposals, of which the enfranchisement of the allies was the key element.

military service   it was the custom for those aspiring to political life to do military service before formally embarking on a political career, though by the late Republic many no longer performed the required ten years: this very brief period of service during the Social War, which – so he claims – he somehow managed to combine with his studies, was Cicero's only military experience until he commanded troops as governor of Cilicia in 51–50.

Sulla   Lucius Cornelius Sulla, consul in 88, commander against Mithradates in the East 87–84 and dictator 82–80.

Pompeius Strabo   Gnaeus Pompeius Strabo, consul in 89, father of Pompeius Magnus ('the Great'); a man of ambivalent character and reputation, he died of illness in 88, having connived at the death of a successor.

Marsi   the Italian people who were the core and leaders of the rising against the Romans in 91–89; initially they gave their name to the Marsic war; it was later known as the Social War (from the Latin socius meaning 'ally').

In 90 and 89 BC laws were passed to give the Italians citizenship and, though sporadic fighting continued, the Romans ended the war by conceding the demands of their allies. The nobility tried to minimize the consequences by restricting the voting power of the new citizens; thus there was another cause of political dispute. But the enfranchisement of all Italy south of the river Po was a watershed in the history of Rome, and the consequences were to be worked out gradually over succeeding generations. Regional differences in identity, ethnicity and language continued to exist and it was only in the nineteenth century AD that Italy became a united nation state. One immediate consequence of the Social War concerned the army: recruits, who were in the main drawn from rural Italy, were now no longer allies but Roman citizens, and their payment devolved upon the Roman treasury.

> • The twenty-first century is witnessing diverse tendencies: on the one hand there is the continued growth of the European Community, 27 states in 2007, while on the other hand there is some pressure to break up into nations (e.g. the push in Scotland and Northern Ireland for greater independence from the United Kingdom, and similarly for independence for Quebec in Canada, the Basques in Spain, the Kurds in Iraq). What was so special about Roman citizenship that led the Italian peoples to fight so vigorously to obtain it?

Wartime education: oratory, law and philosophy

Cicero's late teens were disturbed times for Rome and Italy: there was hostility towards the allies and disagreements about how to handle their demands. While he tried to continue his studies in law, politics and rhetoric for a career in public life, he had been obliged to do military service, but the description of his life at this period, which he wrote in the *Brutus* in 46 BC, makes no mention at all of his time in the army. We must presume he did not find it or the period congenial; he certainly hated war and always sought to resolve political disputes by negotiation. He does, however, recall the practice of military training when defending a protégé, in 56.

When I was a young man, one year was set aside for **keeping our arms in our togas** and we used to undergo physical exercise and training in the *campus* in our tunics; and if we began our military service immediately, it was the same procedure in camp and on active service.

Cicero, *Caelius* 11

---

keeping our arms in our togas   no extravagant gestures, under military discipline, on probation.

campus   military training ground in the Campus Martius outside the walls of the city.

At a time when a young man of Cicero's age and background would normally be active in law and politics, Cicero was devoting himself wholly to study so that he would enter the forum fully trained; it was an unusually long apprenticeship and one may wonder whether he was as uninvolved in affairs as he states. Anyone who has had the misfortune to experience education in wartime might well wonder how accurate Cicero's memories were.

303
304

305

I entered the forum when **Hortensius'** reputation was growing, after **Crassus** had died, when **Cotta** was in exile and the courts were interrupted by war. In the first year of war Hortensius was on active service as a foot-soldier; in the second year he was a **military tribune** and **Sulpicius** was a *legatus*; M. Antonius too was absent. One court alone was in operation under the **Varian statute**, while 5
all the rest were suspended because of war; I often attended it, although those who were speaking in their own defence were not leading orators … The others, who were reckoned leading orators of the time, were magistrates and I listened to them almost daily at *contiones* … The first blow that struck me when I was really eager to listen to orators was the banishment of Cotta. I was gripped with keen 10
enthusiasm and frequently listened to any who were there; although I was writing, reading and declaiming daily, **I was not satisfied merely with rhetorical exercises.**

Cicero, *Brutus* 303–5

> • What would be the modern equivalent to Cicero's education for public speaking?

Hortensius   Quintus Hortensius Hortalus, soon to be the leading advocate in Rome.

Crassus   Lucius Licinius Crassus, Cicero's teacher, who died in 91.

Cotta   Gaius Aurelius Cotta, consul in 75, and the tribune **Sulpicius** are reckoned by Cicero to have been the leading orators in the period between Antonius and Crassus, and Hortensius and Cicero himself. Cotta went into exile, condemned under the **Varian statute**.

military tribune   one of six officers in a Roman legion.

Sulpicius   P. Sulpicius, noble, tribune in 88, who enacted a statute distributing the new citizens equally among the tribes, bitterly opposed by the nobility to which he belonged, and arranged the transfer of the command against Mithradates from Sulla to the aged Marius. As a result Sulla, with his consular colleague Pompeius, marched on Rome. Marius escaped but Sulpicius was hunted down and killed while still in office; he was a talented orator.

legatus   military assistant to the commander of an army.

Varian statute   Q. Varius, tribune in 90, enacted a law establishing a treason court to investigate those alleged to have had dealings with the allies just before the outbreak of the Social War. A number of nobles were condemned and went into exile. Varius was later condemned in the same court.

contiones   mass meetings (singular *contio*) of Roman citizens summoned by a magistrate.

I was … exercises   besides regular practical and theoretical study of public speaking, Cicero wished to hear orators 'live'.

306   For the study of **civil law** I attached myself regularly to Q. Scaevola the augur, the son of Quintus; although he did not make himself available to anyone for teaching, nevertheless by his responses to those who consulted him he taught those who were eager to learn from him. The following year **Sulla and Pompeius were consuls.** That was the time when I got to know intimately the full range of P.   5 Sulpicius' public speaking when he held *contiones* daily during his tribunate; at the same time, when **Philon, the leader of the Academy**, and many of the Athenian nobility had fled from Athens because of **the Mithradatic War** and come to Rome, I devoted myself totally to him, since I was taken with a remarkable enthusiasm for philosophy. I dallied with this subject all the more intensely – the variety and the   10 immense scope of the subject-matter had an intense fascination for me – because it appeared that **the operation of the courts had now been abolished for ever.**

307   **That year** Sulpicius had been struck down; in the following year three orators, **Q. Catulus**, **M. Antonius** and **C. Iulius**, were most cruelly killed.

Cicero, Brutus 306–7

civil law   the law that had to do with Roman citizens; it was derived from statutes, decrees of the plebs, decrees of the senate and the authority of jurists; Cicero perhaps considered a career as a jurist.

Sulla and Pompeius were consuls   88 BC; Lucius Cornelius Sulla and Quintus Pompeius. The latter opposed the tribune Sulpicius and was sent to take over the army of Pompeius Strabo, whose soldiers killed him with the connivance of their commander.

Philon, the leader of the Academy   the last head of the Academy, the school of Plato, in Athens. The Mithradatic War spilled over into Greece and many leading Athenians and intellectuals fled to Rome. Philon probably remained for the rest of his life (he died in 84 or 83 BC) in Rome, where he taught both philosophy and rhetoric. Cicero became a devoted pupil of Philon. In the ancient world philosophy was considered the training ground for good citizenship. Cicero considered it important for the orator and advocate and would himself write extensively on philosophical themes.

the Mithradatic War   the wars waged by the Romans against Mithradates VI, king of Pontus, which, with varying fortunes on both sides, continued until the death of the king in 63 BC.

the operation ... for ever   Cicero feared that the chaos and lawlessness of the period 88–87 would put an end to the operation of the lawcourts and to his intended career.

That year   88 BC.

Q. Catulus   Quintus Lutatius Catulus, noble, consul in 102 with Marius, defeated the Gauls in 101. He opposed Marius in 88/87 and committed suicide.

M. Antonius   the orator and teacher of Cicero, opposed Marius and was killed in the pogrom following his return to Rome in 87/86.

C. Iulius   Gaius Iulius Caesar Vopiscus, half-brother of Catulus, famous as a wit and orator, killed in the same Marian pogrom.

Annus horribilis, 88 BC

Sulpicius, tribune in 88 BC, wished to distribute the new citizens and freedmen equally among the 35 tribes; the ruling oligarchy opposed him bitterly and declared a halt to public business, but Sulpicius, unwilling to tolerate opposition, did a deal with Marius: Marius supported the citizenship proposal with force while Sulpicius enacted the transfer of the eastern command against Mithradates from Sulla to Marius. In the face of violence from the tribune and Marius, the consuls and oligarchy were powerless. Sulla had to consent to the resumption of public business, and Pompeius was wounded in the violence. Sulla escaped, retiring to his army at Nola, where he was still fighting the Samnites and Lucanians in the Social War. He explained to his soldiers what had happened and they clamoured for him to lead them against Rome; most of Sulla's officers refused to join him but one, the noble L. Lucullus, joined in the march, as did Pompeius, his consular colleague. They rapidly captured Rome.

Having scattered and struck down the party of his enemies, Sulla occupied Rome and under arms summoned the senate, passionately desiring that C. Marius be declared a public enemy with all speed. None dared oppose his will except **Scaevola**, who when the question was put to him refused to give an opinion. Furthermore when Sulla truculently insisted, this is what he said: 'You may show me your troops of soldiers with which you have surrounded the senate house; you may threaten me repeatedly with death, but for the sake of my small stock of aged blood you will never get me to judge Marius, who saved Rome and Italy, a public enemy.' 5

Valerius Maximus, Memorable Doings and Sayings 3.8.5

Marius and Sulpicius were outlawed and Sulpicius' legislation annulled. He was hunted down and killed while Marius escaped to Africa. Having enacted some laws and conducted elections, Sulla left Rome for Nola to join his army for the East and the Mithradatic War. The loyalty of soldiers not to the *respublica* but to their commander – one consequence of recruiting landless volunteers – had been revealed; it would bring about the collapse of the Roman Republic.

Cicero must surely have been influenced by the example of his teacher Scaevola and perhaps remembered him in the last months of his own life in 43 BC. Sulpicius he knew personally and rated highly as an orator. He makes the following comment on his tribunate.

Scaevola the augur, who died shortly after this incident.

He proceeded in his tribunate to deprive of all *dignitas* those with whom he had lived in the closest association when he was a private citizen; at the time when he was approaching the very peak of eloquence his life was snatched away by the sword and the penalty was paid for his rashness, causing the *respublica* great damage.

Cicero, On the Orator 3.11

He approved of Sulpicius' oratory but not of his politics.

The obligations of the young

Cicero sets out how the aspiring young noble should behave and the expectations he should seek to satisfy; they precisely define his own experience.

It is the duty of a young man to show deference to his elders and to attach himself to the best and most approved of them, so as to receive the benefit of their counsel and influence; for the inexperience of youth requires the practical wisdom of age to strengthen and direct it.

Cicero, On Duties 1.122

Young men win a good reputation most easily and most favourably if they attach themselves to men who are at once wise and renowned as well as patriotic advisers in public affairs. And if they constantly associate with such men, they inspire in the public the expectation that they will be like them, since they themselves have selected them for imitation.

Cicero, On Duties 2.46

---

1   What obligations might be proposed for young people today?

2   Who are the 'role models' in the modern world? You should consider this on a worldwide basis: think, for instance, of young people in the United States, in Cuba, in Brazil, in South Africa, in Pakistan, in North Korea, in Iraq and so on. (In Britain, the former Beatle Paul McCartney is said to be a contender for the title of 'the nation's greatest living icon'.)

---

2 Sulla and Italy

Rome in the 80s BC

Following the departure of Sulla for the East, there was another year of chaos, warfare and killing; in 86 BC Marius and Lucius Cornelius Cinna seized control of the *respublica*. After the death of Marius in January, Cinna dominated the state until his murder in 84. Cicero viewed the regime with uncompromising hostility: the *respublica* was without law and without dignity. Cicero continued to keep his head down in the study of rhetoric and philosophy with a resident guru.

308 **For about three years** the city was free from armed force; but whether because of the death, absence or exile of orators ... Hortensius held the leading place in pleading cases ... During all this time I spent my days and nights engaged in
309 studying every subject. I was with **Diodotus the Stoic**, who resided in my house and lived with me; he died recently in my house. Besides other subjects he gave me 5 the most thorough training in logic ... I devoted myself to him and to his many
310 varied subjects but let no day pass without practising public speaking. I often prepared speeches and declaimed – for that's what they call practising speeches now – every day with **M. Piso** and **Q. Pompeius** or with someone else. I practised frequently in Latin, but more often in Greek: partly because Greek, offering more 10 resources for stylistic embellishment, enabled me to develop a similar practice

---

For about three years 86–84 BC, the period of Cinna's domination. Cicero suggests he withdrew into a world of study and did not engage in politics. Notice his study in Greek *and* Latin. Many upper-class Romans were by this time almost attaining a bilingualism, and a period of study in Athens was not uncommon.

Diodotus the Stoic 'Diodotus, who was blind, lived for many years at my house. When blind – almost incredibly – he occupied himself far more untiringly than he had previously; he played upon the harp in the fashion of the Pythagoreans, and he had books read to him aloud by night and day, for in studying them he had no need of eyes. He also did what seems scarcely possible without eyesight: he continued teaching geometry, giving his pupils verbal instructions from which and to which point to draw each line' (Cicero, *Tusculan Disputations* 5.113).

M.Piso, Q. Pompeius Marcus Pupius Piso and Quintus Pompeius Bithynicus, said to have been close associates of Cicero, friends and companions in their rhetorical studies and exercise; more details can be found in Cicero, *Brutus* 236, 310 (Piso), 240, 310 (Pompeius).

in speaking Latin, partly because the top teachers could not, **unless I spoke in Greek**, correct my faults or teach me.

Cicero, Brutus 308–10

Then seeing that the whole state was **splitting into factions** and that the result of this would be the **unlimited power of one man**, he retired into the life of the scholar and philosopher, going on with his studies and associating with Greek scholars until the time came when **Sulla seized power** and it looked as though the political situation had become more settled.

Plutarch, Cicero 3.2

Plutarch here follows the line that Cicero himself recorded above in the *Brutus*, but it is hard to believe that Cicero was wholly uninvolved in political affairs of the 80s, especially as he was closely associated with Scaevola *pontifex* during this period. He probably followed the line of his teacher, remaining in Rome but playing no active part in events. If so, it was a valuable lesson for later life. Cicero continues his history of Roman oratory interwoven with personal details.

311   Meanwhile in **restoring the *respublica* disorder broke out**; there occurred the cruel deaths of three orators, **Scaevola**, **Carbo** and **Antistius**; the return of **Cotta**,

---

unless I spoke in Greek   the best teachers of public speaking and the philosophers were all Greek, so that fluency in that language was essential for students; there were now some schools where the teaching was in Latin but these had in 95 BC earned the displeasure of the censors.

splitting into factions   primarily those who supported Marius/Cinna versus supporters of Sulla.

unlimited power of one man   Cinna.

Sulla seized power   83–82 BC.

restoring ... out   this delicate phrase refers to Sulla's return to Italy, the ensuing civil war, the capture of Rome and systematic slaughter of his enemies; 'restoring the republic' was a regular claim of political reformers, Cicero included, and its greatest and most successful claimant, a 19-year-old youth, C. Octavius, the future emperor Augustus. 'Restoring democracy' might be the modern equivalent.

Scaevola   the *pontifex*.

Carbo   orator, said to have spoken rarely in the 80s.

Antistius   an orator with a daily increasing reputation in the 80s.

Cotta   C. Aurelius Cotta, strong supporter of Sulla, consul in 75.

Curio, **Crassus**, the **Lentuli** and **Pompeius**; law and courts were established, the *respublica* was restored … It was at this time that **I first began to take on private and public cases**; it was not my aim to learn in the forum, something a good number 5 have done, but to come there as fully trained as I had been able to make myself. At the same time I devoted myself to study with **Molon**; for while Sulla was dictator he had come as a *legatus* to the senate about payments to the Rhodians.

Cicero, Brutus 311–12

312

The list of those who returned to Rome reveals some of Sulla's supporters in his campaign against the regime in Rome; some had been with him in the East, members of a sort of senate or government in exile, others had remained in Italy, active for the regime or waiting upon events.

Sulla's return to Rome

Sulla landed with his army at Brundisium in 83 BC. He had made his position clear: the *respublica* had been hijacked by a clique with whom he would have no dealings. He regarded those who joined him as friends, those who opposed him as enemies. By the end of 82 he had overcome most of his enemies either by negotiation or in battle, and those who remained were systematically exterminated through the proscriptions. Italy experienced war, fire and great slaughter. Campania and Etruria were ravaged, wealthy landowners were proscribed, towns and districts which had supported Sulla's opponents were devastated or settled with Sulla's veterans. Inhabitants lost their citizen rights, though Cicero would claim this was unconstitutional. Volaterrae, in Etruria, held out until 80. The harvest of the Sullan era – proscriptions and destruction – were long remembered. Cicero does not say much about Sulla and his times. He clearly hated the violence and cruelty.

Curio   C. Scribonius Curio, served with Sulla in the East, consul in 76; his son was tribune in 50.

Crassus   M. Licinius Crassus, consul in 70 and 55; renowned for his wealth, he was killed in 53 campaigning against the Parthians.

Lentuli   brothers, C. Cornelius Lentulus, consul in 72; P. Cornelius Lentulus, consul in 71, executed as a Catilinarian conspirator in 63.

Pompeius   Gnaeus Pompeius Magnus, consul in 70, 55 and 52, dominant political and military figure of the 60s and 50s.

I first began … cases   Cicero's first case was a civil action in 81; in 80 he defended Roscius in a criminal action.

Molon   Apollonius Molon, famed as a teacher, public speaker and grammarian, taught on Rhodes and at Rome.

The **proscriptions** of the rich, the destruction of the *municipia*, which brings to mind that harvest of the Sullan era.

Cicero, Paradoxes of the Stoics 6.46

Now it had ceased to be the case that any action against our allies might seem wrong since such enormous cruelty had been inflicted on citizens. This was so in the case of Sulla, that a victory that was not honourable followed a cause that was.

Cicero, On Duties 2.27

- What possible justification is there for attacking one's own country, as Sulla did?

Sulla's restored *respublica*

Sulla was appointed dictator 'for writing laws and establishing a *respublica*' in 82 BC and set about a programme of comprehensive reform. What his aims were we do not know exactly, since his memoirs have not survived; we have to assess his aims from the arrangements he made:

- The rights of the new citizens were respected.
- Power was restored to an enlarged senate of 600 members; new members were recruited from the *equites*.

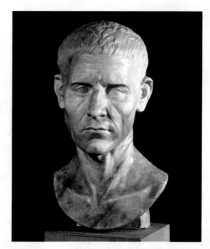

The sharp and powerful gleam of his grey eyes was said to be more fearful because of the complexion of his face – a mixture of coarse red and white blotches.

---

proscriptions the publication in the Roman Forum of the names of Roman citizens who were declared outlaws, whose property was confiscated, whose descendants were debarred from public office. In total perhaps some 40 members of the senate and 1,600 *equites*, many of whom were victims of greed and corruption, were proscribed. Note that Cicero connects proscriptions with greed and a desire to acquire wealth. Sulla needed money and land to reward his troops. The proscriptions were Sulla's most notorious legacy to Rome. Cicero was clearly ambivalent in his attitude towards Sulla, whom he called 'the master of three deadly vices – luxury, greed and cruelty'.

- Membership of the senate became automatic upon election as quaestor.
- All proposed legislation must have the approval of the senate.
- Tribunes must first submit proposals for approval of the senate; their rights of veto were restricted and they might hold no further political office.
- The number of praetors was increased from six to eight and quaestors from 12 to 20; there could thus be a regular turnover of provincial governors and officials.
- Provincial governors were subject to stricter regulations on the conduct of their office.
- The holding of magistracies was strictly controlled: quaestorship and praetorship were obligatory before being eligible for election to the consulship at the age of 42.
- The courts were reformed and the panels of jurors selected exclusively from the senatorial order.

The success of this reform depended upon the senate, but Sulla's senate lacked tradition because so many of its senior members had been victims of the murderous 80s. Roman nobles fought fiercely for their personal interests while the interest of the *respublica* required their support and goodwill. There were at least two structural weaknesses in the system:

- The senate lacked the power to deal with insubordinate and disobedient provincial governors.
- Sulla failed to deal with the army: the mass of the soldiery, Roman citizens recruited from the rural poor, required money and land upon completion of their service. Since the state failed to provide for them, the soldiers relied upon their commanders, and the army became a political force – with dire consequences for the *respublica*.

These reforms can be seen as a conservative attempt to restore traditional senatorial government and to reflect Sulla's own experience of disruptive tribunes. On the other hand, they can be viewed as an attempt to make his seizure of power legitimate and to secure his constitution by filling the enlarged senate with his supporters and by depriving potential opponents of the means to threaten the system through stripping the tribunes of their power to cause trouble. It depends on one's point of view.

The case of Sextus Roscius of Ameria

Sextus Roscius of Ameria was accused of having murdered his father. His father was a 'local notable' with distinguished connections in Rome, where he was murdered when returning from a dinner party. He was a staunch supporter of the Sullan nobility and had no fear of proscription, but he did have a long-standing feud with two other Roscii of Ameria: Titus Roscius Capito and Titus Roscius Magnus, disreputable villains according to Cicero.

Now **Sextus Roscius**, my client, was in Ameria, while T. Roscius Magnus here was in Rome; the son was busy all the time on the farms and had been devoting himself to the family estates and to life in the country in accordance with the wishes of his father, while Magnus was in Rome all the time. Sextus Roscius senior, returning from a dinner, was murdered near the **baths of Pallacina**. I hope this fact itself 5 makes it quite clear upon whom suspicion for the crime falls: but if the facts themselves do not make absolutely clear what up till now has been a suspicion, then you are welcome to judge **this man** here to be implicated in the crime.

Cicero, *Sextus Roscius of Ameria* 18

Note the contrast between the dutiful son on the country estate and the 'criminal' relative, Magnus, who is first suspected and now clearly implicated in murder. His presence in Rome seems sufficient to prove his guilt.

When Sextus Roscius was murdered, the first person to bring the news to Ameria was one Mallius Glaucia, an impoverished freedman, a client and associate of Magnus here. He did not bring the news to the house of the son but to that of his enemy, T. Capito; although he had been murdered an hour after nightfall, the messenger reached Ameria just about dawn; in ten hours during the night he 5 winged his way for the 56 miles with swift transport, not only to be the first to bring the longed-for news but also to show off the blood of his enemy, still as fresh as could be on the weapon only recently pulled from his body.

Cicero, *Sextus Roscius of Ameria* 19

The fascination for macabre details of crime has not changed through the ages. Read any popular newspaper or watch the news on television.

Sextus Roscius   Cicero's client, Sextus Roscius the son, accused of parricide.

baths of Pallacina   Pallacina was a district in Rome, which is thought to have been at the north-east end of the Circus Flaminius.

this man   Sextus Roscius, the defendant.

This bronze statue of an orator, in Italian the Arringatore (compare English 'harangue'), dates from around 80 BC and portrays one of the leading citizens of Perusia (modern Perugia). He wears the broad-bordered toga and the footwear of a municipal aristocrat. He is famous for his arresting pose.

Four days after these events, the matter was brought before **Chrysogonus** in the camp of **L. Sulla at Volaterrae**. The magnitude of Sextus' wealth was pointed out; the excellent quality of his estates – for he had left 13 farms which almost all bordered on the Tiber; and 5 the helplessness and isolation of my client. They pointed out that since Sextus Roscius, a man of such distinction and influence and the father of this man here, was murdered without any difficulty, his son could be quite easily removed from the scene since he did not suspect 10 anything and was a countryman and unknown in Rome. They promised their services in this business.

Cicero, Sextus Roscius of Ameria 20

Not to detain you any longer, members of the jury, a partnership was formed. Proscription was no longer mentioned, since even those who had been afraid before were now returning and thinking they were out of danger. But the name of Sextus Roscius, one of the 5 staunchest supporters of the nobility, was inserted into the lists. Chrysogonus became the purchaser; three farms, probably the best, were handed over to Capito as his own property and he is in possession of them today; Magnus over there moved in on all the rest of 10 the property in the name of Chrysogonus, as he himself says. All these things were done, members of the jury, I know for certain, **without the knowledge of Lucius Sulla**.

Cicero, Sextus Roscius of Ameria 21

Cicero depicts Chrysogonus as an evil, greedy and powerful minion of the dictator. If he was as powerful as Cicero makes out – and this has been doubted since he only appears in this speech and never in Plutarch's *Life of Cicero* – then Cicero was taking a brave risk. Cicero may, however, have created a monster to serve his case.

Chrysogonus freedman and chief administrator of the dictator Sulla.

L. Sulla at Volaterrae Sulla was still dealing with resistance at Volaterrae in Etruria.

without the knowledge of Lucius Sulla Cicero carefully exonerates Sulla of any involvement in the case; he was too busy with high affairs of state to know what his minions were up to.

Meanwhile that T. Roscius Magnus, an excellent fellow, the agent of Chrysogonus, came to Ameria and marched into the estates of this man here. Unhappy, overwhelmed with grief, he had not yet completed the proper funeral rites for his father. Magnus threw him naked out of his house and drove him head first from his ancestral hearth and the gods of his household, members of the jury, 5 and became the master of the huge estate. A man who had been the most tight-fisted when it was a matter of his own estate behaved, as often happens, without restraint when it involved what belonged to someone else. He openly carried off many of the contents to his own house while he secretly made off with a lot more. He gave away no small amount as gifts to those who had helped him and sold off 10 the rest by public auction.

Cicero, *Sextus Roscius of Ameria* 23

The inhabitants of Ameria were outraged by the fate of Sextus Roscius, father and son, and the arrogant behaviour of Magnus. They decided to send an official delegation to Sulla to report what had happened and to complain about the actions of Chrysogonus. T. Roscius Capito managed to get himself included in the delegation.

25   The delegation reached the camp. It is fully accepted, members of the jury, as I have said previously, that these outrageous crimes were committed without Lucius Sulla's knowledge. Now Chrysogonus came to the delegation at once; he authorized some nobles to beg the delegates not to go and see Sulla and to promise
26   that he would do everything they wished. He had become so thoroughly alarmed 5 that he would rather have died than have Sulla be made aware of this affair. The delegates were men of an old-fashioned sort and imagined everyone else to be like themselves. When Chrysogonus assured them he would remove the name of S. Roscius from the lists and would hand over the farms unoccupied to the son, and when Capito, who was among the delegates, added his promise that this would be 10 done, the delegates believed them. They returned to Ameria without having put their case before Sulla.

Cicero, *Sextus Roscius of Ameria* 25–6

Note the contrast between the good old-fashioned country nobles and the devious Greek freedman of the dictator. Needless to say, Chrysogonus did not keep his word nor did the Roscii hand over the estates; instead they began to plot the murder of Sextus Roscius, the son, as the solution to their difficulties. He escaped to Rome, where he sought the help of a noble patron.

As soon as Sextus realized the danger, on the advice of friends and relatives he fled to Rome and took himself to **Caecilia**, the sister of Nepos and daughter of Balearicus, whom I mention out of respect, who was a good friend of his father. That woman, members of the jury, even now retains traces of an old-fashioned sense of duty, something which everyone has always appreciated. She is an example 5 to others. She took Roscius into her home. He was destitute, thrown out of his home and expelled from his estates, fleeing the weapons and threats of criminals. She gave help to a friend when he had been overwhelmed and everyone else had given up hope for him. It was because of her courage, her loyalty and her devoted attention that his name was entered among the list of the accused while he was 10 still alive rather than among the list of the proscribed when he had been killed.

Cicero, *Sextus Roscius of Ameria* 27

Cicero won the case and Sextus Roscius was acquitted. His is a case with human interest, which reveals social relationships, vice and virtue, the links between city and country, and the sorts of nefarious activities that can prosper in a dictatorship. It allows us to gain some idea of what life was like in the countryside of Italy following the 'settlement' of Sulla. It is a speech well worth reading in full. (Berry's translation can be recommended – see the Further reading section.)

Cicero tells us that this first success set him on the path to fame.

My first public case was spoken in defence of Sextus Roscius and gained such favourable notice that no subsequent case seemed beyond my capacity as an advocate. From then on came a succession of cases which I brought to court worked out in great detail and, so to speak, pored over with the midnight oil.

Cicero, *Brutus* 312

Cicero made it his regular practice to act as advocate for the defence and explains why.

Defence brings the greatest glory and influence. This is all the more likely if the speaker happens to be helping a client who appears to be oppressed and persecuted by someone in power. This is the sort of case I have often taken on, for example, when as a young man I spoke for P. Sextus of Ameria against L. Sulla when he was in power. The speech survives, as you are aware.

Cicero, *On Duties* 2.51

Caecilia Caecilia Metella, a grand lady; her father was consul in 123, her brother in 98, and her three uncles had all been consuls. She belonged to one of the great political families, which was linked with and supported Sulla. Well could Cicero 'mention her out of respect'.

Sulla resigned the dictatorship by the end of 81 BC, becoming consul with Quintus Metellus Scipio in 80. He then retired into private life in 79 and died in 78. His retirement intrigued contemporaries, and Caesar thought he did not know his political ABC in laying down the dictatorship.

1 Is there justification for dictatorship?
2 How is political change managed in the modern world?
3 Are there modern parallels for Chrysogonus?
4 How would Cicero fare in a modern court of law?
5 Can you detect anything illogical in the prosecution case?
6 How successfully are politics and law kept separate in contemporary society?

3 Entering upon public office

Cicero in Athens and Rhodes, 79–77 BC

Cicero's successful defence of Roscius in 80 BC brought him many more cases, but the physical strain wore him down. He was advised to cease practice but decided to go on an extended trip to Athens and the East. He was away from 79 until 77 and describes his experiences in an autobiographical passage of the *Brutus*.

The Acropolis of Athens.

314   Although friends and doctors urged me to give up pleading cases, I thought I ought to run whatever risk rather than give up my hope of renown in public speaking. But I reckoned that by relaxing and restraining the use of my voice and by changing my style of speaking I could avoid the danger and speak with greater moderation. To change my normal style of speaking was the reason for 5 my setting out for Asia. So it was that I departed from Rome, when I had been involved in cases for two years and my name was already well known in the forum.

315   After my arrival in **Athens**, I spent six months with **Antiochus**, the most distinguished and learned philosopher of the old Academy, and with him as my teacher and adviser I renewed my **study of philosophy**, a subject I had taken up 10 in my early youth; I had never entirely given up but had regularly added to my knowledge of it.

Cicero, Brutus 314–15

After six months in Athens studying philosophy and gaining regular practice in public speaking, Cicero travelled eastwards to the Roman province of Asia for further oratorical practice and at Rhodes renewed acquaintance with the master teacher Apollonius Molon.

I came to Rhodes and attached myself to that same Molon **to whom I had listened in Rome**. He was outstanding as both a practising advocate and a writer of speeches. He was also particularly good at identifying and noticing mistakes in speaking, an expert in teaching and instructing … I returned two years later not only better trained but almost a changed person. The excessive strain on my voice 5 had disappeared and my speaking had become more restrained, while my lungs had gained added strength and my body was in reasonable shape.

Cicero, Brutus 316

- Cicero defines Molon's qualities as a teacher. How does Cicero's assessment compare with what you consider to be the requirements of a good teacher?

Athens   the cultural centre which elite young Romans regularly visited at this time to further their studies in rhetoric and philosophy.

Antiochus   he had studied under Philon (see note, p. 17), but left his school and founded his own school, the old Academy.

study of philosophy   Cicero believed that a study of history and what the philosophers taught about the rules of behaviour and conduct in life, about personal and social relationships – ethics and morality – were required for the fully trained and ideal orator.

to whom I had listened in Rome   Apollonius Molon and his visit to Rome (see p. 22).

The Sullan constitution in the 70s BC

During the 70s BC, when Cicero first entered public office, the constitution which Sulla had put in place and the senate to which he had entrusted it faced a number of political and military challenges; some change was inevitable:

- Tribunes were permitted to hold further office in 75.
- Subsidized grain was allocated to the plebs in Rome in 72.
- There were demands for changing the senatorial jurors in the courts.

The military problems were more pressing:

- A brief insurrection in Etruria, the consequence of Sulla's harsh measures, was quickly put down in 78.
- A revolt in Spain, led by Sertorius, an opponent of Sulla, became a virtual alternative *respublica* and endured for more than a decade before it was defeated by Metellus Pius and Gnaeus Pompeius in 72.
- A revolt of slaves in 73, led by Spartacus, caused extensive disorder and damage in Italy and the Romans suffered a series of military defeats. M. Crassus was given a special command in 72 and within a year Spartacus and his slaves were finally defeated.

Pompeius was summoned from Spain by the government and rounded up fugitive slaves, claiming responsibility for rooting them out from Italy. This gratuitous insult to Crassus blighted relations between them for the rest of their lives. Given the important roles each played during the next two decades, this personal animosity was a significant feature of Roman politics.

During 71 Crassus and Pompeius declared their intention to stand for the consulship of 70. Crassus was fully eligible, having held the required offices of the *cursus honorum*, while Pompeius was below the required age and not even a member of the senate. He had held no political office. He boasted in 70 that he had carried out the required military service 'with himself as commander-in-chief'. The majority of the senate recognized the magnitude of his service to the *respublica* and he was exempted from the regulations.

Crassus and Pompeius had announced before the elections that if they were elected they would see to it that the full rights of the tribunes were restored. Once elected they carried out their promise. Modern scholars disagree about how damaging this tribunician restoration was for Sulla's constitution.

This destroyed the barrier to popular legislation Sulla had devised; the Sullan system was now in ruins, all the more so because clamour and violence on the streets, which the senate lacked the military force to put down, could be used to overcome legal obstacles to further measures which the masses desired.

P. A. Brunt, *Fall of the Roman Republic*, p. 472

Adjustment rather than breakdown was the hallmark of the 70s ... By 70 the senatorial leadership was more secure and more firmly in control than before. The Sullan constitution had been altered only slightly in form, not at all in intent.

E. S. Gruen, pp. 45, 46

Quaestor in Rome and Sicily, 75 BC

When Cicero returned to Rome in 77 BC he was 29 years old and approaching the age at which he was eligible to seek election to the office of quaestor, the first step on the ladder of public office. He stood in the first possible year, 76, and was elected, thus becoming the first in his family to enter the senatorial order. Quaestors served in various administrative roles in Rome or in the provinces as assistants to governors. In 75 Cicero served as quaestor at Lilybaeum in western Sicily under the governor **Sextus Peducaeus**, where he oversaw payments to farmers for their corn.

It was one year after my return from Asia, when I was an advocate in some cases involving *nobles*, that I was a candidate for the quaestorship, **Cotta** for the consulship and Hortensius for aedile; at that point I was elected quaestor.

Cicero, Brutus 318

I considered that office had not only been given me but entrusted and committed to my care. I carried out my office of quaestor in Sicily thinking that the eyes of all were concentrated upon me alone, that I and my quaestorship were being played out on some world stage. I denied myself all enjoyable pleasures, not only the excessive desires of the present age but those which are natural and necessary.

Cicero, Verrine 2.5.35

A Sicilian anecdote

Cicero clearly took public office with high seriousness, which may not perhaps have been typical of the age – but it was not all official business:

When I was quaestor I tracked down the grave of Archimedes, which was unknown to the Syracusans – they totally denied its existence – and found it enclosed all round and covered with brambles and thickets; for I remembered some verses inscribed, so I had heard, upon his tomb, which stated that a sphere along with a cylinder had been set up on top of his grave. [65] Accordingly taking a good look around … I noticed a small column arising above the bushes, on which there was a figure of a sphere and a cylinder. I said at once to the Syracusans – their leading men were with me – that I believed it was the very thing I was searching for. Slaves were sent in with sickles to clear the ground of obstacles; [66] when a passage was opened we approached the pedestal in front of us. The epigram was traceable with about half the lines legible, as the latter part was worn away. So you see, one of the most famous cities of Greece, once indeed a great school of learning, would have been ignorant of the grave of one of its most learned citizens, if a man of Arpinum had not pointed it out.

Cicero, Tusculan Disputations 5.64–6

Sextus Peducaeus   praetor in 77, he governed Sicily in 76–75 and carried out a census there.

Cotta   C. Aurelius Cotta, consul in 75 (see note, p. 16).

Cicero discovers the tomb of Archimedes, *a painting by Thomas Christian Wink (1781).*
Archimedes was a mathematician and inventor, and a native of Syracuse. He was said to have
invented clever machines to use against the Roman forces besieging his city and was killed in
212 BC when the Romans sacked it. 'Give me a place to stand and I will move the earth,' he
boasted.

More than twenty years later, defending a colleague before the court for
electoral bribery in 54 BC, Cicero proudly recalls his performance as quaestor
in Sicily.

64 I am not afraid, members of the jury, that you may think I am making some
undue claim for myself if I say something about my quaestorship. Although it
went very well, the fact that I later held the highest offices has, I think, meant
that I have not needed to claim all that much glory for my quaestorship. I am
quite confident that no one will dare to assert that anyone else has been more   5
appreciated or more famous for his quaestorship in Sicily. Indeed I will say that
at that time I imagined people in Rome were talking about nothing else but
my quaestorship. At a time when the price of corn was very high I had sent a
considerable quantity to the city. I was polite to the businessmen, fair to the
merchants, generous to the people of the *municipia*, and I showed restraint to the   10
provincials. All considered me most conscientious in every aspect of my post.
The Sicilians devised some unheard-of honours for me.

65   Thus I was leaving the province expecting and imagining that the Roman people would grant me what I wanted without my asking.

Cicero, Plancius 64–5

He was in for a big surprise.

On my way back from my province I arrived at Puteoli, intending to make my way back from there to Rome at a time when there are usually many fashionable people in **that resort**. I almost collapsed, members of the jury, when one of them asked me what day I had left Rome and whether I had any news from the city. When I replied that I was on my way back from my province: 'Of course, I believe   5 you're coming back from Africa.' 'No, from Sicily actually,' I replied with disdain and indignation. Then one know-all declared: 'Why yes, didn't you know he was quaestor at Syracuse?' I said no more. I stopped being indignant and pretended I was one of those who had come to take the waters.

Cicero, Plancius 65

Cicero confessed that he learnt a valuable lesson from this experience. It was not the ears but the eyes of the Roman people that were important. He would from then on make it his business to be seen in Rome and to make his name in the forum. He was only absent of necessity when an exile in 58–57 BC and a provincial governor in Cilicia in 51–50.

The view over the bay at Puteoli, looking down to Cape Misenum.

that resort   Puteoli was a place where rich and smart Romans went to take the waters during the season when the heat of Rome became unbearable.

4 A corrupt governor

Gaius Verres was praetor in 74 BC and governor of Sicily from 73 to 71, when he administered the province with unparalleled corruption. He ransacked public places and private homes with equal rapacity to satisfy his liking for art.

He used to claim he would never be convicted of plundering his province because he had the promise of support from a powerful friend. He was not making money just for himself, but had planned his three years' governorship of Sicily so that he would consider himself doing very nicely if he could put one year's profit into his pocket, could hand over the second to his patrons and the men who were going to 5 defend him, and could keep back the entire profit of his third year, the richest and most lucrative of all, for distribution as bribes to the jurors.

Cicero, *Verrine* 1.40

Corruption in politics and in the courts

In the elections of 70 BC friends of Verres gained office and one of them, M. Metellus, was appointed to preside over the court where Verres was to be accused. When the results of the elections were known, Verres was congratulated because he now had the certain prospect of acquittal.

18
19   Hortensius, the consul-designate, was being escorted home from the **Campus** by a huge crowd of people. **C. Curio** met them by chance … He saw Verres in the crowd by the **arch of Fabius**. He called him by name and in a loud voice congratulated him … He stood with Verres, embraced him and told him he need have no fear. 'I tell you,' he said, 'you have been acquitted by yesterday's elections' 5
21   … Now at this very moment the praetors-designate **were conducting the lot**.

Campus   the Campus Martius, where elections were held.

C. Curio   Gaius Scribonius Curio, consul in 76, supporter of the Sullan constitution.

arch of Fabius   an arch at the bottom of the Via Sacra, near the temple of Vesta (see map, p. 47), dedicated to Q. Fabius Maximus, the great Roman opponent of the Carthaginian Hannibal.

were conducting the lot   when the eight praetors were elected, they conducted the lot to decide which judicial functions they would carry out during their year of office.

It fell to M. Metellus to preside in the **extortion court**. I was told that Verres had been given such hearty congratulations that he sent slaves home to tell his wife.

22 Now this certainly did not please me; I little understood what I had to fear in the result of the lot. I learned from certain informers, from whom I gathered 10 all my information, that a fair number of moneybags full of Sicilian money had changed hands from a certain member of the senate to a Roman *eques*. Some ten of these had been left with that senator for the business of my election. He had

23 summoned **agents** from all **the tribes** by night. One of these, who thought he ought to spare no effort on my behalf, came to me that same night. He revealed 15 what Verres had said: he had recalled how generously he had treated the agents when he himself had been a candidate for the praetorship and then in the recent consular and praetorian elections; he immediately promised as much money as

24 they wanted to prevent my election as aedile ... I was faced with great problems and anxieties within one very short period of time. The **elections** were fast 20 approaching and I was being attacked with big money.

Cicero, Verrine 1.18–24

> • Can you give examples of money being used to buy votes or to block candidates in the modern world?

That was when I first heard the Sicilians had been issued with a summons by Hortensius to come to his house. The Sicilians were obviously free agents. When they learned why they were being summoned they did not come. Meanwhile my election was beginning. Verres thought that he was the master of this as he had been of the other elections in this year. This magnate, with his bland and 5 charming son, went round all the tribes. He called and assembled all the family friends, that is, the agents. When the Roman people recognized and understood this, it exercised complete freedom of action.

Cicero, Verrine 1.25

> • Hortensius would not long remain a counsel in modern law if he sought to bribe persons involved in the case. But are there other ways to bring about corrupt verdicts?

extortion court literally the court 'for claiming back money/property acquired illegally'; it was the court where free citizens from the provinces of the Roman empire, through their patrons, sought redress against corrupt Roman officials.

agents persons employed to distribute bribes at elections.

the tribes all Roman citizens were allocated to one of 35 tribes, which were the voting units in elections for aediles and some other magistrates.

elections after Sulla these were usually held in summer, in the month Quintilis (July). There were also games in honour of Apollo to attract and entertain the crowds of voters. They would assume special importance in 44 BC (see p. 160).

Cicero was elected aedile and proceeded with the prosecution of Verres. Even though he was prosecuting, something he did not normally do, his action in this case can be seen as a defence of the interests of the Sicilians, whose friendship he had gained while he was quaestor. The defence attempted all manner of tactics to delay proceedings, hoping Verres might not appear in court before 69 BC, when he would have friends present. The trial commenced on 4 August 70, when Cicero made a first brief speech outlining the aims of his case and warned the jurors of the consequences of acquitting Verres. Hortensius could offer little in response and Cicero proceeded at once to witnesses and evidence. Verres was effectively condemned. The second part of the trial never took place and only the first speech was ever delivered. Some of what Cicero intended to say follows.

The governor of the province greets his fleet

29 When the height of summer arrived, when all governors of Sicily are usually travelling around because that is the time when the grain is on the threshing-floors, and the province can be best inspected; because the families of slaves are gathered together and the numbers of slaves can be clearly seen and the hardship of their work is most irksome … At this time of year, I repeat, when all other governors 5
are going their rounds, this new-style commander was setting up stationary camp
30 in the most beautiful place in Syracuse. At the very entrance of the harbour …
He erected grand tents constructed of linen sheets. He withdrew entirely from his governor's headquarters so that throughout that period nobody was able to see him outside this compound. No one had access to the actual compound unless 10
he was a companion or tool for his debaucheries. All the women with whom he consorted assembled here – and it is amazing how many of them there were in Syracuse. Men suited to this creature's friendship, suited to his way of life and revelry, gathered here too. His son, now a grown man, also mixed with men and
31 women of this sort … During this time, when this creature, **dressed in a purple** 15
Greek cloak and a tunic reaching to his ankles, was engaging in revelries with his lady-friends, people were not put out or annoyed that the chief magistrate was absent from the forum, that law was not being administered, that the courts were not sitting; that compound on the shore was all the time resounding with the voices of women, with singing and music, while in the forum there was total 20
silence and the absence of lawsuits and law, but men were not annoyed; for it was not the law and the lawcourts that seemed to be absent from the forum but violence, cruelty and the savage and unprovoked plundering of their property.

Cicero, *Verrine* 2.5.29–31

---

dressed … ankles   not only was his behaviour unbecoming for a Roman governor, but his dress was quite outrageous for a Roman citizen.

Syracuse island and the harbour.

> • This is a masterly piece of defamation which no judge today would allow. How does Cicero seek to make the jury hostile to Verres?

Verres was very fond of Nike, the wife of Cleomenes of Syracuse. He dismissed his Roman deputy and appointed Cleomenes to command the fleet, thus getting rid of the husband and keeping the wife in his company. The fleet sailed from Syracuse.

Cleomenes sailed out of Syracuse harbour in a **quadrireme** from **Centuripae** followed by ships from **Segesta, Tyndaris, Herbita, Heraclea, Apollonia** and **Haluntium** – an impressive fleet to look at but weak and ineffective because **so many marines and rowers had been given a discharge.** This conscientious governor watched the fleet under his command while it sailed past one of his lewd 5

---

quadrireme   a ship having four rowers to each bench.

Centuripae … Haluntium   cities of Sicily.

so many … discharge   Cicero alleges that Verres allowed many of the marines and rowers to buy their discharge from him for his own gain, thereby enfeebling the fleet.

parties. Although Verres himself had not been seen in many days, he did allow himself to be seen by the sailors for a short while. There he stood on the shore, the governor of the Roman people, in sandals, in a Greek purple cloak with a tunic down to his ankles, leaning on a fancy girl; a good many Sicilians and Roman citizens had often seen him in this dress before.

10

Cicero, *Verrine* 2.5.86

However, there is other evidence. The historian Sallust, no fool and no respecter of persons, whose *Histories* only survive in fragments, records: 'C. Verres strengthened the coastline close to Italy' (4.28). Modern scholars associate this fragment with the slave uprising of Spartacus and possibly too with the pirates of the eastern Mediterranean, who were in league with the revolt of Sertorius in Spain (see p. 32). Despite all Cicero's accusations, this fragment should give pause for thought: Verres may not have spent all his summer hours carousing and looting Sicilian property.

What price Roman citizenship?

Roman citizenship was a prize possession which set its holders apart from other men and in theory guaranteed them freedom from violence and abuse at the hands of magistrates. But Gavius of Consa did not find it so.

160   Although Gavius of whom I speak was a citizen of **Consa** and a Roman citizen, he had been thrown into prison by Verres but had secretly escaped by some means or other from the stone quarries. He reached **Messana** … where he began to complain and say that he, though a Roman citizen, had been thrown into prison. He was going straight back to Rome and would be there ready for Verres' arrival. 5 The poor chap didn't realize that it made no difference whether he spoke in Messana or before that creature in his governor's headquarters. … Gavius was immediately put under escort and brought before the magistrate of Messana. Verres arrived by chance in Messana that very day. He was brought the news that a Roman citizen was complaining he had been in the Syracusan stone quarries. He 10 had been detained and brought back by the magistrate as he was on the point of boarding a ship, uttering dire threats against Verres. Verres himself could consider the best course and therefore decide what he wanted to do with the man. …

161   Inflamed with rage and breathing evil, Verres came into the forum. His eyes were ablaze, his whole face a picture of cruelty. Everyone was waiting to see how 15

Consa   a *municipium* in southern Italy, whose inhabitants possessed Roman citizenship.

Messana   a city on the straits between Sicily and Italy, modern Messina, was one place which supported Verres at this trial, under duress according to Cicero, and because citizens there had abetted his crimes; hence it was an unwise place for Gavius to declare his intentions.

The stone quarries at Syracuse.

far he would go and what he was going to do. Without warning Verres ordered Gavius to be dragged out, stripped naked and tied up in the middle of the forum, and the rods to be made ready. That poor man cried out that he was a Roman citizen, a citizen of the *municipium* of Consa. He had served in the army under a distinguished Roman *eques*, L. Raecius, who was engaged in business at 20 Panormus. Verres might learn these facts from him. At this Verres replied that he had discovered that Gavius had been sent to Sicily to spy by the **leaders of the slave revolt**. There was no informer of this fact, no shred of evidence, and no suspicion whatsoever. He then ordered **the man to be flogged** in the most brutal fashion from every angle. There in the middle of the forum of Messana a 25 Roman citizen, jurors, was beaten with rods; all the time amid the pain and crack of blows, no groan, no words were heard from that poor wretch except 'I **am a Roman citizen**'. By this mention of his citizenship he thought he would fend off the blows and rid his body of torture; but not only did he fail to obtain escape from the violence of the rods, but when he continued his entreaties more urgently and 30 asserted his Roman citizenship, a cross – I repeat, a cross – was got ready for that unfortunate and suffering man who had never seen such an abomination till then.

Cicero, *Verrine* 2.5.160–2

162

- What techniques does Cicero use here to get his point over effectively to his audience?

---

leaders … revolt   Spartacus and the slaves.

the man to be flogged   a Roman citizen was legally immune from such physical punishment.

I am a Roman citizen   the utterance of these words (*civis Romanus sum*) was the most powerful statement of status and privilege that a Roman citizen could utter.

How sweet the word 'freedom'! How special our rights as citizens! ... Have things come to such a low point that in a Roman province, in a town linked by treaty, a Roman citizen could be bound and flogged in the forum by a man who owed his rods and axes to the favour of the Roman people? When fire, hot irons and other instruments of torture were brought out, if his agonized appeals and his pitiful 5 cries could not restrain you, were you not even moved by the tears and the loud groans of the Roman citizens who stood by? Did you dare to crucify someone who said he was a Roman citizen?

Cicero, *Verrine* 2.5.163

1 Read the episode about the mistreatment of St Paul recorded in the Acts of the Apostles, 22.22–9. How does this contrast with the treatment received by Gavius?

2 Consider the rights of citizenship set out on the inside pages of passports today. The United Kingdom passport states: 'Her Britannic Majesty's Secretary of State Requests and requires in the Name of Her Majesty all those whom it may concern to allow the bearer to pass freely without let or hindrance and to afford the bearer such assistance and protection as may be necessary'; the United States passport reads: 'The Secretary of State of the United States of America hereby requests all whom it may concern to permit the citizen/national of the United States named herein to pass without delay or hindrance and in case of need to give all lawful aid and protection.'

The first stage of the trial finished on 13 August. When Verres failed to show for the second stage, he was condemned and went into exile in Massilia (Marseilles), where he lived until his death in 43 BC. He was clearly a corrupt governor and should not be seen as typical, just as Cicero, a model governor of Cilicia in 51–50, was not typical. Perhaps more typical was Cicero's predecessor in Cilicia, Appius Claudius (see Chapter 10). As throughout history, it is the extremes that attract notice and stir the imagination. Imperialism has both a noble and a dark side, be it fifth-century Athens, republican Rome, Victorian Britain or the contemporary United States.

1 Is the adversarial practice in courts – prosecution and defence – effective in ensuring that justice is served?

2 There are societies or countries which do not use the adversarial system. How is justice administered in such places?

3 Are there examples where juries can be influenced by 'star performers' such as Cicero? Are there cases which should be conducted without juries?

5 The 'new man' progresses in politics

Aedile, 69 BC

Cicero was elected one of the four aediles and held office in 69 BC. The aediles took care of the city and the grain supply, and they supervised a number of the regular festivals. This was the first stage to the higher offices of praetor and consul.

I am now aedile-elect and fully conscious of the responsibility which the Roman people have laid upon me. I must put on, with greatest reverence and care, the holy games for **Ceres, Liber and Libera.** I must win the favour of our mother **Flora** for the Roman people and the plebs by providing well-attended games. I must put on with the greatest dignity and solemnity the ancient games for **Jupiter, Juno and Minerva,** games which were the earliest ones to be described as Roman. I must look after the sacred temples and protect the whole city. I have been given certain benefits in return for the effort and concern which these duties require: **precedence in being asked my opinion in the senate,** the purple-bordered toga, the **curule chair** and the right to hand down a **portrait mask** of myself to posterity.

Cicero, Verrine 2.5.36

(marginal line numbers: 5 at line "I must put on with the greatest dignity…"; 10 at "bordered toga, the curule chair…")

Ceres, Liber and Libera old Italian agricultural and fertility deities whose games were held on 19 April.

Flora Italian agricultural goddess in origin, worshipped as a goddess of fertility. Her games on 27 April were the responsibility of the two plebeian tribunes, of which Cicero was one. These games were attended by a certain licence and indecency.

Jupiter, Juno and Minerva the Capitoline trinity honoured in the Roman games from 5 to 19 September.

precedence … senate the consuls decided the order of speaking in the assembly and one's position in the order was a matter of great importance and prestige.

curule chair the folding ivory chair used by certain magistrates.

portrait mask such death-masks were hung in the first main room of a Roman house.

This frieze from the early first century BC shows a purification ceremony being performed with the sacrifice of a bull, a sheep and a pig. A priest stands with his young attendants at the altar. To the left of the altar stands a soldier, with boys bringing a bowl and cloth for the purification. The monument, which is in the Louvre Museum, Paris, is known as the Altar of Domitius Ahenobarbus.

Public religion in ancient Rome involved the performance of ritual and was in the hands of four great colleges of priests and certain magistrates, such as aediles. The senate, which had always to meet in a consecrated area, dealt with religious matters. 'It provided the principal link between men and gods and controlled men's behaviour towards the gods' (M. Beard and M. Crawford, p. 34). The Romans believed that the gods supported the well-being and growth of the Roman state and, provided the appropriate rituals were carried out properly and without error, would continue that support. Assemblies and meetings of the senate must always be preceded by ritual to ensure the approval of the gods. It is crucial to appreciate the public nature of all this activity. Whether Romans believed in the gods and what they believed in private is to a large extent unknowable.

Cicero discusses the expenses of being an aedile and how the rich showed off their wealth in the splendour of their games. It was also an investment in future political success – election to praetor and consul.

57 I realize that in the good old times the custom developed in our state that magnificence in their aedilician games was demanded of the best men. P. Crassus, who not only had the surname 'Rich' but actually *was* rich, put on splendid games
58 when he was aedile … Now if this is demanded by the people, good men must do it with approval even if they do not want to. But they should act within their 5 means as I myself did.

Cicero, *On Duties* 2.57–8

When Cicero was aedile the Sicilians came bringing many different products from the island out of gratitude to him. Cicero gained no personal profit but used the kindness of the islanders to lower the market prices in Rome.

Plutarch, *Cicero* 8.2

Praetor, 66 BC

We see here how Cicero's quaestorship and his prosecution of Verres paid dividends in gratitude from the Sicilians. In 67 BC Cicero sought election as praetor, in the first year when he was eligible, and was successful. He now for the first time addressed the Roman people assembled in the Roman Forum, and described how he had three times come top of the poll.

There were **several reruns** of the election. I was formally declared three times over by the votes of all the **centuries**, the first of the candidates to be elected to the praetorship. It was then made very clear to me, citizens, what you thought about me 5 personally and what message you were sending out to others.

Cicero, *Cn. Pompeius* 2

Gnaeus Pompeius Magnus. The locks of hair rising over the middle of his forehead are said to be styled in the manner of Alexander the Great.

Cicero had decided to speak in support of a tribunician proposal that Pompeius replace Lucullus in command against Mithradates. Pompeius was the popular hero of the moment because he had very recently, in a Mediterranean-wide command, cleared the sea of the pirates who had been interfering seriously with the corn supply to Rome and attacking Italy. That command had not been without critics and the same *optimates* now opposed Pompeius' replacement of Lucullus.

Cicero had to speak with care. He had to support Pompeius and the wishes of the Roman people but not at the same time alienate such *optimates* as Catulus and Hortensius, whose support he would require if he were to seek and gain the consulship – a good example of the dilemma a potential candidate might face in politics, the more so if he were a 'new man' such as Cicero. Cicero deals with the optimate objections very politely but firmly and here regards Quintus Hortensius not as a fellow advocate but as an optimate politician of considerable influence and importance. We are not yet in a world where there is a rigid distinction between lawyers, advocates and politicians.

---

several reruns   obvious irregularities in the conduct of the elections required holding three ballots.

centuries   the 193 centuries, voting divisions of the centuriate assembly which elected the eight praetors (see Introduction, p. 2).

52 What does Hortensius say? If overall command is to be given to one man, Pompeius is the most worthy, but such command should not be put in the hands of one man. That argument is now obsolete, proved wrong by what has happened more than by words. You used your great oratorical ability and your unrivalled eloquence, Q. Hortensius, and spoke at length in the senate with weight and style 5 against the courageous **A. Gabinius** when he had promulgated a law appointing one commander against the pirates. You spoke at considerable length here in the

53 forum in similar vein against that same proposal. Now I ask you, by the immortal gods, if your influence had carried greater weight with the Roman people than their safety and true interest, would we today possess our present glory and our world 10 empire? Did you think that our empire was in this position when *legati*, quaestors and praetors were being taken captive, when we were being prevented from public and private communication with all our provinces, when all seas had been closed to us so that we were no longer able to transact private or public business abroad?

Cicero, *Cn. Pompeius* 52–3

The Roman people, Q. Hortensius, then reckoned you and all of like view spoke with good intentions, but where the safety of all was concerned, the same Roman people gave heed to its own distress rather than to your influence. Thus **one law, one man, one year** not only freed the Roman people from distress and disgrace but also created the situation where you appeared at last to rule all peoples and 5 nations by land and sea.

Cicero, *Cn. Pompeius* 56

I still ought to speak, I think, about the influential opinion of **Q. Catulus**. He asked you, supposing you put everything in the hands of Pompeius alone, in whom you would put your hopes if anything happened to him. He received a considerable tribute for his courage and his dignity when you declared, almost with one voice, that you would put your hopes in Catulus himself. Indeed he has such quality that 5 nothing seems too great or difficult for him. He has the discretion to control the command, the integrity to take charge of it and the ability to complete it.

Cicero, *Cn. Pompeius* 59

A. Gabinius   tribune in 67, who proposed Pompeius should be given command against the pirates.

one law, one man, one year   the law of Gabinius; Cn. Pompeius (the man); 67 BC (the year) – in reality three months sufficed. This command of Pompeius, which gave him unprecedented power and influence, solved the immediate problem of the pirates. It illustrates how the administration of the Roman empire could no longer be run on a city-state basis. New structures were required but the senate and the *optimates* were wedded to traditional ways. Others would emulate Pompeius' example and contribute to the fall of the Republic.

Q. Catulus   Quintus Lutatius Catulus, consul in 78, staunchest supporter of the Sullan constitution.

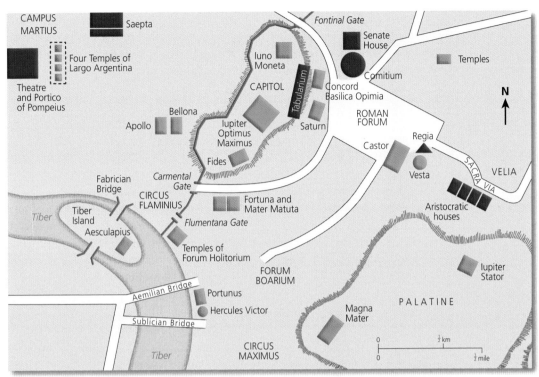

The political centre of Rome at the end of the Republic. The Saepta was the voting area, the Tabularium was the public record office and the Temple of Saturn was the Treasury.

We witness here:

- a political meeting held outdoors in the forum for the people to make decisions;
- question and answer in a public meeting in the case of Catulus;
- the power of the Roman people to make decisions *in their own interests*;
- the optimate opposition to extraordinary commands, which illustrates the 'level playing field' character of aristocratic politics, where each individual, here a tribune Manilius on behalf of Pompeius, seeks to achieve predominance while others, here Hortensius and Catulus, seek to prevent it and to keep everyone at the same level.

Cicero then supports Pompeius by describing his extraordinary career. Remember where he is speaking and his audience. It is not likely that he would have spoken in this way in the senate.

Was anything so unheard of as that a young man **should raise an army** for the *respublica* at a time of crisis? He raised one. That he should be in command? He was in command. That he should achieve outstanding success under his own

---

should raise an army Pompeius raised an army from his ancestral estates in Picenum against the regime in Rome in support of Sulla on his return to Italy in 83.

command? He did. What was so wholly opposed to custom than that a mere youth whose age was well below that required for membership of the senate should be 5 given command and an army, that he should be put in charge of **Sicily and then Africa** and the conduct of war there? He demonstrated in these spheres of duty outstanding integrity, dignity and ability. He ended a major war in Africa and brought home the victorious army. Was it so unheard of that a **Roman *eques* should hold a triumph**? Yet the Roman people not only saw this event but thought 10 everyone ought to attend the celebrations and join in with enthusiasm.

Cicero, Cn. Pompeius 61

62   Was it not remarkable that he should be **exempted from the laws** by a decree of the senate and become consul before he had been legally entitled to hold any curule magistracy? Was it not incredible that a Roman *eques* should by a decree of the senate hold **a second triumph**? Such innovations have been established in individual cases from the beginning of our history but they are not as many as 5

63   we have witnessed in the case of this one man. The numerous and unparalleled innovations in the case of Pompeius have all received the support of Q. Catulus and other distinguished men of the same standing.

Cicero, Cn. Pompeius 62–3

---

1   Can you find any evidence of democracy in this episode?

2   The pirate threat led the Roman people to set aside the regular arrangements of the constitution and to appoint Pompeius to an extraordinary command. Can you give modern examples where threats to a state justify extraordinary measures?

Cicero emphasizes the extraordinary military career and consequent dominant position of Pompeius. At this moment he was a *popularis* hero because his successful campaign against the pirates had secured the free and uninterrupted flow of corn to the city of Rome from Sicily, Africa and Egypt. A large proportion of the urban plebs depended upon it for their survival.

Sicily and then Africa   Sulla appointed Pompeius to deal with remaining opponents in those two provinces, which he speedily accomplished; his actions in executing opponents of Sulla brought him the taunt of 'adolescent butcher' (Valerius Maximus 6.2.8).

Roman *eques* should hold a triumph   Sulla had ordered Pompeius to dismiss his troops and return to Italy, but he led his victorious army back and demanded a triumph, which Sulla casually granted. Cicero obviously does not speak about it in this way.

exempted from the laws   Pompeius was not a member of the senate, had not been quaestor or praetor, and had not reached the required age. Nevertheless the senate exempted him from these statutory requirements.

a second triumph   Pompeius held a first triumph on 12 March 81 or 80 and a second on 29 December 71.

The case of C. Licinius Macer

As praetor Cicero was president of the extortion court and in a letter to Atticus he describes one case that came before him.

Here in Rome I have settled the case of C. Macer and the people have shown me quite remarkable and incredible support. Though I was sympathetic to him, I have gained far greater benefit in the eyes of the people from his condemnation than I should have gained in thanks from the man himself if he had been acquitted.

Rome, first half of 66 BC

Cicero, *Atticus* 1.4.2 (9)

Valerius Maximus gives an alternative version of the case

In a similar haste to death, C. Licinius Macer, on trial for extortion, a man of praetorian rank, the father of Calvus, climbed onto a balcony when the votes were being sorted. When he saw M. Cicero, who was presiding in that court, laying aside his magistrate's toga, Macer sent a message to him to say that he had died not a condemned man but a defendant on trial and that his goods could not be put up for auction. Forthwith with a sweat rag, which he happened to have in his hand, he blocked up his mouth and jaw, stopped his breathing and anticipated punishment by death. When Cicero learnt of this, he made no pronouncement. Thus the son, an orator of shining talent, was protected from family poverty and from the reproach of a conviction in the family by the unusual manner of his father's demise.

Valerius Maximus, *Memorable Doings and Sayings* 9.12.7

While the details of the case are unknown, it is clear that Cicero's conduct as judge and Macer's suicide meant that the provincial citizens never recovered what had been wrongfully taken from them.

The campaign for the consulship

After his praetorship Cicero, mindful of his experience following his quaestorship in Sicily, did not take an overseas province but began to concentrate on his forthcoming campaign for the consulship of 63 BC.

Cicero wrote to Atticus in July 65 about his prospects for the consular elections in 64 to decide the consuls of 63.

C. Macer   C. Licinius Macer, *popularis* tribune in 73, praetor in 68, and a historian. The details of his case are unknown.

1   The position about my candidature, which I know is of the greatest concern to you, is as follows so far as can be currently foreseen. One person, P. Galba, is canvassing but he is being given a straightforward 'no' without deceit or disguise. People's general impression is that his premature canvassing is not unfavourable to my prospects. They are commonly saying no [to Galba] because they are under 5 obligation to me. I hope this will be of some benefit to me when news gets around that my friends are turning up in very large numbers. I was thinking of making a start on my canvass precisely when Cincius says your boy is setting out with this letter – that is, on 17 July at the tribunician elections in the campus. Candidates who seem certain are **Galba, Antonius** and **Q. Cornificius**. I think you will have 10 laughed or groaned at the last. Now **strike your forehead**, some even think of Caesonius. But I do not think **Aquilius** will be a candidate. He has said he will not, has declared illness and urged his monarchy in the courts as an obstacle. **Catilina** will definitely be a candidate if the jury finds that it is not light at midday. About Aufidius and Palicanus I do not think you are waiting for me to write. 15

2   **Caesar** is thought a certainty among those currently canvassing. Thermus is reckoned to be contending with **Silanus**. They are so lacking in both friends and reputation that it seems to me not impossible that **Turius** will slip in ahead of them, but no one holds this view except me. In my calculations it seems it would be most advantageous for Thermus to be elected with Caesar. For there 20 is no one among those who are now campaigning who, if he were to drop back into my year, would seem to be a stronger candidate. Thermus is overseer of the

---

Galba   Publius Sulpicius Galba, patrician, seen as lacking in energy.

Antonius   Gaius Antonius, supporter of Sulla, expelled in 70 from the senate. He had started on his career again and was praetor with Cicero in 66 and would be his colleague as consul in 63. A disreputable character, he was a son of Cicero's old teacher, M. Antonius.

Q. Cornificius   a candidate with Cicero in 64.

strike your forehead   a dramatic gesture used by some orators in the courts; others included clapping one's hands, stamping on the floor and striking thigh and chest.

Aquilius   C. Aquilius Gallus, colleague as praetor in 66 and friend of Cicero, the most eminent jurist of the day. He claimed weak health and his pre-eminent position ('monarchy') in advising the courts prevented him from being a candidate. Cicero is being ironical; Aquilius was a weak candidate.

Catilina   L. Sergius Catilina, praetor in 68, who was facing extortion charges for his governorship in Africa in 65. Cicero was confident Catilina would be found guilty.

Caesar   L. Iulius Caesar, elected consul for 64.

Silanus   D. Iunius Silanus, consul in 62, contending with Thermus for the other consular post.

Turius   a man of small ability but great energy, a frequent speaker, who came within a few centuries of reaching the consulship; so reports Cicero, *Brutus* 237.

Flaminian Way, which will easily have been completed by that time. I should happily add him on to consul Caesar now. This is my informed thinking so far on the candidates. I shall show the greatest diligence in carrying out every function 25 of a candidate. Since **Gaul** seems to carry great influence in the voting, when court business in the forum in Rome has slackened, I shall perhaps make an expedition in September as a *legatus* to **Piso**, to return in January. When I perceive the views of the *nobiles* I shall write to you. All other matters I hope are running smoothly, at least as far as the candidates here in the city go. See that you take responsibility 30 on my behalf for that **band of Pompeius**, our friend, since you are not too far away. Tell him I shall not be angry with him if he does not come for my election.

Rome, July 65 BC

Cicero, Atticus 1.1.1–2 (10)

What makes this letter interesting is that we know what happened and can see how well Cicero forecast. For the elections of 65 BC he was right about L. Iulius Caesar, who was elected with a C. Marcius Figulus. The *Brutus*, written in 46, shows that Cicero may not have been too far wrong about L. Turius. For the elections of 64, when Cicero was a candidate, the three certainties Galba, Antonius and Cornificius were all candidates, together with Catilina.

Not long afterwards Cicero wrote again to Atticus.

1   At this moment I am thinking of defending Catilina, who is a fellow candidate. We have the jury we want, with full agreement of the prosecutor. If Catilina is acquitted, I hope he will associate more closely with me in arranging the campaign. But if it turns out otherwise, I shall put up with it like a man.

2   I need you to return home early. There is a distinctly widespread impression 5 among people that your friends, the nobility, are going to oppose my holding office. I can see you will be of the greatest benefit to me in winning over their support. See, therefore, you are in Rome at the beginning of January, as you have arranged.

Rome, shortly after the previous letter

Cicero, Atticus 1.2.1–2 (11)

- Why does Cicero think of defending Catilina? What might the victims of Catilina's misdeeds in Africa think of Cicero's action and of Roman courts?

Flaminian Way   Rome's Great North Road, 219 miles in length, leading from the city to Ariminum (Rimini) on the Adriatic coast.

Gaul   that part of Gaul south of the river Po.

Piso   C. Calpurnius Piso, consul in 67, governor of Transalpine and Cisalpine Gaul, staunch supporter of the Sullan constitution and stern opponent of the *populares*.

band of Pompeius   Pompeius and his army in the East, mentioned in jocular vein.

After what Cicero wrote in the first of these letters, it is surprising to find him contemplating the defence of Catilina. The prosecutor was Publius Clodius. Cicero did not in the end defend Catilina – it is not known why. The opposition of the *nobiles* is a symptom of their dislike of a 'new man'. Atticus might be a Roman *eques* but his influence and connections were invaluable to Cicero and to his many friends.

Advice on electioneering

Among the manuscripts of Cicero's letters to his friends (*Friends*), there exists a lengthy essay in the form of a letter, the *Commentariolum Petitionis*, 'A Handbook of Electioneering'. It purports to have been written to Marcus Cicero by his brother Quintus to give him advice, as a 'new man', on the conduct of his campaign for the consulship in 64 BC. The authorship continues to be disputed. The author, however, fully understood the context and workings of late republican politics and it is a key document. LACTOR 3, *A Short Guide to Electioneering*, provides a complete translation of the *Commentariolum Petitionis*, selections from which follow.

The author states that there are three key issues to consider for the campaign (2) and then proceeds to advise on the importance of friends (3) and the need to convince the *nobiles* that one is of optimate and not *popularis* sympathy (5).

2   Consider what city this is, what you are seeking, who you are. As you go down to the forum almost every day, you must keep the following in mind: '"I am a new man". I am seeking the consulship. This is Rome.' …

3   Make sure you show off how many and how varied your friends are. Few 'new men' have as many as *you* have. They include all the **publicani**, virtually the 5 whole equestrian order and many **municipia** closely connected with you. Then there are many men of all ranks whom you have defended in the lawcourts and several *collegia* …

---

publicani   men involved in state contracts, especially collecting taxes, members of the equestrian order.

municipia   the towns of Roman citizens in Italy.

collegia   a group of men having a common interest, e.g. trade, craft, or living in a particular neighbourhood. In 64 BC the consuls passed a decree in the senate outlawing such groups as politically disruptive.

5   You must canvass the *nobiles* and **consulars** with care. You must send friends to
     persuade them that our political sympathies have always been with the *optimates*;   10
     we have been in no way *popularis* in politics. If we have ever **spoken in a *popularis***
     manner, we did this to gain the support of Cn. Pompeius in order to have a man
     of great power friendly to our canvass or at least not opposed.

                              (Q. Cicero), *Commentariolum Petitionis* 2, 3, 5

>   This is clear evidence of the jealousy and snobbishness of the elite towards
>   the 'new man'. Elsewhere it is recorded that the nobles thought the consulship
>   polluted if obtained by a 'new man'. Cicero would experience aristocratic
>   *hauteur* frequently in his political career, especially in the 50s.

Since I have explained what assets you possess to counterbalance your lack of
nobilitas, I think I ought now to speak about the importance of the election
campaign. You are a candidate for the consulship. All think you deserve that office,
but some begrudge your holding it. You are by origin a member of the equestrian
order and you are seeking the highest position in the state. It *is* the highest and   5
an office that confers much more distinction on a man who is brave, eloquent
and upright than on any others. Do not imagine that those who have held this
office fail to see how much *dignitas* you too will enjoy once you have obtained it.
I suspect that those born of consular families who have not attained the position
of their ancestors are jealous of you, except in the case of any individuals who are   10
particularly fond of you. Even 'new men' who have been praetors do not, I think,
like the idea of your reaching higher office than they, unless they are obliged to
you for some act of kindness.

                              (Q. Cicero), *Commentariolum Petitionis* 13

>   The author considers the issue of friendship at length, how to win friends
>   and who one's friends are (16), and the support and favour of friends and the
>   people (21). Note how the word friend is stretched for election purposes – 'we
>   are all friends now'.

16   An election campaign for public office may be divided into *two* sorts of activity:
     one is concerned with *securing the support of friends*, the other with *securing the*
     support of the people. The support of friends must be won by acts of kindness,
     which may be spontaneous or through some obligation, long acquaintance, charm

---

nobiles and **consulars**   those of consular families and ex-consuls, crucial supporters in the
canvass.

spoken in a *popularis* manner   a reference to the speech on behalf of Pompeius, and the
need to beware of populist utterances.

and an attractive personality. But this word 'friends' has wider application during 5
an election campaign than at any other time in one's life. Anyone who shows any
degree of goodwill towards you, who pays attention to you, who visits your house
regularly, must be included in the category of 'friends'. It is a particular advantage
to be popular and well liked among those who are friends for genuine reasons.
They are relations through blood or marriage, members of some club, or some 10
other close connection.

21   Three main inducements lead men to display goodwill and to give enthusiastic
support to a candidate in a campaign. They have received favours, they look for
future prospects, or they have a similar outlook and point of view. See how to
provide for each of these factors. 15

(Q. Cicero), *Commentariolum Petitionis* 16, 21

The author notes the importance of appearing in the forum with crowds
of supporters (36) and then suggests ways of winning over the people (41).
Above all he stresses the need to avoid any specific political statement and to
satisfy everyone (53).

36   As far as possible, go down to the forum at fixed times: a large gathering escorting
you every day creates an excellent impression and brings prestige.

41   Now I have said enough about establishing friendships, I must speak about the
other part of the election campaign which involves one's dealings with the people.
This requires remembering names, ingratiating behaviour, being constantly in the 5
public eye, generosity, publicity, putting on a show and having political prospects.

53   In this electioneering you must make absolutely sure there is an eager anticipation
and a positive view of your political prospects. You must not adopt a political
position while campaigning, either in the senate or in a meeting of the people.
You have to keep in mind that the senate must judge that, on the record of your 10
life, you will be an upholder of its authority. The Roman *equites*, the *boni* and the
men of wealth must reckon from your past life that you will be devoted to peace
and quiet times. The masses must reckon you will be favourably inclined to their
interests, since you have adopted a *popularis* line at least in public meetings and
in the courts. 15

(Q. Cicero), *Commentariolum Petitionis* 36, 41, 53

Finally he discusses the perils of electioneering in the city of Rome.

The third point remains: 'This is Rome.' It is a city made up of a mixed mass of peoples where trickery, deceit and vice of every kind are to be found in plenty and where we will have to put up with arrogance and insolence, spite and pride, hatred and interference of many people. It is obvious to me that a man who is operating amid these deep-rooted and widespread evils, which involve so many people, requires great skill and tact to avoid stumbling, scandal and trickery, and to prove to be the one man capable of dealing with so great a variety of characters, opinions and feelings. 5

(Q. Cicero), *Commentariolum Petitionis* 54

---

1 How much of this is relevant or irrelevant to modern elections? In considering the question you should attempt a worldwide view and not restrict your response to western democracy. Think in particular about the United Nations.

2 In one of his speeches Cicero declares that just as one looks for certain qualities when purchasing an estate manager, so the Roman people 'choose their magistrates as the estate manager of the *respublica*. They are quite satisfied if magistrates possess quality and integrity but if they have some skill in addition so much the better' (Cicero, *Plancius* 62). What qualities are sought in political candidates in modern society?

Catilina and Antonius had formed an electoral compact but did not succeed in the consular elections of 64 BC. Cicero was elected at the head of the poll and Antonius was elected second, while Catilina suffered a rebuff. Cicero's achievement was considerable: he was a 'new man', without consular or praetorian ancestry, he came from a *municipium*, and he was elected to the consulship at the earliest possible age with the support of every century in the centuriate assembly. The 'new man' had reached the pinnacle.

6 Catilina and Clodius

A 'popularis' consul, 63 BC

Cicero assumed the office of consul on 1 January 63 BC. As he had been elected first, he presided at meetings of the senate in January and arranged the order of speakers. After the first meeting of the senate Cicero addressed the Roman people in the forum and, having set out at length his credentials as a 'new man', declared he was going to be a *popularis* consul.

6
7   But I am going to declare here that I shall be a *popularis* consul. I realize I have not been elected with the support of powerful men or with the overwhelming influence of a few men but through the judgement of the entire Roman people. I was placed so far ahead of men of the noblest birth I must inevitably appear *popularis* in this office of consul and in the whole of my life. But I badly need   5
you to understand the precise meaning and significance of this word. Now there is a serious error currently abroad because of the deceit and pretence of certain people; they are attacking and obstructing not only the interests but also the well-being and security of the people. They want by means of their speeches to get themselves considered *popularis*.   10

Cicero, *Agrarian Law* 2.6–7

9   I declared in the senate that in this office I would be a *popularis* consul. For what is so *popularis* a thing as peace? … What is so *popularis* a thing as liberty? … What is so *popularis* a thing as tranquillity? It is so pleasurable that you, your ancestors and all the bravest men think they must undertake the greatest tasks so as to be able one day to enjoy tranquillity, especially if they exercise authority and enjoy   5
dignity. Moreover, it is for this reason that we owe our forebears especial thanks and praise, because it is as a result of their labour that we are able to enjoy tranquillity without risk. How can I not be *popularis*, citizens, when I see all these things – peace abroad, the liberty proper to your race and name, tranquillity at home, in a word all the things which are dear and precious to you, assigned to my trust and, in   10
10   a way, to the guardianship of my consulship? Citizens, you must not reckon **a promulgation of free handouts** as something *popularis* and desirable. It can create a fine impression in a speech but in reality can achieve absolutely

---

a promulgation of free handouts promulgation of proposed legislation meant putting the text up in public in the forum and leaving 17 days to elapse before voting was permitted. Here Cicero refers to the proposal of the tribune Servilius Rullus for a programme of extensive land reform, which aimed to satisfy the widespread demand for land and to relieve poverty in Rome and Italy. The evidence comes from Cicero's

nothing except to bankrupt the treasury. Disruption of the lawcourts, overruling decisions of the courts, restoration of the condemned are not to be considered *popularis* – these are usually the last resort of states which are tottering on the brink of ruin. And you must not reckon those who are promising lands to the Roman people to be *popularis*: either they are plotting some secret scheme or they are putting on a fine show, creating false and specious optimism. 15

Cicero, Agrarian Law 2.9–10

> • In this speech, Cicero argues that his opponent Rullus is proposing measures that are popular in the short term but ruinous to the state in the long term. What modern controversies centre on popular but questionable vote-winning proposals?

A case of 'high treason'

In the year 100 BC the activities of the tribune Saturninus and his associates had caused the senate to pass the so-called 'final decree'. In the ensuing tumult Saturninus was killed. Rabirius, now an old man, had been involved with many others in the tribune's death and was in 63 (37 years later) prosecuted for 'high treason' by a tribune, Labienus, with the assistance of Iulius Caesar. The procedure was archaic and the details are complex and obscure. It is likely that Cicero was defending Rabirius before an assembly of the Roman people.

Rabirius has been brought to court on a capital charge, not because he is guilty of some offence, not because people envy him his life, nor because citizens have long-standing, justifiable and intense hostility towards him. The aim is to remove from the *respublica* **that crucial source of help** to our sovereignty and our empire, which has been handed down to us by our forefathers, so that hereafter no 5 resolution of the senate, no executive power of the consuls, no unanimity of the *boni* shall be strong enough to confront the ruin and destruction of the state. In these endeavours to overthrow the state, you will find the reason why an attempt has been made upon the life of one weak, lone old man.

Cicero, Rabirius on a Charge of High Treason 2

speeches in the senate and before the people in opposition to the proposal – 'masterpieces of misrepresentation' (D. Stockton, p. 88). Cicero calls himself 'a people's consul' but proceeds to argue that what on the surface would seem to be wholly in the people's interest is nothing of the sort. His hypocrisy is revealed in his letters but his oratory was so successful that the proposal never came to the vote and Rullus disappears from history; the problem, however, most certainly did *not*.

that crucial source of help Cicero is here referring to the so-called 'final decree'.

boni the politically sound, loyal conservatives, supporters of the senate.

This attack required all to carry out their responsibilities loyally to the *respublica*.

3   It is the responsibility of a loyal consul, when he sees all the resources of the *respublica* being undermined and torn apart, to bring help to his country and to bring rapid assistance for the safety and good fortune of all; to plead for the loyalty of the citizens and to rate his personal safety secondary to the safety of the community. It is at the same time the responsibility of loyal citizens, such as 5 you have shown yourselves to be at all times in the history of the *respublica*, to block approaches that lead to political discord, to strengthen the defences of the *respublica* and to consider the executive power of the consuls and the decision of the senate of supreme importance. You must judge that **the man who has followed such a course of action** is worthy of praise and honour rather than condemnation 10 and punishment.

5   In this situation there is something that I must do first of all: in so serious a conflict which involves the life, the reputation and the fortunes of all, **I ask for the blessing and favour** of Jupiter, the Best and Greatest, and of all the immortal gods and goddesses whose help and support govern this *respublica* far more than the reason 15 and counsel of men. I pray to them that they may allow this day to have dawned so as to preserve the safety of this man and to establish the *respublica* securely.

Cicero, Rabirius on a Charge of High Treason 3, 5

---

1   Can you suggest modern examples of where those in power (governments, dictators, victors in war) use or abuse the law in their own interests?

2   How do modern states try to ensure that the poor get a fair trial?

This case was important because the prosecution by the *populares*, Labienus and Caesar, was seeking to challenge the use of the 'final decree'. From an optimate point of view the decree was the last defence against revolution; the *popularis* view saw it rather as the nobility operating lynch law in their own interests.

---

the man ... course of action   Gaius Rabirius.

I ask for the blessing and favour   we see here how important Cicero believes it to be that his defence of Rabirius should enjoy the blessing and favour of the gods, and should be in harmony with their will since they protect the Roman state and empire. The corollary, of course, is that his opponents in the case, Labienus and Caesar, do not enjoy such blessing and favour and that their prosecution is not in harmony with the will of the gods. Obviously they would not see it in that light.

Iulius Caesar is elected *pontifex maximus*

In 64 BC Quintus Caecilius Metellus Pius, the *pontifex maximus* (High Priest), died. The *pontifex maximus* presided over Roman state religion. The people elected a successor from among the 15 members of the college of priests and he was normally a senior member and an experienced and distinguished political figure. The office of the priests, where records were kept, was the Regia (see p. 47).

Caesar campaigned for the post of *pontifex maximus* with massive bribery. Reflecting on his enormous debts from the campaign, when he set out early in the morning to go down to the election, he is said to have kissed his mother and warned that he would not return except as the *pontifex*. He had two very powerful competitors who were much older and more distinguished; he defeated them, 5 taking more votes in their tribes than either of them took in all the other tribes.

Suetonius, Iulius Caesar 13

---

1   What role do you think religious figures should have in modern society? Should it be limited to personal matters or extend to public issues as well?

2   Does money play a significant role in the outcome of modern elections? If so, what is the source of the money (the candidate's own resources, party coffers or lobbyists' contributions)?

At the probable time of the election, Caesar was a candidate for praetor. His opponents Quintus Servilius and Quintus Catulus had been consuls in 79 and 78 BC respectively. The use of massive bribery may seem surprising, but priests in republican Rome were not ordained and were as much state officials and politicians as they were priests. Much of their priestly activity involved state and political affairs; they were thus wholly different in character and function from a modern clergyman. No one sought a *pontifex* for personal or spiritual advice and counselling. With Caesar's election the *populares* had gained a significant victory.

The consular elections of 63 BC

Shortly before the elections for the consulship of 62 BC, the noble Lucius Sergius Catilina spoke privately to some of his associates about the state of affairs in Rome. When his words became known, Cicero summoned the senate and attempted to delay the elections. Cicero recalls the occasion when, later in the year, he defended L. Licinius Murena, one of the successful candidates.

Now you remember the occasion when the words of that wicked gladiator [Catilina] became publicly known, words which it was said he had spoken at a meeting in his own home: no trustworthy champion, he said, of the poor could be found unless he were himself poor; those who were poor and unfortunate ought not to trust the promises of the well-off and fortunate. And so those who wished to replace what they had spent, to recover what had been taken away from them, ought to look at how much he owed, how little he possessed, how great the risks for which he was prepared; the person who was going to be the leader and standard-bearer of those who were wretched and unfortunate ought to be the least afraid and the most wretched and unfortunate.

Cicero, *Murena* 50

Here is the Roman noble and patrician claiming to be the champion and patron of the poor and unfortunate – a type known throughout history.

You will also remember that, having heard these words, I [Cicero] proposed that a decree of the senate be passed that the elections should not be held the following day, in order that we could deal with these matters in the senate. On the following day in a crowded meeting of the senate I called upon Catilina and prevailed upon him to say whatever he wished about the matters which had been reported to me. As open as ever, he did not justify himself but incriminated and entangled himself. For he then said the *respublica* had **two bodies**, one feeble with a weak head, the other strong but without a head; if the latter were to be worthy of him, it would never lack a leader while he was alive. The crowded senate groaned but **did not, however, pass a decree of sufficient severity** to match his outrageous remarks. Some members were reluctant to decree bold action because they had no fear, others because they were afraid of everything. Catilina rushed out of the senate in joyful triumph. He ought not to have left that meeting alive, particularly since a few days previously courageous Cato had threatened to bring him before the court. Catilina had then replied that if any fire were started against his fortunes, he would put it out not with water but by **utter ruin**.

Cicero, *Murena* 51

two bodies   the first is the senate and nobility, the *boni*, with Cicero at their head while the second is the urban and rural plebs to whom Catilina is offering himself as leader.

did not ... severity   it is fairly clear that Cicero was wanting the senate to pass the 'final decree' but that the majority, for whatever reason, was not convinced by his speech and that he suffered a rebuff. It is important to remember throughout this episode that Catilina was one of the nobility, whereas Cicero was a 'new man'.

utter ruin   Catilina means he will bring about chaos and destruction in Rome, in the manner of a modern-day terrorist.

The character of Lucius Sergius Catilina

In 56 BC Cicero, in defending his protégé Caelius, has to rebut accusations that his client was an intimate friend of Catilina.

12 Catilina possessed, as I think you remember, very many traces of the highest quality, which were not fully developed but sketched only in outline. He enjoyed the company of many criminals while he pretended he was also devoted to men of the highest quality. He often induced people to vice; he encouraged them as often to industry and hard work. The flames of lust blazed in him but he had 5 an active interest in military matters. I do not think there has ever been such an extraordinary creature on earth, a person made up of such contrary, diverse
13 and mutually conflicting natural talents and passions. Who at one moment was more attractive to men of repute, at another more closely associated with the disreputable? Who at one time was a citizen belonging to **the better party**, at 10 another a more deadly enemy of this state? Who more debauched in his pleasures, who more able to endure toil? Who more rapacious in greed, more lavish in generosity? There were then, jurors, these remarkable qualities in the man: to embrace many people in friendship, to protect them with devoted attention, to share what he had with all, to be of service to all his friends in their times of 15 need with his money, influence, physical toil, even crime if necessary, and reckless daring; to change his personality and to control it according to circumstance, to twist and turn this way and that, to live soberly with serious people, congenially with the free and easy, with dignity among the elderly, affably with the young,
14 recklessly with criminals, and without restraint with the depraved. With this 20 varied and complex personality he had gathered all the wicked and reckless men from everywhere but at the very same time he kept hold of many good and brave men because he appeared to possess in some degree a quality that looked like virtue.

Cicero, Caelius 12–14

The historian Sallust gives a similar description of the complex nature of Catilina in his *Catilina* 5, as a preface to his analysis of the decline of morality and the corrupt nature of the late Republic.

The supporters of Catilina

In a speech to the Roman people in the forum Cicero purports to give a description of the followers of Catilina. It requires careful reading and thought.

---

the better party the *optimates*.

17   I will set out for you, citizens of Rome, from what sort of men forces are being recruited; next I shall offer each individual category whatever remedy I can with words of advice.

18   *One category* consists of men who possess estates far larger than the great debts they have run up; they are so attached to their estates that they can in no way be 5 parted from them. These men appear most honourable – for they are wealthy – but their intentions and their case are utterly shameless …

19   *A second category* consists of those who are weighed down with debt but hope for domination; they want absolute control of affairs and think that, when the *respublica* has been thrown into chaos, they can gain the public offices that they 10 have no hope of getting when it is at peace …

20   *The third category* is made up of men who are quite old but toughened through years of training. Manlius – Catilina is now taking over from him – belongs to this category. These are men from the colonies which Sulla established. As a whole I think these colonies are made up of the best and bravest men, but there are 15 colonists who in their sudden and unexpected wealth have flaunted that wealth too extravagantly and without restraint. They build like grandees, take delight in choice estates, huge households of slaves, exquisite banquets; they have fallen into such enormous debt that, if they want to be solvent, they will have **to summon Sulla up from the dead.** 20

21   *The fourth category* is quite a varied, mixed and troublesome lot; they were overwhelmed long ago, they never rise above the surface, they are staggering under long-standing debt, some through idleness, some through bad management, and some through extravagance. Very many of them have become discouraged by summonses and judgments of the courts, by confiscation and sale of their 25 properties, and are said to be taking themselves to that camp.

22   *The fifth category* comprises killers and assassins, in short criminals of all sorts … *The final category*, which is last in order but also in character and style of life, comprises those closest to Catilina, intimate companions of his own choosing, his nearest and dearest; you see them with their neatly combed hair, beautifully 30 groomed, beardless or with long beards, dressed in sleeved tunics down to their ankles – veils not togas; the exertions of their whole life and the toil of all their

23   waking hours are spent upon banquets that last till dawn. All the gamblers, adulterers, homosexuals and perverts are to be found amid this troupe. These boys, so charming and effeminate, have learned not only how to love and be loved, 35 to dance and sing, but also how to use knives and sprinkle poisons. If they do not

---

to summon Sulla up from the dead   these insolvent Sullan colonists can only hope to survive if Sulla the dictator returns from the dead to provide them with the wealth and land he had first given them.

leave the city, if they do not die, even if Catilina dies, know for sure that this group
will be a seedbed of Catilinas in the *respublica*. But what do these poor creatures
want for themselves? Surely they are not going to take their lady-friends with
them to camp? But how will they be able to do without them, especially during 40
these winter nights? How will they endure the frosts and snows of the Apennines?
Perhaps they think that because they have learnt to dance naked at their banquets,
they will therefore more easily withstand the winter.

Cicero, Catilina 2.17–23, selections

> 1 Try making a list of the supporters of Catilina without any of Cicero's value
>   judgements. Is there any common factor?
> 2 Is there any genuine sympathy for the poor from either Cicero or Catilina?
> 3 In modern states what views do governments and political parties have
>   about poverty and the ways to eliminate it?

*Relief of the temple of Iupiter Stator, where at the heavily guarded meeting
of the senate Cicero denounced Catilina in his first Catilinarian speech.*

In the event the consular elections were only briefly postponed. Cicero presided and was escorted to the Campus Martius by a bodyguard of *equites* and wore a breastplate conspicuous beneath his toga so as to protect himself from the alleged violence of Catilina and his associates. For the second year running Catilina was not elected. Whatever backers he had now deserted him and he was driven to desperate measures. The Senate passed the 'final decree' on 21 October instructing the consuls to take measures to protect the *respublica*. On 27 October Manlius rose in open revolt in Etruria and the senate learned of this uprising around the beginning of November. Catilina met with his associates on the evening of 6 November and a plan was made to assassinate Cicero the following day. Cicero received information and the plan failed. On 7 November there was a meeting of the senate. Catilina attended and Cicero denounced him to his face.

Confrontation in the senate

1   How much longer, Catilina, are you going to exploit our patience? How much longer will that madness of yours play games with us? To what length will that unbridled effrontery of yours flaunt itself? Have you in no way been affected by the nightly defence on the Palatine, by the night guards in the city, by the fears

Cicero denounces Catiline. *This famous painting by Cesare Maccari (1840–1919) hangs in the Palazzo Madama in Rome, which has been the seat of the Italian Senate since 1871.*

of the people, by the rallies of all loyal citizens, by **this heavily fortified location** 5
for the meeting of the senate, by the looks and countenances of all around you
here? Do you not realize that your plans are known? Do you not see that your
conspiracy is contained since all here know about it? Do you think that any one
of us does not know what you did last night or the night before, where you were,

2 whom you met, what plans you made? What a changed world and times we live 10
in! The senate realizes these facts, the consul sees them; yet this man remains alive.
Alive, did I say? More than that, he comes into the senate, he takes part in public
debate, he makes a note and marks down each one of us with his eye for slaughter,
while we, brave men that we are, seem to be doing enough for the *respublica* if we
avoid his madness and his weapons. You ought long ago, Catilina, to have been 15
led to your death on the order of the consul; the destruction which you have long
been scheming for all of us, should have been directed upon yourself.

Cicero, *Catilina* 1.1–2

9 Immortal gods! Where in the world are we? What sort of a *respublica* do we
inhabit? In what city are we living? Here, conscript fathers, here among our
number in **this most august and important council in the world,** there are men
planning the death of us all, the destruction of this city and of the whole world as
well. I, the consul, see them; I ask them their opinion about the *respublica*; those 5
who ought to have been slaughtered with the sword, I do not yet wound even with
my tongue! **You were, Catilina, at the house of Laeca last night, I believe;** you
allocated the parts of Italy, you decided where you wanted each person to go; you
picked those to leave behind in Rome, those to lead forth with you; you arranged
the areas of the city for burning, you confirmed that you yourself were about to 10
depart, and you said you had to delay a little longer because I was still alive. Two
Roman *equites* were found to free you of this anxiety and to promise they would

10 kill me in my bed before dawn. I learnt all this almost before your meeting had
broken up; I strengthened and fortified my house with more guards, I shut out
those whom you had sent to greet me the next morning. Indeed those same men 15
arrived at my house at the time when I had predicted to many prominent citizens
that they would.

Cicero, *Catilina* 1.9–10

---

this heavily … senate   the senate met in the temple of Iupiter Stator (the stayer) on
the Palatine, near the house of Cicero, and was guarded by a body of armed *equites*.
Catilina's presence must have surprised many but did not unnerve Cicero.

this most august … world   the senate, whose members were addressed as 'conscript
fathers'.

You were … I believe   this information was relayed to Cicero through Fulvia, the mistress
of one of the conspirators; 'I believe' is ironic – for Cicero knew full well the plans Catilina
had made.

In this situation, Catilina, if you are not willing to face death, then you cannot surely hesitate to go off to some other land and entrust to exile and solitude that life of yours which has been snatched from so many just and deserved punishments? **'Put the matter before the senate,'** you say. That is what you demand; and, if the members of this order decree that you go into exile, you say you will obey. I shall not put this demand to the senate – that is something not in keeping with my practice; however, I shall see that you realize what those here think of you. Leave the city, Catilina, free the *respublica* from fear, and go off into exile, if those are the words you are looking for. So – what are you waiting for? Do you not notice the silence of all here? They are not stopping you, they are not saying anything. Why are you looking for them to express their opinion when you can see clearly what they want from their silence?

Cicero, Catilina 1.20

Sallust records the occasion and makes the following comment.

31.6   Then the consul Marcus Tullius, either because he was afraid of his presence or moved by anger, made a speech, brilliant and useful for the *respublica*. He later
7   wrote it up and published it. When he sat down, Catilina, ready to be wholly deceitful, with his head downcast, began to demand with the words of a suppliant that the fathers should not believe anything about him without good reason: such was the family from which he came, such was the way of life he had established from his youth that his prospects were all good; they should not think that he, a patrician, whose own and whose ancestors' services to the Roman plebs were very many, needed the ruin of the *respublica*, while M. Tullius, an **immigrant in the**
8   **city of Rome**, was saving it. When to this he began adding other insults, they
9   all protested loudly, calling him an enemy of the state and a murderer. At this point, beside himself with rage, 'Since I am surrounded by enemies,' he replied, 'and driven over the top, I shall put out the fire which threatens me by wholesale
32.1   demolition'. Then he rushed out of the senate house and went home.

Sallust, Catilina 31.6–32.1

'Put the matter before the senate' evidence of an interruption by Catilina during Cicero's speech; that Cicero was not willing to put the issue to the vote in the senate on this occasion reveals that many members were not convinced by the consul's evidence and preferred to support the patrician noble.

immigrant in the city of Rome a wounding remark delivered by the proud noble to Cicero, the citizen from the *municipium* of Arpinum, a mere 70 miles from Rome. In contemporary Britain or the United States such a remark uttered in a public place would certainly occasion public uproar and possibly legal action.

Catilina left Rome that same evening and went to join Manlius in Etruria. Around the middle of November Catilina and Manlius were declared *hostes* (enemies of the state), while towards the end of the month Cicero was obliged to defend Murena, one of the successful candidates for the consulship of 62 BC, on a charge of electoral bribery. He was accused by Sulpicius Rufus, a distinguished jurist and an unsuccessful candidate, and by Porcius Cato, the rigid and uncompromising Stoic. Murena was almost certainly guilty, but for Cicero it was absolutely essential for the security of the *respublica* that there should be two consuls in office in January 62.

A last appeal from Catilina

Sallust claims that Catilina, on his departure from Rome, wrote a letter to some ex-consuls and *optimates* declaring that he had been wrongly accused by his enemies and was now going into exile at Massilia (Marseilles), without any admission of guilt. He wrote a rather different letter to the leader of the *optimates*, Quintus Catulus, which Sallust here reproduces. P. McGushin, in his edition of Sallust (p. 123), notes that this letter contains several non-Sallustian words and phrases, which suggests at least some element of authenticity. It is a wonderful example of the scorn and wounded pride of a Roman noble.

1 'Lucius Catilina to Quintus Catulus. Your outstanding loyalty, which I know from experience and which I have appreciated in my great dangers, has given confidence
2 to this appeal of mine. I have therefore decided not to prepare a defence of **this new plan of action**. I have decided to set out an explanation not through any
3 consciousness of guilt. Upon my word, you may know it to be true that I was 5 provoked by wrongs and insults, because I was deprived of the rewards of my hard work and effort and **I did not get a position of *dignitas*.** I undertook, as was my custom, the cause of the poor as a whole not because I was unable to pay debts in my name from my own estate – and the generosity of **Orestilla** and of her daughter would pay off all the debts in other people's names – but because I saw **unworthy** 10 **men** honoured with public office and felt that I had been wrongly suspected and

---

this new plan of action   ambiguous: it could mean going into exile or joining Manlius.

I did … *dignitas*   he failed to obtain what he considered his birthright – the consulship.

Orestilla   Aurelia Orestilla, the third wife of Catilina, a beauty but 'no respectable person ever praised her for anything apart from her beauty'. She was alleged to have procured the death of a stepson.

unworthy men   notably, of course, Cicero.

4   treated as an enemy of the state. It is on these grounds that I have pursued **hopes,**
     honourable enough in view of my situation, of preserving what remains of my
5   *dignitas.* Though I should like to write more, news has come that force is being
6   organized against me. I now commend Orestilla to you and hand her over to your   15
     protection. Please protect her from harm, I ask you in the name of your children.
     Farewell.'

Sallust, Catilina 35.1–6

Meanwhile in Rome the associates of Catilina clumsily tried to involve some
Gallic envoys in the conspiracy. Cicero was informed and the envoys were
persuaded to obtain signed statements from the conspirators, which they did.
As they left Rome they were arrested with the incriminating documents; the
conspirators were brought before the senate on 3 December and admitted
their guilt. It now remained to decide their fate.

'The great debate' on the 'immortal Nones'

On 5 December (the Nones) the senate met in the temple of Concord on the
Capitoline Hill surrounded by armed guards, to debate and to decide the fate
of the conspirators. In this meeting there is evidence of genuine debate. Sallust
gives versions of speeches by Caesar and Cato which were pivotal in reaching
the final decision. Cicero delivered his fourth speech against Catilina.

I see that there are so far two proposals: one from **D. Silanus** recommends that
those who have tried to destroy the state should be punished with death; the other
from **C. Caesar** sets aside the death penalty but includes the most severe of other
available punishments. Each of these men, as befits his dignity and the gravity
of the situation, is concerned about the most severe punishment. The one does   5
not think that those who have tried to deprive all of us and the Roman people of
life, who have tried to destroy the empire and to blot out the name of the Roman
people, ought for a single moment to enjoy life and the air we all breathe; he recalls
that this form of punishment has often been employed in this *respublica* against

---

hopes ... situation   the phrase has the same ambiguity as 'this new plan of action'
above.

D. Silanus   Decimus Iunius Silanus, consul-elect, second husband of Servilia and thus
brother-in-law of Porcius Cato. He spoke at first for the 'extreme penalty', meaning
death, but after the speech of Caesar declared that he had meant life imprisonment by
'extreme penalty'.

C. Caesar   Gaius Iulius Caesar, now *pontifex maximus* and praetor-elect, proposed a
penalty of life imprisonment.

wicked citizens. The other considers that the immortal gods have ordained death   10
not for the purpose of punishment but as necessary and natural, a relief from toils
and woes. That is why wise men have never been unwilling to face death and why
brave men have often been quite happy to face it. But imprisonment, and that for
life, is certainly devised as an exemplary punishment for an unspeakable crime.

Cicero, Catilina 4.7

Now before I come back to ask you your views, I shall say a few words about myself.
I see that I have brought upon myself a host of personal enemies; quite as large
as the gang of conspirators – and you can see it is very large. However, I reckon
that gang vile, feeble and despicable. But should that gang ever be roused by the
criminal madness of someone, should it ever become more powerful than your   5
authority and that of the *respublica*, I shall nonetheless never regret, members
of the senate, my advice and my action. Death, which those men are possibly
threatening me with, is at hand for all. Nobody had gained as much glory in life
as I have through **the decrees with which you have honoured me**. In all other
cases you have decreed a public thanksgiving for distinguished achievements, but   10
uniquely in my case for saving the *respublica*.

Cicero, Catilina 4.20

The senate voted to condemn the conspirators to death. They were immediately
escorted to the prison and executed. The deed had been done. It was at once
controversial: no Roman citizen might be legally put to death without first
being tried before his peers, and the senate was not a court of law. However,
the conspirators were adjudged *hostes* (enemies of the state) and therefore
no longer citizens. The senate and the consuls had been acting in a state of
emergency – the 'final decree' had been passed on 21 October. But Cicero had
made enemies and one would soon embarrass him by vetoing the speech with
which he had prepared to celebrate his last day of office.

- In the late Republic it was extremely rare for Roman citizens to be judicially
  executed. The death penalty in the modern world is a controversial and
  much-debated issue. What do you think about the arguments on both sides?
  It would be worth reading Caesar's arguments in full (Sallust, *Catilina* 51)
  before considering the matter.

---

the decrees with which you have honoured me   at the end of the meeting of the senate
on 3 December a decree of thanksgiving to the gods was passed in Cicero's name – the
first ever for a civilian – while Catulus called Cicero 'the father of his country'.

The end of Catilina – the battle of Pistoria

While these events were taking place in Rome, Catilina joined Manlius in camp at Faesulae in northern Etruria; news of the executions demoralized his troops and he decided to make for Gaul, but was blocked by government forces. At Pistoria in early 62 BC he was surrounded and decided to risk battle with an army commanded by Cicero's colleague Antonius, who missed the battle because of an attack of gout. It was a short and hard-fought battle.

1   It was only when the battle was over that you could see clearly how great had been
2   the daring and determination in the army of Catilina. Almost every individual lay
3   dead in the position he had occupied while alive. There were a few in the centre
     whom the **praetorian cohort** had scattered; they had fallen back some distance
4   but all had been wounded on the front of their bodies. Catilina was found far ahead 5
     of his own forces among the corpses of his enemies; he was still breathing faintly,
     his face still retaining that fierce temper which he had shown when he was alive.

Sallust, Catilina 61.1–4

The ceremony of the Bona Dea

Publius Clodius Pulcher belonged to the distinguished noble family of the Claudii, but he adopted the plebeian form of the name. On a night in December 62 BC he had dressed as a woman and gained access to the house of the *pontifex maximus* and praetor Iulius Caesar, where aristocratic Roman women were performing the religious rites of the Good Goddess for the health and prosperity of the *respublica*. The rites were secret and men were strictly excluded. Rumour had it that Clodius was having an affair with Caesar's wife. It was a scandal in high places and the enemies of Clodius were out to destroy him. Clodius was determined not to be destroyed.

I imagine you have heard that when a sacrifice was being conducted at the house of Caesar on behalf of the people a man in woman's clothes entered the house. After the Vestal virgins had conducted the sacrifice afresh, the matter was raised in the senate ... Following a decree of the senate it was then referred to the Vestals and the pontiffs, who declared that it was sacrilege. After that, in accordance with 5
a decree of the senate the consuls promulgated a bill. Caesar sent his wife notice of divorce. The consul Piso, because of his friendship with Clodius, is working hard to have the bill rejected, although it is a bill that he is himself proposing as a result of a senatorial decree on a religious matter. Messalla [the other consul] is so far taking a strong and severe line. 10

Rome, January 61 BC

Cicero, Atticus 1.13.3(13)

---

praetorian cohort   elite troops fighting with the commander of the army.

We see here several features of Roman public religion. A religious ritual, which has been impugned, must first be conducted again. The senate, as the body responsible for relations between the gods and the *respublica*, is consulted and refers the matter to the persons concerned – pontiffs and Vestals. The senate accepts their decision and proposes to establish a court to try a case of sacrilege. The consul of 61 BC, M. Pupius Piso, is embarrassed at having to propose the measure because he is a personal friend of the accused Clodius – a good example of how personal and political issues could clash. Caesar divorced his wife, Pompeia (hence the remark 'Caesar's wife must be above suspicion', derived from Plutarch, *Caesar* 10.9).

The trial of Clodius and its aftermath

Everyone knew that Clodius was guilty and his condemnation was universally expected, but he was acquitted. Atticus has written to Cicero seeking an explanation, which Cicero duly gives.

2 Now if you ask the reason for the acquittal, to go back now to the first point, it was the poverty and the disreputable character of the jurors. It was the idea of Hortensius that caused **this** to happen. He was afraid that Fufius would veto the proposal put forward in accordance with the **senatorial decree**. He did not see that it would have been better had that man been left in disgrace and in the **dress** 5
of a defendant rather than be committed to a weak jury. But his hatred led him into rushing to bring the case to court; he declared that Clodius' throat would be cut even by a **sword made of lead**.

4 When during the preliminary hearings individual matters were brought for decision, the court showed incredible strictness and unanimity. The defendant 10
failed to obtain any request, the prosecutor was given more than he asked for. In short, Hortensius was triumphant because he had had such foresight. There was

---

this Hortensius persuaded people that the tribune Fufius might propose a motion that the jurors be chosen by lot. This would favour Clodius as the selected jurors could then be tampered with.

senatorial decree the senate had proposed that the urban praetor should himself select the jurors, which would have been decidedly unfavourable to Clodius. Hortensius, however, fearing Fufius would veto this proposal and convinced that Clodius could not escape conviction, persuaded people to allow Fufius' proposal.

dress of a defendant defendants in court regularly put on the dress of mourning to excite and obtain sympathy.

sword made of lead even the bluntest instrument would put an end to Clodius, so patently guilty.

no one who did not think that the accused had been convicted a thousand times. When I was brought **into court as a witness** I believe you will have heard from the shouting of Clodius' supporters how the jurors all stood up and surrounded me, 15 how they showed off **their bare throats to Clodius in exchange for my life** …

5   When the jurors shouted out in my defence, just as if I were **the salvation of Rome**, the accused and all his supporters collapsed. The day following, the same sort of crowd gathered at my house as that which escorted me home when I laid down my consulship. 20

Cicero, *Atticus* 1.16.2–5 (*16*)

The jurors asked for protection, which a senatorial decree granted. No one imagined the accused would even reply to the charges.

5   You know that **Calvus … my eulogist** whose speech flattering me I had told you about. He completed the whole business, within two days, through one slave and he was from a gladiatorial school. He summoned the jurors to his house, made promises, stood surety, and made gifts. And then – ye gods, what a shocking business – for some of the jurors there was a bonus to their pay – nights with 5 certain ladies and introductions to youths. Most good men departed, the forum was full of slaves. However, **25 jurors**, although they faced very great danger, were courageous enough and preferred to **face death** than cause universal ruin. There were 31 whose famine moved them more than their fame. When Catulus saw one of them, he asked, 'Why did you ask us for a bodyguard? Was it because you were afraid 10 6   your money would be stolen?' There you have, as briefly as possible, the sort of trial it was and the reason for the acquittal.

Rome, beginning of July 61 BC

Cicero, *Atticus* 1.16.5–6 (*16*)

---

into court as a witness Cicero broke Clodius' alibi, which was to have the most serious consequences for Cicero himself. 'Marcus Tullius himself was questioned and stated that Clodius had come to his house to pay a morning call on the very day that Clodius had claimed he had been at Interamna almost 90 miles from the city; quite obviously he wished it to appear that he had no opportunity to commit adultery in Rome.' So notes a later commentator.

their … life the jurors were prepared to defend Cicero physically, at the risk of their lives, from the supporters of Clodius, the slaves and thugs filling the forum.

the salvation of Rome recalling his handling of the Catilinarian conspiracy.

Calvus … my eulogist Marcus Crassus.

25 jurors the jury consisted of 56 members; 25 voted 'guilty' and 31 acquitted Clodius. We don't know how the jury split, as we do for the trial of Milo in 52 (see p. 122). On this episode see M. Beard, J. North and S. Price, pp. 129–30.

face death at the hands of Clodius' supporters.

7 The 'First Triumvirate'

The background, 61–59 BC

Gaius Iulius Caesar. Note the hair swept forward to disguise his baldness.

Pompeius had returned to Italy from the East in late 62 BC. He had dismissed his troops on arrival at Brundisium; he would be no dictator in the Sulla mould. He was the great *popularis* hero but at the same time he looked for acceptance by the *optimates* – indeed, having divorced his wife Mucia, he sought a marriage alliance within the family of Cato, only to receive a public rebuff. He had two political requirements: he wanted ratification by the senate of the administrative arrangements he had made in the East and he wanted land for his veteran soldiers. He was so resolutely resisted on both fronts by his optimate opponents that by the year 60 neither requirement had been satisfied.

In early 60 Caesar returned from his governorship in Further Spain wishing to celebrate a triumph and to stand for the consulship of 59. His opponents, led by Cato, sought to oppose him on both fronts. Caesar had to wait outside the walls of Rome while the senate considered whether to grant him a triumph. A candidate for the consulship had to appear before the consul presiding at the election in person and when Caesar asked to be freed from this regulation, Cato talked at such length that the senate was dismissed before reaching a decision. Caesar gave up the triumph, entered the city, made his submission and was elected. It was not an absolute victory since his colleague was to be a die-hard optimate, Marcus Bibulus, who was the son-in-law of Cato. Furthermore, in deciding the provinces which the consuls of 59 should have when they completed their year of office, the senate had allocated them the forests and cattle-paths of Italy – an insignificant assignment, if not an insult.

As a result of Pompeius' achievements in the East, the economic situation had improved immeasurably, so that the *publicani* who handled the collection of taxes in the province of Asia looked to make a handsome profit. Competition for the tax contract – it was for a five-year period – had been fierce and the successful company now recognized that it had overbid and was seeking a rebate on the contract. Marcus Crassus strongly supported their request but was resolutely opposed by Cato.

Some time, probably during the year 60, Iulius Caesar, Gnaeus Pompeius and Marcus Licinius Crassus made an informal agreement to aid one another in achieving their objectives. This compact was not made public nor were its terms revealed. It is frequently called the 'First Triumvirate' by modern historians, a convenient shorthand provided one remembers that neither its members nor any contemporaries ever so described it. In hindsight it might appear to have been a *coup d'état* which spelt the doom of the *respublica*.

Cicero's letters to Atticus, 61–60 BC

Cicero writes to Atticus in December 61 BC about two matters which were threatening to cause a split between the senate and the *equites*.

8   I believe you have heard that our *equites* have almost split off from the senate. In the first place they were very annoyed that a bill had been promulgated by decree of the senate **for judicial investigation** concerning those who had taken money to give verdicts. By chance I was not present when the decision had been taken on the matter and I realized that the equestrian order was annoyed, but I 5 did not say so openly. I upbraided the senate, so I thought, with great authority. I

9   was stern and eloquent in a cause that was certainly not respectable. Now another delight from the *equites*, almost intolerable. I have not only tolerated it but even supported it with my eloquence. Those who had purchased the tax contract for Asia from the censors complained that through eagerness they had fallen into 10 error and **paid much too high a price**. They asked that the contract be cancelled. I was the leader among their supporters or actually the second, for Crassus encouraged them to dare make the request. A disagreeable matter, a disgraceful request and an admission of recklessness. There was the greatest danger that

---

for judicial investigation   the equestrian members of juries in the courts were not subject to any legal process for corrupt behaviour, unlike senators; thus they resented this action.

paid much too high a price   with the victories of Lucullus and Pompeius in the East, the prospects for the Asian tax contract had seemed good for the first time in some years; great competition led to overbidding and the successful company now sought a rebate on its contract.

if they had not gained their request they would be openly **alienated from the** 15
senate. In this matter I more than anyone brought them help and arranged that
they might deal with a very full meeting of a generous senate. On 1 December
and the day following I spoke at length about the dignity of the orders and about
unity. The issue has not yet been resolved but the wishes of the senate have been
made clear. One person had spoken against it, **Metellus**, the consul-designate. 20
However, because of the **shortness of daylight** it did not get as far as that hero of
ours, Cato, who was going to speak.

Rome, December 61 BC

Cicero, Atticus 1.17.8–9 (17)

> Cicero begins his catalogue of political woes with the case of Publius Clodius
> and the violation of the rites of the Bona Dea, which was then followed with
> a scandalous trial.

The *respublica* then suffered the disaster of a **bought, debauched trial**. See what
followed next. **A consul** was imposed upon us; none, apart from philosophers
such as we are, could look upon him without a sigh. What a great blow that was!
Then the senate passed a decree on electoral bribery, and on the courts, but no
statute was carried. The senate was bombarded with criticism; the *equites* were 5
alienated because of the proposal: '**whoever in the matter of acting as a juror**'.

---

alienated from the senate, unity   Cicero was keen to try to preserve the 'harmony of the
orders', that unity of the senatorial and equestrian orders which had been formed during
his consulship and which he regarded as essential for the maintenance of the *respublica*.
The action of the senate in blocking equestrian requests threatened that unity. He never
accepted that this harmony was something born of the particular circumstances of 63 and
was unlikely to become permanent.

Metellus   Quintus Metellus Celer, consul in 61.

shortness of daylight   the meeting of the senate was in December, when daylight is
limited; meetings of the senate were permitted only in daylight and a common method
of obstruction was to 'talk out' a proposal until night approached, when the meeting
had to be dismissed.

bought, debauched trial   the trial of Clodius for sacrilege, the corruption of the jury
with money and introductions.

A consul   Lucius Afranius, a military associate of Pompeius with a talent for dancing,
who, as the consul 'imposed' by Pompeius to achieve his two requirements, was a total
disaster.

'whoever in the matter of acting as a juror'   a partial quote from a statute concerning
investigation of jurors who had taken bribes. The *equites* had previously not been subject
to this statute.

Thus in that year the **two foundations of the** *respublica* which I alone established were overthrown: the authority of the senate was discarded and the concord of the orders was broken off.

Rome, January 60 BC

Cicero, Atticus 1.18.3 (18)

> In March 60 BC Cicero writes to Atticus of his actions in checking an agrarian law which the tribune Flavius was proposing with the support of Pompeius in an attempt to achieve one of his requirements. There are some surprising points in this letter: the holding of a public meeting in the forum supporting landowners; the fact that potential beneficiaries of a land law thanked a man who was effectively blocking it; and the way in which Cicero's actions affected his relations with Pompeius.

Affairs in the city are as follows: an agrarian proposal is being vigorously pushed by a tribune Flavius at the instigation of Pompeius. The proposal has nothing *popularis* about it apart from its **proposer/instigator**. With the **agreement of a** *contio* I removed all those items which were to the disadvantage of private landowners. I set aside that land which had been public in the consulship of **P. Mucius and L.** 5 **Calpurnius**; I confirmed the possessions of the Sullan settlers … One clause I did not reject was that land might be purchased with **the windfall money** which is being received from the new revenues over the five-year period. The **senate is opposed** to this whole scheme of an agrarian law, suspecting that some new position of power is being sought for Pompeius. Pompeius is exerting himself vigorously, wishing 10 the proposal to be carried. I, **with the thanks of the beneficiaries of the law**, am

---

two foundations of the *respublica*   Cicero as consul had striven to defend the position of the senate and promoted the union of the senatorial and equestrian orders.

proposer/instigator   the Latin texts have variants, proposer meaning Flavius, instigator Pompeius.

agreement of a *contio*   it is surprising that a public meeting supports the interests of property owners but this needs to be read with the sentence: 'One clause … five-year period', which is the whole aim of Flavius' proposal and which Cicero accepts, despite opposition from the senate. There is an acute analysis of this issue in R. Morstein-Marx, pp. 210–12.

P. Mucius and L. Calpurnius   consuls in 133.

the windfall money   the revenues coming to the treasury as a result of Pompeius' eastern campaigns.

senate is opposed   continuing senatorial and optimate hostility to Pompeius and his pre-eminence.

with … law   again, this needs to be read with the sentence showing Cicero's support for purchase of land. Cicero is securing the rights of property owners, 'his army', but at the same time supporting Pompeius and the potential beneficiaries of the law.

confirming the holdings of all private owners, for as you know they are my army – the men of means. I am satisfying the people and Pompeius (for I want that too) by the purchase. When the details have been fully settled I think the **dregs of the city** can be cleared away and **the desolate parts of Italy repopulated.**   15

Rome, 15 March 60 BC

Cicero, Atticus 1.19.4 (19)

- What is your reaction to Cicero's use of the expression 'dregs of the city'?

Cicero had hoped to play the role of esteemed consular following his handling of the Catilinarian conspiracy, but he felt he was never fully accepted by the *optimates*, who were envious of his success, if not actually hostile. He was distressed by the outcome of Clodius' trial and the potential split between senate and *equites*. In the light of this, he decided he must look for a stronger and more reliable ally: Pompeius. Cicero writes to Atticus about this in June 60 BC.

You reprimand me in a gentle sort of way for my friendship with Pompeius. I would not want you to think that I have become a close associate of his for the sake of protection. But the situation was that if any dissension were to arise between us there were bound to be major political conflicts in the *respublica*. If I have foreseen and taken provision for this, it is not that I have departed from my constitutional 5 position as an optimate but that Pompeius is a **better citizen** and has laid aside some part of the lack of principle characteristic of a *popularis*. I would have you know that, in spite of many people encouraging him to attack them, Pompeius talks publicly in more glowing terms about my achievements than about his own. He declares that he has served the *respublica* well but I have saved it. I am not sure how much benefit 10 his doing this is to me; it benefits the *respublica* at any rate. Furthermore, what if I could make Caesar a better citizen? The winds are very favourable for him at the moment. Am I then doing all that much harm to the *respublica*?

Cicero, Atticus 2.1.6 (21)

---

dregs of the city   Cicero had publicly objected to the tribune Rullus using this phrase of the urban plebs in 63, but here uses it himself in private correspondence. It shows that Flavius' measure included the urban poor together with the veterans of Pompeius. The measure met with such resolute opposition from the consul Metellus that Flavius had him imprisoned. He was released at the instigation of Pompeius and the measure was never put to the vote.

the desolate parts of Italy repopulated   the population of ancient Italy is currently a central topic among Roman historians. The debate can best be followed in N. Rosenstein and R. Morstein-Marx (eds.), ch. 6.

better citizen   more inclined to be an optimate.

1 Do you have the feeling that Cicero is being realistic? Or living in a world of make-believe?

2 How genuine are Pompeius' 'glowing terms' about Cicero likely to have been?

3 Why do you think Atticus may have had reservations about Cicero's friendship with Pompeius?

One might feel that Cicero is exaggerating his own and Pompeius' political importance, and that he is deceiving himself about his influence upon Pompeius. His desire to convert Caesar is fascinating. Caesar admired Cicero much more than Pompeius ever did.

Another point: if no one envied me, if all supported me, as they should do, the medicine would still have to be administered all the same to cure the diseased parts of the *respublica* rather than to cut them off. But as things are, the equestrian order, which I **once stationed** on the Capitoline Hill with you as standard-bearer and leader, has deserted the senate. **Our leading citizens** think they are close to   5 heaven if they have bearded mullet in their fishponds to feed by hand, while they ignore everything else. Don't you think that I am doing enough good if I ensure that **those who are able to do harm** do not want to?

Cicero, Atticus 2.1.7 (21)

> Cicero often complains about envy and lack of support in his efforts to deal with political problems and about the leading citizens who withdrew from day-to-day politics into idle leisure.

As for our friend Cato, your regard for him is no greater than mine; but even though he has the best of intentions and the highest integrity, he sometimes harms the *respublica*. He gives his views as if he were in the **Plato's** *Republic*, not in the **cesspit of Romulus**. It is absolutely right that one who has accepted money

---

once stationed   to guard the meeting of the senate on 5 December 63 to discuss the fate of the Catilinarian conspirators.

Our leading citizens   Cicero's 'fish-fanciers', men such as Hortensius, Lucullus and Philippus who had their fishponds stuffed with the most expensive fish and largely ignored political affairs. It is indicative of a luxurious style of life in the late Republic that was wholly at odds with traditional Roman frugality. Cato enjoyed his wine but is unlikely to have cultivated bearded mullet.

those who are able to do harm   Caesar and Pompeius.

Plato's *Republic*   the famous work of the Athenian philosopher Plato on the ideal state.

cesspit of Romulus   Rome, the city founded by Romulus, described unflatteringly as a sewer, akin to the previous remark of Cicero about removing the 'dregs' from the city.

to give a verdict as a juror should come before a court. Cato proposed this and the 5
senate agreed. The *equites* are at war with the senate house but not with me, for I
was against it. It is the height of impudence for the *publicani* to want to renounce
their contract. We should have put up with the loss so as to keep the *equites* with us.
Cato resisted and prevailed. Now, we have a **consul in prison** and riots occurring
ever more frequently, while **none of those** who used to gather to defend the state 10
when I and my successors were consuls, has breathed a word of support.

Antium (?), June 60 BC

Cicero, Atticus 2.1.8 (21)

> **1** Is the unflinching principle of a Cato possible in modern politics?
>
> **2** Do you feel that politicians are right to compromise to attain desirable ends?

However one regards Cicero's opinions, this letter provides a useful description
of the political figures and some of the issues of the day. One might be tempted
to criticize Cicero in comparison with Cato. The latter was inflexible in holding
to his political principles, while Cicero was prepared to make concessions, as
in the matter of the *equites*. He perceived a greater advantage in maintaining
concord between senate and *equites* in order to defend the *respublica* against
the domination of any individual or faction.

By the end of 60 BC Cicero had to face difficult decisions. Caesar, consul-
elect, had published a comprehensive agrarian proposal and intended to see it
through. It is clear that he had made overtures to Cicero seeking his support.

3   **The matter** requires careful consideration. Either I must put up brave resistance
to the agrarian law, which will mean a stiff fight but one full of credit, or I must
keep quiet, which effectively means burying myself in **Solonium or Antium**.
I can even give my help. They tell me Caesar has not the slightest doubt that this
is what I will do. **Cornelius**, that's **Balbus**, I mean the close friend of Caesar, has 5

---

consul in prison   the tribune Flavius had the consul Metellus Celer put in prison for
opposing his land-law.

none of those   the leading citizens, including the fish-fanciers, sunk in torpor and
idleness.

The matter   what action to take over the agrarian proposal of the consul-elect Caesar,
clearly designed to meet the requirement of Pompeius and thus confirming agreement
between them.

Solonium or Antium   country retreats of Cicero, implying a complete withdrawal from
politics.

Cornelius Balbus   he came from Cadiz in Spain, gained citizenship as a result of service in
the war against Sertorius, was first associated with Pompeius and later became a close
adviser and principal agent of Caesar.

been at my house. He assures me that Caesar will make use of my advice and that of Pompeius on all matters and that he will do his utmost **to reconcile Crassus** **to Pompeius**. The consequences are as follows: close association with Pompeius, with Caesar too if I want it, reconciliation with my enemies, peace with the masses, and security in old age … I do not think I can hesitate. I must abide by what I have 10 always held best: **'one omen is best – to fight for the fatherland'.**

4

Rome (?), late December 60 BC

Cicero, Atticus 2.3.3–4 (23)

Speaking in the senate more than three years later Cicero reported that Caesar had invited him to be involved in the administration of the agrarian law, 'to be one of three men of consular rank most closely associated with himself' (Cicero, *Consular Provinces* 41 – see p. 90); clearly, that is, to join the triumvirate. He had offered Cicero any post as *legatus* that he wanted. Cicero had firmly rejected all these offers as contrary to his political principles, but not without gratitude.

- Why do you think Caesar made so many efforts to win over Cicero?

Caesar's consulship, 59 BC

Caesar became consul on 1 January 59 BC. Events moved rapidly. Caesar brought the agrarian law before the senate, agreeing to amend any clause that was objectionable. None was found but the senate, led by Bibulus and Cato, was obstructive. Caesar then brought the proposal before the people and it was voted into law by the use of force. Pompeius' arrangements in the East were ratified and the *publicani* got their rebate. The pact was strengthened by a political marriage when Pompeius married Iulia, the daughter of Caesar.

---

to reconcile Crassus to Pompeius   the date when the so-called 'First Triumvirate' was formed is a problem. *If* Caesar and his agent are being honest in what they report to Cicero, then the compact of the Three has not yet been formed. Almost certainly Caesar had been supported in his bid for the consulship by Pompeius and perhaps also separately by Crassus, who never failed to back a promising candidate. Crassus and Pompeius, it will be recalled, had been at variance since their consulship in 70. It was Caesar who managed to reconcile them.

'one … fatherland'   words of the Trojan Hector, from Homer, *Iliad* 12.243. Cicero intended to remain loyal in defence of the *respublica*. As often in his letters, Cicero quotes a line in Greek, in which he was fluent as were so many Roman nobles of the period.

The reaction of Bibulus

When Bibulus failed to prevent the enactment of Caesar's first agrarian law, he resorted to religious obstruction, declaring that he was 'observing the heavens', an action which meant that voting assemblies of the Roman people might not be held. Caesar ignored his action and worked through his legislative programme, not without violence. Cicero is here addressing the college of pontiffs in 57 BC in the presence of his enemy Clodius.

It was when **your tribunate was tottering and weakening** that you suddenly became the champion of the auspices. You brought Marcus Bibulus and the augurs before a public meeting. In reply to your question the augurs stated that when 'observing the heavens' is taking place, business cannot be conducted in the popular assembly. In answer to your question Marcus Bibulus declared that he 5 had been observing the heavens.

Cicero, On His House 40

Although Caesar ignored this action of Bibulus and his later attempts at obstruction and withdrawal to his house, the validity of his legislation might thus be called into question at some subsequent time, and attempts made to cancel his measures. Faced with possible threats, the members of the triumvirate would need to continue their compact and remain united.

Cicero defends Gaius Antonius

After his defeat of Catilina, Antonius was proconsul in Macedonia; his performance was on a par with his disreputable character and he was recalled to face prosecution. A reluctant Cicero was obliged to defend his former colleague; but Antonius was condemned and went into exile, much to the delight of former supporters of Catilina. When speaking in 57 BC before the college of pontiffs, Cicero recalled one consequence of remarks he had made in defence of Antonius before the extortion court in 59.

It was around midday when I made some complaints about the political situation in court which seemed to me to have some bearing on my case. I was defending my colleague, Gaius Antonius. Some scoundrels relayed these remarks to certain **worthy persons** in a version quite different from what I had said. At three o'clock

---

your tribunate was tottering and weakening   as the tribunate of Publius Clodius in 58 was coming to its close.

worthy persons   Caesar, or Caesar and Pompeius.

on the very same day **your adoption** took place. The interval in all other legislation 5
must be **three market days**. If an interval of three hours is sufficient in the case of
an adoption, then I find no fault at all.

Cicero, On His House 41

Cicero's ill-timed criticism was a serious personal miscalculation and,
knowing from his letters what he felt about the Three and their actions,
one may wonder how distorted 'the remarks relayed by some scoundrels'
actually were. Caesar, as *pontifex maximus*, presided and Pompeius, as augur,
assisted at the adoption. It seems that the three market days required were
disregarded. Clodius' adoption was to have serious consequences for Cicero
when as tribune in 58 BC he acted against Cicero for his execution of the
Catilinarian conspirators.

Cicero's letters to Atticus, 59 BC

Twenty-two letters from Cicero to Atticus written between April and
September 59 BC survive, many of which contain his reactions and comments
on what was happening in Rome. Cicero initially withdrew from Rome to
his country estates to devote himself to writing, while Atticus was in Rome.
By the time he returned in June, Atticus had left for his estate in Epirus in
north-west Greece. The last eight letters in the series date from this time.
A selection from them follows. In the first, Cicero finds Pompeius' actions
difficult to understand and is critical of him.

I simply do not know what our friend **Gnaeus** is thinking about … how people
have been able to lead him along even to this point. He has up until now been
using sophistries like these: he approves **Caesar's laws**, but Caesar himself, he

---

your adoption   Clodius changed his status from patrician to plebeian, thereby enabling
him to stand for the office of tribune of the plebs.

three market days   by a law passed in 98 such a period – 17 days – had to elapse between
the publication and the voting on a proposed statute, and the same was required for
an adoption. Cicero declares that this certainly did not happen in the case of Clodius'
adoption – it was three hours, not three market days – and thus his adoption and tribunate
were invalid. The purpose of the law in 98 was precisely to prevent such occurrences as
Cicero describes. In the modern world, in government, business and organizations of all
sorts, it is a frequent requirement that notice of proposals or amendments or questions
be given by a specified date before scheduled meetings for just the same reason.

Gnaeus   Pompeius.

Caesar's laws, his actions   Pompeius supported the laws of Caesar, but the manner of
their enactment is a matter for which Caesar was personally responsible.

says, must answer for **his actions**. He approved the **agrarian law**, but whether it might have been **vetoed** or not, he says, was absolutely no concern of his. He approved that the **business of the Alexandrian king** should at last be completed – whether Bibulus had been observing the heavens at that time was not for him to enquire. In **the matter of the** *publicani* he wished to accommodate that order – what would have happened if Bibulus had come down to the forum at that time he could not have divined. But now, **Sampsiceramus**, what are you going to say? That you have arranged **revenue from Mount Antilibanus** and removed it from the **Campanian land**? Well? How are you going to carry that point? 'I shall keep you down,' he says, 'with Caesar's army.' No you won't, I can assure you. It's not so much that army that will keep me down as **those ungrateful men**, who are called *boni* but have never, either with words or with rewards, given me back any benefit or thanks.

Formiae, April/May 59 BC

Cicero, *Atticus* 2.16.2 *(36)*

The regime of the Three was universally detested. Here Cicero writes of another offer from Caesar.

2   You *must* realize that nothing has ever been so infamous, so disgraceful, so universally disagreeable to men of all sorts, orders and ages as the state of affairs that now exists. It is more so, I assure you, than I would have wished, let alone have imagined possible. These *populares* have taught even well-mannered men to hiss.

---

agrarian law, vetoed   Caesar's first agrarian law was vetoed, but the veto was ignored and the law passed by the use of force.

business of the Alexandrian king   the restoration by the Three of Ptolemy Auletes of Egypt to his throne in Alexandria for a vast sum of money.

the matter of the *publicani*   the rebate on the tax contract.

Sampsiceramus   a derogatory nickname given to Pompeius by Cicero in his letters and the name of a king of Emesa in Syria.

revenue from Mount Antilibanus, Campanian land   in return for the eastern revenues – Antilibanus is a mountain range in Lebanon – Pompeius had supported Caesar's second land-law allocating Campanian land. The first law had not produced enough land to satisfy all the prospective settlers.

'I shall … Caesar's army'   the threat is to control the citizen body by the use of military force, the method of modern military dictatorships.

those ungrateful men   Cato, Hortensius and their like. Cicero continually complains of their lack of gratitude and appreciation for his saving of the *respublica* in 63. They were, in his view, envious, but perhaps condescending to a 'new man'.

Bibulus is in the clouds, though I do not know why, but he is praised as if he were 5
'the one man who by delay saved the *respublica* for us'. Pompeius, my hero, has
brought about his own ruin, a fact that causes me very great distress. They have
the goodwill of no one. I fear it may be necessary for them to use terror. Personally
I am not fighting their regime because of my friendship with Pompeius but I am
not approving it either. I do not wish to condemn all my previous achievements. 10
I take a middle way.

3   Public feeling has been made very clear at the theatre and the shows. At the
gladiatorial games both the giver of the show and those who had been invited
were bombarded with hisses, while at the games of Apollo the tragic actor
Diphilus attacked Pompeius savagely: 'To our misfortune thou art great.' He 15
was obliged to give a host of encores. At the lines 'a time will come when you
will bitterly regret that same prowess' the whole theatre erupted with shouts,

---

Bibulus is in the clouds by this time Bibulus had withdrawn to his house and was
contenting himself with issuing stinging edicts which were posted up and read with
amazing enthusiasm and support by people in the city. Cicero doubted his action would
achieve much.

'the one man ... for us' a famous line of the early father of Roman poetry, Ennius,
referring to Quintus Fabius Maximus, who by avoiding pitched battle with Hannibal in
the Second Punic War (218–201 BC) eventually brought about his defeat.

Pompeius ... ruin evidence shows that Pompeius, although he had by this time gained
his objectives, recognized that it had been at the price of unpopularity such as he had
never experienced before. He was most unhappy with himself, an unhappiness Cicero
shared.

Public feeling ... shows this is an important issue of Roman republican politics and
currently a topic of debate among scholars. The action of the Roman people here at the
games and in the theatre shows that the people possessed some political influence. The
elite were not able to arrange political matters simply to suit themselves without taking
any account of the 'voice of the people'. In elections, in legislation, in the courts, the
people could make their views known by reacting *en masse*. They did not possess political
initiative – it was the responsibility of the magistrate to decide who spoke at meetings –
but the people voiced approval or dissent, the latter in this period often accompanied by
violent reaction. This does not mean that Rome was in any sense a democracy like that of
fifth- and fourth-century Athens, but it is clear that the people could not be ignored and
the elite politician who so attempted risked embarrassment, defeat and sometimes worse.
(See F. Millar, *passim*.)

gladiatorial games gladiatorial games put on by Gabinius, who was standing for the
consulship of 58.

games of Apollo these games, put on by the urban praetor, lasted eight days (6–13
July): two days of games in the Circus Maximus with horse-racing, the rest given over to
dramatic productions, as mentioned in Cicero's letter.

great seen obviously as a reference to Pompeius Magnus (the Great).

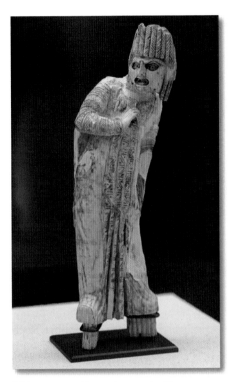

This statuette of a tragic actor is of ivory coloured blue, with the sleeves striped blue and yellow. The actor, whose mouth can be seen through his mask and who is wearing high, stilt-like shoes, is playing the part of a woman.

and similarly with other lines. Such were the lines that you might think they had been written specially by an enemy of Pompeius. When 'If neither laws nor custom can compel' and other lines were spoken there were loud murmurs and shouts of approval. When Caesar entered, the applause died. Young Curio followed. He was applauded just as Pompeius had once been when the *respublica* was in sound health. Caesar was annoyed. A letter is said to be winging its way to **Pompeius in Capua**. The three are hated by the *equites*, who stood up and applauded Curio. They are enemies of all. They threaten the **Roscian law**, even the **corn law**. Things really are in a pretty muddle. Personally I would have preferred that **their regime should go by in silence** but I fear that may not be possible. Men are not willing to endure what they have to endure, like it or not. Now all are speaking with one voice, but that unanimity is based more on hatred than on brute force.

Cicero, *Atticus* 2.19.2–3 (*39*)

Caesar wants me to be his *legatus*; that's a more honourable way of avoiding danger. I am not altogether rejecting it. How so? I prefer to fight. But nothing is fixed. Yet again I say 'If only you were here'. But I will summon you if the need arises …

Rome, July 59 BC

Cicero, *Atticus* 2.19.5 (*39*)

Cicero fears the consequences of public hostility to the Three.

Pompeius in Capua   Pompeius was not present in the theatre: he was in Capua.

Roscian law   Roscius Otho, tribune in 67, passed a law giving the front 14 rows in the theatre to the *equites*. Senators sat in the area in front of the stage, the *orchestra*.

corn law   a law giving corn at a subsidized rate to Roman citizens; precisely which such law is unclear.

their regime … silence   Cicero hoped that with the passage of time the regime of the Three would fade away and that the best response was no action. However, the reaction of the Roman people had been such as to make him fear that the Three would be forced to use violence to buttress their position and secure their legislation; it would thus become like a modern dictatorship.

Caesar wants me to be his *legatus*   Caesar is still attempting to secure the support of Cicero, evidence of the latter's political significance.

---

1   I have no need to write in great detail about the *respublica*; it is in **utter ruins**. It is in a more wretched state than when you left it. At that time it appeared that a despotism had overwhelmed the state, one that was pleasing to the masses and though irksome to the *boni* at least not ruinous; but it is now so disagreeable to all that we shudder to think where it is going to erupt. We have experienced the 5 anger and recklessness of those men, who in anger at Cato have brought about **complete ruin**. They seemed at that time to be using such mild poisons that we could apparently die without pain; but now with the hisses of the masses, the talk of the *boni* and the murmurings in Italy, I fear that they are ablaze with anger.

2   **Personally I had hoped**, as I often said to you, that the wheel of the *respublica* 10 might have turned in such a way that we could scarcely hear its sound, scarcely see the imprint of its track; that's how it would have turned out, if people had been willing to wait for the passing of the storm. They sighed in secret for a long time, then they began to murmur, and finally they all began to speak out and shout aloud. 15

Cicero, Atticus 2.21.1–2 (41)

I do not know what will be the outcome for Bibulus. As things now stand, he has a remarkable reputation. He put off the elections to the month of October. Such action usually upsets the wishes of the people. **Caesar thought** that he could, with a speech, incite a public meeting to march on Bibulus' house. Although he made many highly inflammatory remarks he was unable to raise a murmur. In short, 5 they realize that no section of society supports them. That's all the more reason why we have to fear violence.

Rome, after 25 July 59 BC

Cicero, Atticus 2.21.5 (41)

> •   Throughout history there has been tension between the proponents of silent and of active opposition in the face of tyranny and dictatorship. Consider examples in the history of the twentieth century. In what circumstances, if any, does active opposition seem to you appropriate?

---

utter ruins, complete ruin   in Cicero's view the Three had seized control of the *respublica*. Elections, assemblies, senate and courts were no longer free, being controlled in the last resort by force – by Pompeius' veterans and later by the army of Caesar. Such lack of freedom, ruin in Cicero's words, obviously affected the political class – the senatorial and equestrian orders – but Cicero notes the 'hisses of the masses', so the urban plebs were hostile too. One might wonder why.

Personally I had hoped   Cicero hoped that silent and inactive opposition would not provoke the Three who, having achieved the aims of their compact, would allow the *respublica* to become free again. But that was surely to ignore the aims of their enemies, who intended to overturn all their measures.

Caesar thought   an example of the people voting with their feet, so to speak, to the embarrassment of Caesar.

In August 59 BC Cicero writes to Atticus about the distress of Pompeius.

2   First of all, I want you to know this: **Sampsiceramus**, our friend, bitterly regrets his situation and wants to be restored to the place he occupied before he fell. He shares his distress with me and at times openly looks for a remedy. I don't think any can possibly be found. Secondly, the leaders and associates of **that party** are becoming feeble although they face no opposition. There has never been   5

3   among the whole citizen body a greater unanimity of views and conversation. I personally – I am sure you're keen to know this – take no part in public affairs but am devoting myself to work and business in the courts.

Rome, August 59

Cicero, *Atticus* 2.23.2–3 *(43)*

In the last letter of the series Cicero comments on the situation in Rome.

Concerning affairs here, what can I write except the same as I have often written? Nothing is more hopeless than the state of the *respublica*, none more hated than those responsible. I myself, so I think and hope and guess, **am protected** by the powerful support of people's goodwill.

Rome, September 59 BC

Cicero, *Atticus* 2.25.2 *(45)*

Sampsiceramus   Cicero's nickname for Pompeius, the most powerful member of the Three in 59, who had faced the growing hostility to the Three and suffered the most unpopularity – something he had never before experienced. Pompeius might consider some move towards the nobility and the senate, but Caesar had taken steps to ensure his continuing connection through the marriage alliance. Pompeius had married Caesar's daughter, Iulia, a classic example of the arranged marriage for political ends, which actually turned into a devoted partnership only to be ended by the death of Iulia in childbirth in 54. If only Iulia had survived …

that party   the Three and their supporters.

am protected   in the event, when the crisis came in 58 BC with an assault by Clodius, the protection and goodwill proved a delusion.

Caesar and the senate

According to a speech which Cicero delivered in the senate in 56 BC, the *optimates* had several times in 59 made Caesar an offer to re-enact his laws so that they would be legally valid. This passage is the only evidence for the offer, and it is surprising.

The *optimates* more than once made an offer to C. Caesar that he should put forward the same proposals in another way. By this offer they were respecting the auspices and approving his laws.

Cicero, Consular Provinces 46

It is hard to believe the offer could have been made 'more than once' in 59 BC, and one wonders how Bibulus or Cato reacted. Pompeius might have supported the proposal and the senate did add the province of Transalpine Gaul to Cisalpine Gaul and Illyricum, which Caesar had been given as his province by the law of the tribune Vatinius earlier in the year. But, for whatever reason, Caesar did not take up the offer.

8 Exile and restoration

The tribunate of Clodius, 58 BC

In 59 BC Publius Clodius was elected tribune of the plebs and took up office on 10 December. He at once set about a comprehensive programme of popular legislation. There were bills to provide corn free to the Roman populace, to restore the *collegia* (local or trade associations) outlawed in 64, to prohibit the use of auspices to prevent legislation as Bibulus had tried to do in 59, and to remove the powers of the censors over membership of the senate. With massive popular support and little opposition, the bills were voted into law at the very beginning of January. Late in 59, Cicero wrote to Atticus about the situation in Rome.

Clodius is hostile to me. Pompeius assures me *he* will do nothing against me, but it is dangerous for me to believe him. I am preparing myself for resistance. I hope I will have the **full support of all orders**. I miss you; moreover, the situation calls for you to meet the crisis. You will bring great help in my planning what to do, in my morale, and lastly, in physical defence, if you are here when the crisis comes. 5
Varro satisfies me. Pompeius is an inspired speaker. I hope I shall at least come out of the business with great honour or actually without trouble.

Rome, between September and November 59 BC

Cicero, *Atticus* 2.21.6 *(41)*

Clodius is hostile   Clodius was hostile to Cicero probably because he had destroyed Clodius' alibi in the Bona Dea trial in 61, but his public ground of hostility was the execution of the Catilinarian conspirators on 5 December 63.

Pompeius   Cicero had written previously to Atticus that he had received assurance from Pompeius that Clodius would not say a word against Cicero; in this, so Cicero wrote, Pompeius did not deceive him but was himself deceived.

full support of all orders   the senate and the *equites*. The latter certainly supported Cicero when the crisis came, but the leaders of the senate did not. Cicero was to be sadly disappointed and resentful when he was abandoned. There were a number of factors: the fact that Cicero was a *novus homo* looked down upon by the *nobiles*, his incessant talk of and excessive pride in his actions in 63, the fragile nature of the concord of the orders (see Glossary) achieved in 63, and Cicero's active hostility to the Three. If only Cicero had taken up one of Caesar's offers …

Varro   Marcus Terentius Varro, who served in campaigns with Pompeius and was a very great scholar. He was a close friend of Atticus and currently helping Cicero against Clodius.

I hope   the idea is that he will emerge victorious from a fight with Clodius or that there may be no fight at all.

Cicero and Caesar

Cicero and Caesar enjoyed cordial social relations since they had common interests in language and literature but politically they were poles apart. One might argue that Caesar had the wider vision and looked towards the future, while Cicero's was the narrower and deeply conservative view, that of the tiny senatorial elite.

In his letters Cicero recalled the offers Caesar made to him in 59 BC. They reveal the extent to which Caesar tried to get Cicero on his side, and Cicero's determination to stick to his republican principles and the respect and dignity which he commanded among the 'good men'. In a speech in the senate in 56, Cicero made the following declaration.

41 When Caesar was consul, he carried out measures and wished me to take part in them. Although I did not approve of them, I was nonetheless gratified by his judgement of me. He invited me to be **one of the commission of five**. He wanted me to be **one of three men of consular rank** most closely associated with him. He offered me any *legatio* I wished, with as much privilege as I desired. I rejected all 5 these offers because I adhered firmly to my political principles, but not without a feeling of gratitude…

42 He transferred **an enemy of mine** to plebeian status. Either he was angry with me because he saw that I could not be attached to him even by favours, or he was prevailed upon by constant requests. Not even that act harmed me because 10 he later not only suggested but even asked me to be a *legatus* of his. I did not accept this offer either. It was not that I considered it inappropriate to my dignity, but because I did not suspect how great a criminal assault was threatening the *respublica* from **the consuls** of the following year.

Cicero, Consular Provinces 41–2

---

one of the commission of five an inner subcommittee of the 20-man commission responsible for the administration of Caesar's land-law.

one of three men of consular rank to join the triumvirate, making it a group of four.

an enemy of mine Caesar as *pontifex maximus* had presided at the transfer of Clodius to plebeian status.

the consuls L. Calpurnius Piso, father-in-law of Caesar, and A. Gabinius, close supporter of Pompeius, consuls in 58. Their 'criminal assault' consisted in supporting the legislation of Clodius in return for the provinces of Macedonia and Syria with unlimited powers following their consulships.

1 How do you regard Cicero's refusal to respond to Caesar's offers? Was he to be admired for sticking to his principles, or foolish not to take advantage when the offers were made?

2 'Ponder and understand this hard saying of an upright scholar, who knew the world, though he was not of it – he who is strictly honest and unbending is not fit for the direction of political affairs' (T. Rice Holmes, p. 71; the reference is to Professor G. Long, *Cicero Orations* (1858), vol. iv, p. vi). Can you think of similar examples of modern politicians obstinately sticking to their principles when a more flexible stance might have helped the state?

Cicero and Clodius

Twenty-seven letters that Marcus wrote to his brother Quintus survive. The following letter was written in autumn 59 BC, when Quintus was governing the Roman province of Asia. Cicero writes of his preparations against Clodius and is optimistic about his prospects.

It seems that our cause will not lack supporters. People are giving assurances in a remarkable way, offering personal help and making promises. For my part I have not only the highest hopes but higher spirits too: hopes, in that I am confident we shall prevail, and high spirits with the *respublica* in its present state, in that I do not fear any mishap. The **situation at present** is as follows: if Clodius gives 5 notice of a prosecution, all Italy will assemble to help and we will come out of it with redoubled glory. If on the other hand he tries to proceed by force, I hope with the support not only of friends but also of outsiders that we shall meet force with force. All are pledging themselves, their friends, clients, freedmen, slaves, and their money too. Our old band of *boni* is fired with zeal and affection for 10 us. Those who were previously somewhat unsympathetic or indifferent are now joining with the *boni* through their hatred of the tyrants. Pompeius is full of promises and Caesar too, but I do not trust them sufficiently to curtail any of my preparations. The tribunes-designate are friendly, **the consuls** are showing themselves very favourable, and we have **Domitius, Nigidius, Memmius and** 15 **Lentulus** – praetors who are very friendly and energetic citizens. The others are *boni* but these are singularly so. So you should have courage and good hope.

Rome, October–December 59 BC

Cicero, Quintus 1.2.16 (2)

situation at present   Cicero envisages that Clodius will attack him either through the courts or by force with his supporters from the urban plebs, and either way he expects victory.

the consuls   L. Calpurnius Piso, A. Gabinius, consuls-elect for 58, but their favourable showing did not in fact extend to their year of office.

Domitius, Nigidius, Memmius and Lentulus   four of the eight praetors-elect for 58. The praetors did not support Cicero as he had hoped, but were less hostile than the consuls.

1 What would you say is the tone of this letter?

2 Why should Quintus have 'courage and good hope'?

3 Does Cicero reveal any doubts or uncertainties?

Events turned out rather differently. Clodius was a good deal shrewder than Cicero had imagined. He gained the support of the consuls by a deal on provinces, he dominated the ten tribunes, the praetors were effectively powerless, the army of loyal citizens did not materialize, and the *equites*, who did show support for Cicero, were forced into submission. Crassus as ever remained in the background, Caesar was unsympathetic – after all, he had made several offers to Cicero – and Pompeius betrayed Cicero. An anecdote in Plutarch (*Cicero* 31.3) alleges that when Cicero went to Pompeius' Alban villa to seek his help, Pompeius left the house by another exit because he was too embarrassed to face Cicero.

The actions of the *optimates* were perhaps most galling of all to Cicero. Some even gave support to Clodius – he was one of them – and they perhaps got malicious delight from seeing Cicero's discomfiture. Cato, whose removal from Rome Clodius engineered by a special command to annex the island of Cyprus, advised Cicero to save Rome from factional strife and bloodshed by withdrawing from the city and becoming the saviour of his country for a second time. Cicero was particularly incensed by what he regarded as the betrayal of Hortensius, who counselled him to yield to circumstance and leave Rome. Caesar, so Cicero reports (*On His House* 22), wrote a letter to Clodius congratulating him for having got rid of Cato in such a way that he could never again speak against special commands, and he no doubt felt much the same about Cicero's removal.

Clodius first introduced a bill in February to outlaw anyone who had put Roman citizens to death without trial. Cicero was the obvious target because he had been responsible for the execution of the Catilinarian conspirators though, as Roman law required, he was not personally named in the proposal. Cicero yielded and withdrew from Rome, probably around the middle of March. Clodius then passed a second law exiling Cicero by name and confiscating his property. His house on the Palatine was ransacked and demolished. Clodius then had a temple to 'Liberty' erected and dedicated on part of the site.

Cicero in exile, 58–57 BC

On his way to exile, Cicero seeks help and advice from Atticus.

May I see the day when I can thank you for having forced me to stay alive. So far I wholly regret **that you did**. But I beg you to come to me at **Vibo** without delay. I have altered my travelling for many reasons and am on my way there. If you do come there, I shall be able to make a plan for my whole journey and exile. If you do not do that, I shall be surprised, but I am sure you will.

March 58 BC

Cicero, Atticus 3.3 (47)

Exile was a desperately unhappy time for Cicero, and his letters to Atticus and to the family fully reveal his changing moods. These letters, published after his death in 16 books by his secretary, allow us to know him better than any other figure of ancient times. One could argue that he suffered a mental breakdown – in a letter to Atticus in August 58 BC Cicero writes: 'You say you hear that grief has actually disturbed the balance of my mind. No, my mind is sound enough' (*Atticus* 3.13.2 (*59*)). He settled eventually at Thessalonica in Macedonia where he received kind treatment from the quaestor Cn. Plancius, who had his residence there. He stayed there from May until November 58 and then moved to Dyrrhachium (see map on p. 145) on the Adriatic coast, where he could more easily keep in touch with news from Rome.

Cicero writes to his wife Terentia on his way to exile.

1   I send you letters less often than I can – the reason is that every moment is wretched for me and when I write to you or read your letters I am so overcome by tears that I can hardly bear it. If only I had been less keen to stay alive! Certainly I would have seen no misfortune in my life, or not much. But if fortune has kept me alive for some hope of recovering a happy state, then I have made less of a mistake. 5 But if the present misfortunes are irreversible, then I certainly want to see you, my life, as soon as possible and to die in your embrace. Neither the gods whom you have worshipped with such piety nor the men whose interests I have always served have granted us their thanks in return …

3   What ruin, what despair I am in! Am I to ask you, a sick woman, mentally and 10 physically exhausted, to come here? Should I, then, *not* ask you? Am I then to be without you? I think I should put the matter like this: if there is any hope of my

---

that you did   force me to stay alive.

Vibo   a town in the toe of southern Italy (see map on p. 5).

return, you must give it your support and help the cause. But if, as I fear, it is all over, then arrange to come to me any way you can. Be sure of one thing: if I am with you, I shall not think I have been completely ruined … 15

6   For the rest, my dearest Terentia, bear up as honourably as you can …

Brundisium, May 58 BC

Cicero to his family, *Friends* 14.4.1, 3, 6 (6) with omissions

> Cicero seems to have considered religious piety something peculiar to women and comments elsewhere on Terentia's worship.
>
> He writes to Atticus of his mental turmoil and his mistake.

From the frequent changes in my letters I imagine you see the disturbed state of my mind. This has been brought about not so much as a result of unhappiness, although I have been struck by a singular and unbelievable disaster, as from the recollection of my own fault. You surely see now **whose villainy** constrained me and betrayed me. I wish you had seen it earlier and not surrendered your whole 5 mind to grief at the same time as I did. And so when you hear that I have been stricken and overwhelmed with grief, reckon that I suffer more the penalty of my folly than the outcome itself. I trusted a man whom I did not think to be a scoundrel. Grief for my own troubles and fear about my brother impede my writing. 10

Thessalonica, 29 May 58 BC

Cicero, *Atticus* 3.8.4 (53)

> Not long afterwards, on 13 June, Cicero wrote to Atticus (3.9.2 (54)): 'It was not enemies but the jealous who ruined me.' Atticus tried to exonerate the 'jealous', including Cato. Cicero responded: 'As for your clearing from blame those who I wrote were jealous of me, including Cato among them, I consider him to have been so free from that villainy that I very greatly regret that the pretences of others were more influential with me than his good faith' (Cicero, *Atticus* 3.15.2 (60)). But Plutarch records that Cato advised Cicero to yield to circumstance and become for the second time the saviour of his country (*Cato the Younger* 35.1). Cicero absolved Cato of jealousy and pretence, but not Hortensius and others.

---

whose villainy   the chief culprit was Hortensius, the 'man whom I trusted and did not think to be a scoundrel'.

Cicero spells out his woes in a letter to his brother Quintus.

2   What am I to hope for? **My enemy** is extremely powerful, **my detractors** dominate the state, **my friends** are unfaithful and very many people are jealous of me.

3   Of the new tribunes, certainly **Sestius** is most ready to help me and so, I hope, are **Curtius, Milo, Fadius** and **Atilius**. But Clodius is resolute in opposition. Even when he is no longer in office he will be able to stir up public meetings with the   5 same gang. Then too someone will be found to interpose a veto.

4   Such prospects were not put to me when I was setting out. I was often told I would return with the greatest glory within three days. 'What did you yourself think?' you will ask. Well in my case many things combined to upset my mind: the sudden desertion of Pompeius, the hostility of the consuls, and the praetors   10 too, the timidity of the *publicani*, slaves with weapons. The tears of my family and friends prevented me from going to my death. That would certainly have been the most fitting way to protect my honour and to escape intolerable distress.

Thessalonica, August 58 BC

Cicero, Quintus 1.4.2–4 (4)

Cicero's fears about Clodius and a veto proved fully justified. He sets out the factors that clouded his judgement and led him to leave Rome. He frequently blamed false friends who had betrayed him with their advice. He failed or did not wish to recognize that the decisive factor in his fate was not Clodius' hostility or Hortensius' advice but the attitude of Caesar and Pompeius. Cicero had failed to follow the path he had mentioned in his letters to Atticus in the previous two years (see the letter to Atticus, 2.1.6 (*21*), on p. 77).

Cicero writes to his family of his distress and grief. He acknowledges that the family share a common disaster, but he is the more wretched because he alone is responsible. He should have avoided trouble by taking up Caesar's offer, or by more careful preparation, or by a brave death.

2   Nothing could have been more wretched, more disgraceful and more unworthy of me than *this*. I am overwhelmed with distress and with shame. I am ashamed that I have not provided courage and attention for the best of wives and the sweetest of children. Your wretched state, your grief and your weak health are before my eyes day and night …   5

My enemy   Clodius.

my detractors   Caesar, Crassus, Pompeius.

my friends   Hortensius and others.

Sestius, Curtius, Milo, Fadius, Atilius   tribunes-designate for 57, who had recently been elected. The last named, Sextus Atilius Serranus, when in office, supported Clodius and opposed a motion for Cicero's recall.

5   You write that you will come to me, if that is my wish. Since I know that a large part of this burden is being borne by you, I want you to stay there … Look after your health and be fully assured that nothing is dearer to me or ever has been than yourself.

Dyrrhachium, November 58 BC

Cicero to his family, Friends 14.3.2, 5 (9) with omissions

The fight for Cicero's return

The campaign for Cicero's return began almost as soon as he departed but made little progress while Clodius was in office. With new magistrates in 57 BC the fight began in earnest but Clodius, whose older brother Appius was one of the praetors of 57, was still powerful on the streets, as the events of January show. The consul Spinther proposed in the senate on 1 January that Cicero be recalled. This was generally agreed but two hostile tribunes held up proceedings until 23 January. Cicero recalls the situation in 56 when he was defending Sestius, who was charged with being a party to violence in the campaign to restore Cicero. This passage vividly, even if with some exaggeration, illustrates the violence that was a feature of the late Republic. Cicero is here defending Sestius against their common enemies.

75   At last the day came for the assembly of the plebs to deal with my case, 23 January. The principal sponsor of the proposal, **Q. Fabricius**, a man who was most friendly to me, occupied the **sacred precinct** some time before dawn. On that day **Sestius**, who now stands trial for violence, took no action. This agent and defender of my cause made no move but waited to see the intentions of **my enemies**. Well, 5 what about those who have schemed to bring Sestius here before the court – how did they conduct themselves? They had seized the forum, the *comitium* and the senate house in the dead of night with armed men and a good number of slaves.

They launched an attack on Fabricius, laid violent hands upon him, killed several
76   people and wounded many others … They caused wholesale slaughter in the 10 forum. With drawn swords covered in blood, as one body they cast their eyes over every part of the forum and shouted out for my dearest brother, a man

---

Q. Fabricius   the tribune who first worked for Cicero's recall in 57.

sacred precinct   translates the Latin word *templum* and denotes a space where meetings and assemblies could be held, in this case the rostra.

Sestius   P. Sestius, the tribune of 57, was in the end most active in organizing force to meet the force of Clodius and bring about Cicero's return.

my enemies   Clodius and his gangs.

comitium   a circular area in front of the senate house where the Roman people had originally assembled.

of the greatest courage and my most devoted supporter … He experienced the
monstrous brutality of those criminals and brigands. He had come to beg the
Roman people for the restoration of his brother but was driven from the rostra 15
and lay on the ground in the *comitium*. He covered himself with the bodies
of his slaves and freedmen and protected his life on that occasion by cover of
77 darkness and flight rather than by law and the courts. You recall, members of the
jury, that this was the occasion when the corpses of citizens filled the Tiber and
clogged up the sewers, when blood was wiped up with sponges in the forum. 20

Cicero, *Sestius* 75–7

> - Can you identify various ways by which Cicero tries to influence the jury in
>   favour of his client?

The consuls, the praetors apart from Appius Claudius, and eight of the ten
tribunes supported Cicero's case. Pompeius, for whatever reason, swung
into action on behalf of Cicero, writing to Caesar and travelling around Italy
encouraging the *municipia* to support his recall by their presence in Rome.
Sestius visited Caesar in Cisalpine Gaul to appeal on Cicero's behalf but seems
not to have had much success. Caesar feared Cicero's tongue and required
guarantees about his future conduct. In the event Quintus agreed to stand
surety for his brother. Milo and Sestius recruited gangs to counter the forces of
Clodius and at last, on 4 August 57 BC, an assembly of the centuries was held
which voted for Cicero's return. Cicero recalled that day when he addressed the
college of pontiffs, in the presence of his enemy Clodius, on 29 September.

89 Do you [Clodius] imagine that the Roman people is made up of those who are
hired by pay, who are induced to do violence to magistrates, to lay siege to the
senate, to be eager for daily slaughter, arson and looting? The sort of people you
could not assemble unless the shops had been shut … What a thought that this
was the face and grandeur of the Roman people of whom kings, foreign nations 5
and peoples at the ends of the earth, are in awe – a crowd of people gathered
together from slaves, from hirelings, from criminals and from down-and-outs.
90 No, what you saw in the **Campus Martius** on that occasion when even you had

---

Campus Martius it was the assembly of the centuries that voted for Cicero's recall. It met
in the Campus Martius outside the walls of the city. In this assembly voting was weighted
in favour of the rich. Pompeius had urged the wealthy citizens from the *municipia* to
travel to Rome to support Cicero. They turned out in large numbers – hence Cicero could
joke that the country towns (*municipia*) had been closed. The urban masses were more
influential in the assembly of the tribes – when a large turnout was required shops were
closed – hence the decision of Cicero's supporters to frustrate the influence of Clodius
and the plebs by holding the vote in the centuriate assembly.

the opportunity to speak against the authority and enthusiasm of the senate and all Italy – that was the beauty of the Roman people, that its genuine appearance. 10 That is the people which is the lord of kings, the victor and ruler over all nations; you saw it, you scoundrel, on **that glorious day** when all the leading citizens of our state, men of every order and age, reckoned that they were casting their votes not for the welfare of a single citizen but for that of the whole citizen body. They had come to the Campus not because the shops had been closed but because the 15 *municipia* had been closed.

Cicero, On His House 89–90

Cicero is making an explicit contrast between the assemblies Clodius can summon in the forum and that assembly which voted for his recall. A careful reading will enable you to extract and list the contrasting features.

The return of Cicero, 57 BC

As soon as Cicero got back to Rome he wrote to Atticus about his general position and his return to the city. He had recovered his prestige with the public, his standing in the senate and his influence with the *boni*, but his private affairs were in a considerable mess, for which he was seeking Atticus' help and advice.

4 … I set out from Dyrrhachium on 4 August, the very day the law concerning me was put to the vote. I reached Brundisium on 5 August … On 11 August, while I was at Brundisium, I learned from a letter from my brother Quintus that the statute [for my recall] had been carried in the **assembly of the centuries** with magnificent support from all ages and orders and an incredible gathering of the 5 people of Italy. I was most handsomely honoured by the people of Brundisium and then began **my journey** from there. All along the way delegations gathered to meet me with congratulations.

5 When I got to the city, my arrival was such that no one of any order known to my **nomenclator** failed to come out to meet me – apart from those enemies who 10 could neither conceal nor deny the fact that they were enemies. When I reached the **Porta Capena**, the steps of the temples had been filled by the humblest

---

that glorious day   4 August 57, when the vote for Cicero's recall took place.

assembly of the centuries   see Glossary.

my journey   Cicero describes his journey almost as if he were returning to Rome after a victorious campaign to seek a triumph.

nomenclator   a slave employed to tell his master the names of people he met.

Porta Capena   a gate in the south-east of the city wall through which the Via Appia enters Rome.

The Via Appia, the road along which Cicero returned to Rome from exile.

plebeians. They showed their joy and congratulations to me by loud applause; similar crowds and applause accompanied me right up to the Capitol and in the forum and on the Capitol itself there was an amazing crowd. On the following 15 day, which was 5 September, I made a **speech of thanks in the senate**.

Rome, September 57 BC

Cicero, *Atticus* 4.1.4–5 (*73*)

> Cicero was at once involved in political affairs. His grateful support of Pompeius would hardly endear him to the conservative *optimates*. In the following letter Cicero records his proposal that Pompeius be put in charge of the corn supply for Rome.

The **price of grain** had risen very sharply and people had gathered in great numbers first **at the theatre** and then at the senate. At the instigation of Clodius they were shouting that the scarcity of grain was my doing. The senate was meeting during those days to discuss the corn supply and people – not only the plebs but the *boni* too – were calling upon Pompeius to take charge of the matter. He himself wanted 5

speech of thanks in the senate   the speech *On his Return in the Senate*, which survives.

price of grain   grain had been expensive in July, then the price dropped, only to soar in September when Cicero's return brought large numbers to the city; hence Clodius' accusation.

at the theatre   the Ludi Romani, the oldest and most famous games, held 5–19 September in honour of Iupiter.

this and the crowds were demanding that I personally should propose it. **Two days later** I put the proposal and spoke in detail about it. The **consulars**, apart from Messalla and Afranius, were absent, because they alleged that it was not safe for them to state their view in public. On my proposal a decree of the senate was passed that Pompeius should be invited to undertake the business and that a   10 statute should be enacted. The decree of the senate was read out immediately. The crowd applauded in that new and stupid manner when my name was read out. I then **made a speech** at the invitation of all the magistrates apart from **one praetor** and **two tribunes** of the plebs.

Rome, September 57 BC

Cicero, *Atticus* 4.1.6 *(73)*

The argument over Cicero's house

When Cicero left Rome in March 58 BC, his house on the Palatine was ransacked and demolished and his country villas were looted. As we have seen, Clodius constructed a temple to Liberty on part of the Palatine site; when Cicero returned he sought to regain possession of the site and asked for permission to rebuild and for costs for the demolished house and his country villas. Clodius naturally opposed this tooth and nail. There was a 'tremendous struggle'. Cicero addressed the college of pontiffs on 29 September.

The **pontiffs** came to the verdict that 'if the person who claimed to have consecrated that part of the site had not been authorized by name either by order of the people or by resolution of the plebs and had not been so ordered either by order of the people or by resolution of the plebs, then it was their view that there could be no religious objection to its restoration to me'. I was at once congratulated, for no   5

Two days later   on 7 September when the senate met on the Capitol.

consulars   their absence showed their dislike of a proposal to grant Pompeius extraordinary powers. Messalla, consul in 61, and Afranius, consul in 60, supported the Three.

made a speech   not the surviving speech, *On His Return to the People,* which mentions neither corn nor Pompeius.

one praetor, two tribunes   Appius Claudius (praetor), Atilius Serranus and Numerius Rufus (tribunes).

The pontiffs   there were 15 members of the pontifical college, 14 of whom Cicero probably addressed. The *pontifex maximus*, Caesar, was absent in Gaul. The names of all the rest are given in Cicero's speech *On the Responses of the Haruspices* 12, where they are listed in order of seniority. They advised the senate and magistrates on all religious matters and sacred law and, most importantly, controlled the calendar. Note the heavy legal language of their judgment.

one doubted that the house had been legally assigned to me. Then all of a sudden Clodius got up in a public meeting that **Appius** arranged for him. He announced to the people that the pontiffs had decided in his favour and that I was trying to get possession by force. He encouraged them to follow him and Appius and to defend **their Liberty**. Even among the dregs of his supporters some were amazed, 10 while others laughed at his utter folly …

Cicero, Atticus 4.2.3 (74)

> The pontiffs explained their decision and then Marcellinus, the consul-designate, proposed that the Palatine site be restored to Cicero and compensation be paid for his house there and his villas at Tusculum and Formiae. Clodius tried to filibuster while Atilius Serranus interposed his veto. Cicero describes the meeting of the senate in a letter to Atticus.

4   On 1 October there was a crowded meeting of the senate. **All the pontiffs** who were members of the senate were called in. **Marcellinus**, who was one of my keenest supporters, was called upon to speak first. He asked the pontiffs to explain the reasons for their decision. **M. Lucullus** then replied about the thinking of all the pontiffs. They were the judges of the religious issue, the senate was the judge 5 of the law. He and his colleagues had reached a decision on the religious issue and they would now decide in the senate about the law together with members of the senate. Each member [of the senate], asked in turn for his opinion, spoke at length supporting my case. When it came to **Clodius' turn**, he wanted to use up the whole day and there was no stopping him. However, when he had spoken for almost three 10 hours the senate became angry and noisy and he was finally forced to wind up his speech. While a decree of the senate on the motion of Marcellinus was being put to the vote, with the agreement of all but one, **Serranus** interposed his veto. Both

---

Appius   the praetor, Appius Claudius, older brother of Clodius.

their Liberty   the temple dedicated to Liberty which Clodius had constructed on the site of Cicero's house.

All the pontiffs   13 of the 14 pontiffs in Rome were members of the senate, the exception being the brother-in-law of Clodius, L. Pinarius Natta. The *pontifex maximus*, Iulius Caesar, was, as we have seen, away in Gaul.

Marcellinus   Cn. Cornelius Lentulus Marcellinus, consul-designate, and thus the first to speak.

M. Lucullus   M. Terentius Varro Lucullus, consul in 73, not the senior pontiff, but the order of speaking for the year was determined by the senior consul.

Clodius' turn   Clodius attempted to filibuster and talk the session out before a vote could be taken.

Serranus   Atilius Serranus, the tribune, allegedly bribed at the start of his tribunate and now continuing in his support of Clodius. On the consuls referring the use of the veto to the senate, see the note on p. 134.

consuls at once prepared to refer the matter of the veto to the senate. There were some impressive speeches. It was the wish of the senate that my house should 15 be restored to me; that a contract be put out for the **portico of Catulus**; that the authority of the senate should be defended by all the magistrates. If any violence occurred, the senate would take the view that this had occurred as a consequence of the action of the person who had vetoed the decree of the senate. Serranus took fright ... and asked for a night's delay. Members of the senate did not want 20 to concede this, for they **remembered 1 January**. However, reluctantly but with 5   my goodwill the concession was made. The following day the decree of the senate, which I am sending you, was passed.

Rome, October 57 BC

Cicero, Atticus 4.2.4–5 (74)

Violence on the Palatine

The priests might decide, the senate might decree, but that did not stop Clodius from violent obstruction. In the absence of any police force, gang warfare prevailed.

2   On 3 November the workmen were driven off our site by armed men ... my brother Quintus' house was first damaged by stones thrown from my site and then set on fire on Clodius' orders. The city looked on as firebrands were thrown; there were noisy complaints and groans – not may I say from the *boni*, I tend to think there aren't any – but from all and sundry. Clodius had rushed about like a 5 madman even before this, but after this outburst of madness he thinks of nothing but the slaughter of his enemies, he goes around street by street, he openly offers slaves the hope of freedom ...

3   On 11 November when I was going down the **Via Sacra**, he pursued me with his followers. Shouts, stones, clubs and swords: and all this without warning. 10 I retreated to the forecourt of Tettius Damio's house. Those who were with me easily prevented his roughs from entering. Clodius could have been killed ... On 12 November he tried to storm and set fire to Milo's house, which is on the

---

portico of Catulus the elder Catulus, consul in 102, constructed a portico on the Palatine, which Clodius destroyed and replaced by one which extended into Cicero's property. The contract was for the reconstruction of the original.

remembered 1 January on the first day of 57, when the matter of Cicero's recall was about to be voted on, the tribune Serranus asked for a night's delay to consider whether to use his veto, and then proceeded to delay the vote until 23 January. It was feared he would attempt a repeat performance.

Via Sacra the 'Sacred Way' that led down from the Velian Hill to the east of the forum to the forum itself and continued to the Capitol.

Cermalus, in broad daylight about eleven o'clock, bringing up men with shields and drawn swords and others with lighted firebrands. He himself had taken over 15 **P. Sulla**'s house as his camp for this assault. Then **Q. Flaccus** led out some toughs from **Milo's Annian house**. They killed the most notorious of Clodius' band of thugs and went after Clodius himself, but he took refuge in the recesses of Sulla's house.

Senate on 14 November. Clodius at home. Marcellinus outstanding, the rest full 20 of vigour. **Metellus** used up the time for speaking by **cunning practice**, with the help of Appius, and even that **close friend** of yours. Your letter is absolutely right about the consistency of his lifestyle. Sestius was furious. Clodius later threatened the city if **his elections** were not held. Milo posted up **Marcellinus' proposal**, which the latter had read from the script. It was to embrace the whole of my case 25 – building site, acts of arson, the danger that I had faced in person – Clodius to be brought to trial and all these matters to be put ahead of the elections. Milo declared that he would watch the sky for omens on all **comitial days**. Speeches were made, disruptive by Metellus, reckless by Appius and quite mad by Publius. However, the upshot was that elections would take place unless Milo declared unfavourable 30 omens in the Campus.

4

Rome, November 57 BC

Cicero, *Atticus* 4.3.2–4 *(75)*

Cermalus   north-west part of the Palatine.

P. Sulla   Publius Cornelius Sulla, kinsman of the dictator, elected to the consulship in 66 but removed with P. Autronius for electoral bribery. He was defended in 62 by Cicero when charged with complicity in the conspiracy of Catilina.

Q. Flaccus   he is otherwise unknown.

Milo's Annian house   a house on the Capitoline which Milo had inherited from Titus Annius.

Metellus   Quintus Metellus Nepos, consul in 57, who supported Clodius in his election campaign and tried to obstruct the tribune Milo in his attempt to delay elections so Clodius could be prosecuted.

cunning practice   a filibuster.

close friend   probably Hortensius.

his elections   Clodius was a candidate in the elections for curule aedile, which should have been held in July and were not in fact held until January 56, when Clodius was elected.

Marcellinus' proposal   that Clodius should stand trial forthwith for violence before the elections.

comitial days   days on which assemblies of the Roman people could be held. In November 57, apart from market days, the 21st and 29th, every day from the 18th until 29th, the end of the month, was possible.

Marcellinus wanted to bring Clodius to trial for the recent violence, while Clodius wanted elections to be held first, because election to the office of aedile would render him immune from prosecution. The tribune Milo sought to prevent the consul Metellus from holding the elections by declaring unfavourable omens on every possible occasion. The elections were not held in 57 BC, nor was Clodius prosecuted. When they were held in January 56, Clodius was elected and he proceeded to institute legal proceedings against Milo for violence.

9 Cicero the realist

In December 54 BC Cicero wrote to Lentulus Spinther, the consul of 57 who had played a leading role in his recall: 'I owed the greatest debt to Pompeius as you stated publicly and testified' (Cicero, *Friends* 1.9.6 (*20*)). He had clearly come to recognize who had been responsible for his recall, but he might have added Caesar, whose agreement had been vital and who had required guarantees that Cicero would not oppose the Three. His brother Quintus had given them. In the euphoria of his return Marcus apparently failed to realize that he would no longer have the political independence which he had previously enjoyed and which all the *boni* considered their prerogative. He also faced political embarrassment over the Egyptian problem, which provides another good example of how personal obligations might conflict with political issues.

The Egyptian problem

The Egyptian king Ptolemy, whose citizens had driven him out of Alexandria, arrived in Italy in autumn 57 BC and lodged with Pompeius at his villa in the Alban hills south of Rome. He wished Pompeius to restore him and engaged in bribery and murder to achieve that aim. Pompeius was keen to obtain the command, but Crassus too was interested and opposed Pompeius. The *optimates* were, as ever, opposed to the ambitions of Pompeius, and the senate, on the motion of the consul Lentulus, decreed in late 57 that the governor of Cilicia should restore the king. Lentulus was to govern that province in 56. Cicero had obligations to Pompeius and to Lentulus.

On 13 January 56 Cicero wrote to Lentulus, who was now on his way to govern Cilicia and Cyprus.

1

3

Hammonius, the envoy of the king, is **attacking us openly with money** ... the king's supporters, and there are not many of them, want the task put in the hands of Pompeius. The senate approves the **sham of a religious objection** not on religious grounds but through spite and dislike of the king's bribery ... What

---

attacking us openly with money   the king wanted Pompeius, not Lentulus, to restore him. He borrowed money to achieve that aim and had his agent distribute it openly.

sham of a religious objection   Gaius Cato, tribune in 56, was bitterly hostile to Pompeius. He had persuaded the senate to pass a motion declaring that it would be dangerous for the *respublica* for the king to be restored with an army. This removed the possibility of an attractive military command.

---

has happened up to 13 January – I'm writing this the same morning – is that the motion of Hortensius, myself and Lucullus concedes the religious point about an army, for there's no way that point can be gained. But in accordance with the decree of the senate **which was passed on your motion** it decrees that you restore the king provided you can do this to the benefit of the *respublica*. While the religious point excludes an army, the senate would keep you as the person responsible.

Rome, 13 January 56 BC

Cicero to Lentulus Spinther, *Friends* 1.1.1, 3 (*12*)

- How do modern politicians solve conflict between personal and public interests?

Cicero was walking a tightrope. In a letter of 17 January to his brother Quintus describing the struggle between Lentulus and Pompeius for the command to restore Ptolemy, he wrote: 'In this matter I fulfilled my obligation to Lentulus remarkably and I satisfied the wishes of Pompeius brilliantly' (Cicero, *Quintus* 2.2.3 (*6*)). He noted, however, that Lentulus appeared to have been removed from the task and was himself quite upset. No decision was reached and by June or July Cicero advised Lentulus that he should decide the matter himself.

The trial of Milo in 56 BC

Clodius was elected aedile in January 56 BC and proceeded to indict **Milo** for violence before the people. A preliminary hearing on 7 February provides a vivid illustration of the conduct of public affairs in the open air. Pompeius was defending Milo.

Pompeius spoke, or rather tried to. As soon as he stood up, Clodius' gangs raised loud shouts and this continued throughout his speech. He was impeded not only by shouting but by insults and abuse. He came to the end of his speech – he was certainly courageous and not deterred; he said all he wanted and at times even in silence, when he won through by his authority. When he had finished Clodius got up. Such a noise greeted him from our side, for we thought we ought to return the thanks, that Clodius could not control his thoughts, words or tongue. This

---

which was passed on your motion   the senatorial decree authorizing Lentulus, as governor of Cilicia, to restore Ptolemy.

Milo   T. Annius Milo, tribune in 57, who had taken a lead in organizing force to procure Cicero's recall.

continued right up to around two o'clock – Pompeius had spoken until midday – with all manner of abuse and the **most obscene verses being uttered against Clodius and Clodia**. Clodius was beside himself, pale with fury, and amid the shouts asked: 'Who is starving the people to death?' His gangs replied: 'Pompeius.' 'Who wants to go to Alexandria?' They replied, 'Pompeius.' 'Who do you want to go?' 'Crassus,' they replied. Crassus was there to support Milo but with no enthusiasm. A little after two o'clock as if on a given signal the Clodians began spitting on our people. Tempers rose. They pressed forward to move us from our position. Our side charged. The gangs fled. Clodius was thrown from the rostra. At that point I too fled, fearing what might happen in a riot. The senate was summoned to the senate house. **Pompeius stayed at home**. I did not go to the senate. I did not want to stay silent about so grave an occurrence and I did not wish to upset the sensitivities of the *boni*. Pompeius was criticized by **Bibulus, Curio, Favonius and young Servilius**.

Rome, 12–15 February 56 BC

Cicero, Quintus 2.3.2 (7)

> Notice how political issues are mixed with a court case, how Clodius throws out questions to the crowd and how the crowd responds by attacking Pompeius, and how the meeting ends in violence, which no organized police force exists to control or prevent. The senate is then summoned to discuss what has happened. The trial was postponed but in fact never took place.

The trial of Sestius – a political statement

> In March 56 BC, as we have seen, Cicero defended Publius Sestius, who as tribune in 57 had played a leading role in support of his restoration. It was Sestius' organization of forces to counter Clodius and his gangs which had led to the indictment for violence. Sestius was unanimously acquitted. Within the speech, Cicero took the opportunity to issue a statement of his political beliefs. He begins by defining the *optimates*.

Who, then, are all these *best men*? If you ask their number, they are countless; otherwise the state could not remain stable. They are the leaders of state policy,

---

most obscene ... Clodia   Clodius and his sister Clodia were alleged to have had incestuous relations. Clodia was a notorious figure in elite Roman society. Cicero attacked her in his defence of a young aristocrat, Marcus Caelius; see Cicero, *Defence Speeches* (trans. D. H. Berry) and, for a brilliant evocation of her social milieu, T. P. Wiseman.

Pompeius stayed at home   perhaps for personal security, but holding *imperium* for the corn supply prevented him entering within the walls of Rome.

Bibulus ... Servilius   *optimates* hostile to Pompeius.

they are those who follow that line, they are the members of the **leading orders**, to whom the *curia* is open, they are the Romans from the *municipia* and from the countryside, they are those engaging in business, they are even freedmen *optimates*. The number of this group, as I have said, is spread far and wide and of varied background; but, to remove misunderstanding, the group as a whole can be briefly outlined and defined: *optimates* are all those who are not guilty of crime, not naturally evil, not raving lunatics, not burdened by domestic debt. They are, therefore – this breed as you have termed them – men innocent of crime, of sound mind, and with their domestic affairs in a flourishing state. Those who, in governing the *respublica*, serve the wishes, the interests and the views of these men, the defenders of the *optimates* and the *optimates* themselves, are reckoned the most important and the most distinguished citizens and leaders of the state.

Cicero, *Sestius* 97

> This definition is unrealistically wide and exaggerated. The best men were, in Cicero's view, drawn from the leaders of the senatorial order, from ordinary members of the senate, from the equestrian order, including some of the elite of the country towns of Italy – men from families such as that of Cicero himself. Cicero then considers their aims and objectives.

What then is the objective of these men who govern the *respublica*, on which they must concentrate their attention and towards which they must direct their action? It is what stands far above all else and is most desirable for all men of sound mind, all the *boni*, all the well-off – it is *otium* with *dignitas*.

All who want this are *optimates*; those who bring it about are thought the foremost men and the saviours of the state. It is neither right nor proper that men should be so carried away by the *dignitas* of playing a part in public affairs that they do not make provision for *otium*, nor that they should concentrate on *otium* which is incompatible with *dignitas*.

Now these are the foundations of this *otiosa dignitas* [peaceful dignity], these are the components which must be guarded by the leaders and defended even at the risk of their lives: **religious observances**, the auspices, the powers of magistrates,

---

leading orders   the senatorial and equestrian orders.

otium with *dignitas*   peace with dignity, peaceful dignity; this idea may be defined as the social standing appropriate to a person as a result of his status and service to the *respublica*, combined with tranquillity and harmony within the *respublica* – which together allow all citizens to lead their lives in freedom. The topic is one that has been the subject of considerable study, most recently in R. A. Kaster (ed.), *Cicero, Speech on Behalf of Publius Sestius*.

religious observances   the performance of public religious ritual by the appropriate persons in proper form without any error or fault, such as had occurred at the rites of the Bona Dea in December 62.

the authority of the senate, the laws, **the customs of our ancestors**, the courts, jurisdiction, **trust**, the provinces, the allies, the great glory of the empire, the military, the treasury.

15

Cicero, Sestius 98

The Campanian land

In December 57 BC a crowded meeting of the senate had listened in silence to a speech from Rutilius Lupus, one of the new tribunes, on the matter of the Campanian land, but no further action was then taken since Pompeius was not present. This land was among the most fertile in Italy and had been a valuable source of income to the treasury before it was allocated and settled under Caesar's land-law. Despite the additional income accruing from the eastern provinces, the treasury was still short of the moneys Pompeius needed for ensuring the corn supply. At the same time there was a widespread belief that the compact of the Three was in terminal decline, Crassus and Pompeius being seriously at odds. An attack on the legislation of 59, seeking to reclaim the Campanian land for the treasury, might succeed. Debate began in earnest in April 56, as Cicero reports to his brother Quintus.

1   … On 5 April a decree of the senate gave Pompeius 40 million sesterces for the corn business. On the same day there was a heated debate in the senate about the Campanian land, with shouting almost as at a *contio*. The shortage of money and the high price of corn had made the problem more acute …

3   … I had dinner that night at **Crassipes'**. After dinner I was carried over to 5 Pompeius' villa. I had not been able to see him during the day because he had been away. I wanted to see him because I was going to leave Rome the next day and he was to journey to Sardinia. I met the good man and asked him to restore you to us as soon as possible. He replied 'forthwith'. He was about to leave on 11 April, so he said, in order to board ship from either **Salebro or Pisae**. 10

Rome and on the way to Anagnia, April 56 BC

Cicero, Quintus 2.6.1, 3(10)

---

the customs of our ancestors   the traditional, conservative way of doing things handed down from generation to generation which had been most famously stated by Q. Ennius, the father of Roman poetry: 'On ancient customs and men of old the Roman state stands firm.'

trust   this may refer to financial probity, creditworthiness or being true and honest to one's word, able and willing to do what one says for oneself and others.

Crassipes   Furius Crassipes, the second husband of Cicero's 23-year-old daughter, Tullia, whose first husband Piso had died in 57.

Salebro or Pisae   ports on the coast of Etruria.

Pompeius gave no sign of annoyance with Cicero's stance over the Campanian land, nor did he say he intended to meet Caesar and Crassus at Luca before going to Sardinia. Cicero failed to mention to Quintus that he had proposed that a debate on the Campanian land be held on 15 May.

In his letter to Lentulus in 54, Cicero explained how he had proposed a debate in the senate about the Campanian land, and its repercussions.

8   When **that proposal of mine** was uttered, a great stir of emotion occurred not only **among those where it should have** but with **those to whom I never thought it would**.

9   The senate had passed a decree in accordance with my proposal; Pompeius, although he had not revealed to me that he was in the least offended, **set out for** 5
Sardinia and Africa and on his journey went to meet Caesar at **Luca**. There Caesar made many complaints about my proposal. He had seen **Crassus beforehand at Ravenna** and had been stirred up by him against me. It is generally agreed that Pompeius was **quite annoyed by it**. Although I heard this from others I discovered it principally from my brother. Pompeius met him within a few days 10
of leaving Luca. 'You're just the man I want,' he said. 'Nothing could have been more opportune. Unless you take your brother properly in hand, you will have to pay over **what you guaranteed** me on his behalf.' In short he made serious complaints, mentioned his services, recalled the frequent dealings he had with my brother about Caesar's legislation and the assurances my brother had given 15
him concerning me. He called upon my brother to witness that his efforts for my restoration had been done with Caesar's goodwill; he asked Quintus to commend Caesar's cause and *dignitas* to me; if I were unwilling or unable to defend them, I should not attack them.

---

that proposal of mine   Cicero's proposal that a debate be held in the senate on the Campanian land on 15 May.

among those where it should have   Caesar and, perhaps, Crassus.

those to ... would   Pompeius.

set out for Sardinia   to superintend the corn supply.

Luca   southernmost town of Caesar's province on the Ligurian coast.

Crassus beforehand at Ravenna   the southernmost town of Caesar's province on the Adriatic coast. Crassus and Cicero shared a mutual dislike.

quite annoyed by it   annoyed by the complaints of Caesar against Cicero.

what you guaranteed   Quintus had promised Pompeius, and through him Caesar, that Marcus would not attack the Three.

10   My brother brought me this news and furthermore Pompeius sent **Vibullius** to   20
me with instructions that I should keep the matter of the Campanian land on
hold until his return. I then came to my senses.

Rome, December 54 BC

Cicero to Lentulus Spinther, *Friends* 1.9.8–10 (*20*)

What precisely was decided at Luca we do not know, and can only guess from
what happened later. 'Caesar must have shown masterful tact in composing the
differences between Crassus and Pompeius' (M. Gelzer, p. 121). Throughout
his time in Gaul, Caesar kept in constant touch with friends and affairs in
Rome, dispensing large sums of money to further his interests. A later source
says there were 120 **lictors** and two hundred or more members of the senate
in attendance at Luca.

Face to face with political reality

Cicero had enjoyed political distinction and independence and found having
to face political reality after Luca an unpleasant experience. He moaned to
Atticus.

1   Moreover – for I've long been nibbling at what must be fully consumed – I
thought my **palinode** slightly dishonourable. So, farewell to principle, honesty
and honour in politics. The **treachery is unbelievable in those leading citizens**,
for that's what they want to be and would be if they had any honesty. I saw it, I
knew it. They led me on, abandoned me and threw me out. Even so I was minded   5
to agree with them in politics. But they were the same as always. Now at long last,
with your advice, I have regained my senses.

Vibullius   he had been a prefect of engineers with Pompeius and was not a senator but
employed by Pompeius on diplomatic missions.

lictors   the attendants on magistrates invested with authority; the large number present
indicates almost an alternative seat of government.

palinode   a recantation, generally reckoned to have been the speech *On the Consular
Provinces*, though not all scholars agree. It was clearly some speech or statement widely
known so as to bind Cicero without any chance of backsliding. Alternative suggestions
lack evidence.

treachery … citizens   the familiar and bitter complaints about Hortensius and others.

2   You will say you advised me what to do, not that I should put it in writing as well. But I actually wanted to bind myself of necessity to **this new alliance** and not to allow any possibility of slipping back to those who even when they ought to feel   10 sorry for me don't give up being jealous of me ... Since the powerless don't want

3   to be my friends, let me do my best to make myself liked by the powerful. You will say you wish I had done that sooner. I know you wanted me to do so, and that I have been a proper ass. But now it's time to be friends with myself since I cannot in any way be friends with them.   15

Antium, June 56 BC

Cicero, *Atticus* 4.5.1–3 (*80*)

Cicero supports Caesar in the senate

Caesar had been honoured by the senate in 57 BC for his Gallic campaigns with a public thanksgiving of an unprecedented 15 days. Cicero thought this was making Caesar more supportive of the senatorial order. Then in 56 after Luca came a request for moneys for his additional legions and an increase in the number of his officers. Cicero, 'having regained his senses', moved both proposals, illustrating publicly 'the new alliance'.

The matter of the payment of Caesar's army has recently been put before us. Not only did I vote in favour of it but I also worked hard that you should vote in favour. I replied at length to those who disagreed. I was present at the drafting ... when the matter of the ten *legati* was decided. Some resolutely refused to grant them, others wanted precedents, others delay, others to grant but without any   5 expression of congratulation. On this issue I spoke in such a manner that all understood I did what I felt was for the good of the *respublica* more handsomely because of the *dignitas* of Caesar.

Cicero, *Consular Provinces* 28

The political situation in summer 56 BC

Cicero could publicly proclaim his support for the Three but his letters tell another story. He tells Lentulus of the situation in Rome and advises him to have regard for both dignity and security.

You say that you wish to know what the state of the *respublica* is: opposition is intense, but the conflict is unequal. For those who are **stronger in resources, arms and power** have, it seems to me, actually managed to attain a greater authority

---

this new alliance   Cicero's agreement not to attack the Three.

stronger in resources, arms and power   Caesar, Crassus and Pompeius.

because of **their opponents' stupidity and lack of determination**. Thus they
have gained everything through the senate with little opposition, when they did 5
not think they could gain it even through the people without disorder. Pay and
ten *legati* have been decreed to Caesar; that in accordance with **the Sempronian
law** there should be no successor has been arranged without difficulty. **I write to
you somewhat briefly** because the situation of the *respublica* does not please me.
However, I *do* write in order to advise you that while your affairs remain in good 10
shape you may learn the lesson which I, who have been devoted to every branch
of literature from childhood, have come to realize more through experience than
through learning. We must not take thought for our security without *dignitas* nor
for our *dignitas* without security.

Rome, late June or July 56 BC

Cicero to Lentulus Spinther, Friends 1.7.10 (18)

The consular elections of 56 BC

The elections of 56 BC were delayed. One candidate, Domitius Ahenobarbus,
had announced his intention to have Caesar succeeded in Gaul. After
nominations had closed, Crassus and Pompeius announced they wished to
be candidates. The consul Marcellinus refused to accept their candidacy so
they proceeded to block the elections for the rest of the year. In January 55
there was an **interregnum** and an *interrex* nominated Pompeius and Crassus.
They were elected – Domitius persevered but was driven off by force – and
then proceeded to control the elections of other magistrates to ensure that
their intended legislation – presumably the plans agreed at Luca – was not
opposed. Writing to Atticus, Cicero laments the position of Domitius.

Concerning Domitius … his situation is just like mine. The **same people** have
brought it about, it has the same unexpectedness and the same total absence of

---

their … determination   Cato and the *optimates*, whose selfishness, lack of direction and
unity Cicero deplores.

the Sempronian law   the law of the tribune, Gaius Sempronius Gracchus, 123/2 BC, which
required the senate to name the consular provinces before the elections of their potential
holders. Since the senate did not name Caesar's Gallic provinces in 56, he was secure.

I write to you somewhat briefly   so briefly that he did not tell Lentulus of his part in
supporting Caesar in the senate.

interregnum   when elections could not be held in any year, an interregnum occurred and
an *interrex* was appointed, who held office only for five days; after the first *interrex* of
the year, any successor might nominate two consular candidates and elections were held
immediately. A sign of the disordered times, this happened in 55, 53 and 52.

same people   Caesar, Crassus and Pompeius.

boni; there's just one difference – **he deserved it**. As for the actual misfortune, I tend to think he came off better. But what can be more distressing for a man who had been **consul-designate for so many years** than not to be able to become consul, especially when he has no competitors, or at least only one other? If it is true, as I am inclined to think it is, that in the columns of their little notebooks the lists of the future consuls are no less long than those of previous consuls, then what can be more distressing than his fate except that of the *respublica*, for which it is not even possible to hope for anything better?

Antium or Tusculum, mid-November 56 BC

Cicero, *Atticus* 4.8a.2 (*82*)

> A tribune, Trebonius, then passed a law giving five-year commands in the provinces of Syria and Spain to Crassus and Pompeius. They themselves then arranged a five-year extension of Caesar's command. Crassus departed for Syria and his campaign against the Parthians before the end of the year.
>
> In early February 55 BC Cicero, writing to his brother, declared: 'they control everything and they want everyone to know it' (*Quintus* 2.8.3 (*13*)). At about the same time he wrote to Lentulus.

3   I have another consolation. All concede that I more than all others should be allowed to support Pompeius' wishes or remain silent or **return to my literary studies**, my greatest pleasure. I shall certainly do that **if his friendship allows me**. I have performed the **highest offices and faced the greatest ordeals. I had expected to enjoy dignity in giving my opinions in the senate and independence in politics** but that's all been removed from me as from everyone else. One must either assent to a few without dignity or dissent without avail.

---

he deserved it   it is not at all clear why Cicero says this, or what Domitius had done to deserve rejection.

consul-designate for so many years   Domitius was one of those *optimates* said to have been born to the consulship. One doubts whether he would have considered his misfortune on a par with Cicero's.

return … studies   throughout his career Cicero engaged in literary and philosophical studies, but particularly when, as now, he was not able actively to engage in politics.

if his friendship allows me   Cicero was to find that Pompeius would require him to be active in the courts defending his friends, who were not always Cicero's friends.

highest offices … ordeals   the consulship of 63 and exile in 58–57.

I had expected to enjoy … politics   the summit of senatorial ambition, after having held the consulship, though not in Cicero's case a great provincial governorship. He aspired to an honoured place within the senate, giving advice and instituting policy, enjoying the political independence of the leaders of the *respublica*.

4   … The pattern of things has changed completely: senate, lawcourts, and the *respublica* as a whole. *Peace* is what we must hope for and those who control things seem likely to provide it so long as **certain persons** are able to put up with 10 their domination with greater patience. There's no point in thinking about the consular dignity characteristic of a brave and resolute member of the senate. Its loss is the fault of those who **alienated from the senate** the order most closely connected with it and the man of greatest distinction.

Rome, February (?) 55 BC

Cicero to Lentulus Spinther, Friends 1.8.3–4 (19)

Cicero's life in the later 50s BC

Three themes reasonably define Cicero's life in the later 50s BC: lawcourts, literature and lack of political independence. He remained an avid observer of the political scene but no longer an active participant.

Lawcourts: Cicero is forced to defend Gabinius

Aulus Gabinius returned to Rome in 54 BC after his governorship of Syria, where he had controlled the activities of the *publicani* to their annoyance and, at the instigation of Pompeius, restored Ptolemy Auletes to his throne in Alexandria. His enemies were lining up to prosecute him on various charges but Pompeius was determined to defend him, as Cicero would discover. His case is a good example of the interplay of politics and personalities in the late Republic. Cicero writes to Quintus, who in 54–53 was on Caesar's staff in Gaul.

Gabinius has not yet been charged with extortion because **Cato** is ill. Pompeius is putting a lot of pressure on me for a reconciliation. So far he has got nowhere and he never will if I keep a scrap of personal liberty.

Arpinum and Rome, September 54 BC

Cicero, Quintus 3.1.15 (21)

---

certain persons   Cato and associates.

alienated from the senate   Cato and colleagues, who in 61–60 had caused a split between the senate and the *equites* and who had treated Pompeius, 'the man of greatest distinction', with jealousy and hostility, as they continued to do.

Cato   he was praetor in 54 and presided over the recovery (extortion) court.

In the event, Gabinius was first charged with *maiestas* (treason) because, in restoring Ptolemy, he had gone outside the limits of his province without the authority of the Roman people. Cicero neither prosecuted nor defended but gave evidence against Gabinius, who declared afterwards that he would make amends if he were allowed to remain within the state. Fears of a dictatorship and the extraordinary efforts of Pompeius brought Gabinius acquittal but he faced further trials and was next charged with extortion. Pompeius pulled out all the stops. Cicero was obliged to defend, witnesses were summoned from Alexandria, Pompeius himself spoke in support and a letter came from Caesar, but in vain. The jurors were implacable and Gabinius went into exile. In either 54 or 53 BC Cicero spoke on behalf of C. Rabirius Postumus, an equestrian banker, who had lent money to the Egyptian king, and he found it necessary to explain his defence of Gabinius.

32   **My reason, Memmius, for defending Gabinius was our reconciliation.** And indeed I do not regret that with me enmities die whereas friendship endures
33   for ever. Now if you think that I took up his case unwillingly to avoid offending the feelings of Pompeius, I am afraid you have absolutely no understanding of Pompeius or me. *He* would not have wished me to act against my will just to   5 please himself while I, who have treasured the freedom of all citizens most highly, would not have put my own at risk.

Cicero, *Rabirius Postumus* 32–3

Cicero viewed all these proceedings with dismay: there was no *respublica*, no senate, no courts and no dignity in anyone.

Literature: Cicero, *On the Orator*

At various periods in his life when, as now, Cicero could not play an active part in politics, he turned to the study of literature and philosophy, and to writing. He writes to Lentulus about his work on oratory.

My reason ... reconciliation   an interesting point – had Cicero not been reconciled with Gabinius, would he have defended him? It is hard to believe that Cicero is being wholly honest in what he says here. Personal feelings are not expected to be an issue in English courts, where defence barristers take on cases according to their professional competence. In the United States lawyers are not supposed to accept or reject potential clients according to personal feelings. A statement such as Cicero makes here would therefore be unthinkable within today's legal system.

I have written … three books consisting of debate and dialogue *On the Orator*, which I think will not be without use for your [son] Lentulus. They steer clear of the ordinary rules and encompass the whole oratorical theory of **Aristotle** and **Isocrates**.

Rome, December 54 BC

Cicero to Lentulus Spinther, *Friends* 1.9.23 (*20*)

Having completed his study on oratory, Cicero turned to a work on politics.

Cicero, *On the Republic*

Cicero writes to Atticus about his progress in writing *On the Republic*.

Now I shall proceed to the other points. **Varro**, about whom you write to me, will be included at some point provided there is a place. You know the format of my dialogues: as in my oratorical works, which you praise to the sky, those who are in the discussion cannot mention anyone unless they have known or heard that person. I have given the discussion concerning the *respublica*, on which I 5 have begun work, to the persons of **Africanus, Philus, Laelius and Manilius** and I have included some young men … Since I have made use of introductions in the individual books as Aristotle does … I am thinking of arranging one so that I have a reason to introduce him [Varro] by name. I realize this is something which will please you. I hope I can finish what I have attempted. I have taken on a huge 10 subject – which will not escape your notice – and one that needs a lot of free time, which I dearly need and do not have.

Rome, July 54 BC

Cicero, *Atticus* 4.16.2 (*89*)

Aristotle   fourth-century Greek philosopher, master and teacher, of the greatest significance, who had written on the topic.

Isocrates   fourth-century Athenian orator and teacher of rhetoric, of central importance in education. The best study of this work is E. Fantham, *The Roman World of Cicero's* De Oratore.

Varro   Marcus Terentius Varro, the polymath, who does not appear anywhere in the surviving parts of the *De Republica*. It is probable that Cicero did not find a place for him.

Africanus, Philus, Laelius and Manilius   all leading Roman statesmen of the second century BC. The best introduction to this much-discussed work is probably J. E. G. Zetzel, *Cicero, On the Commonwealth and On the Laws*.

Cicero began work on the *De Republica* (*On the Republic*) in 54 BC, and it was published in 51. 'It was the tops with everyone,' Caelius reported to Cicero. The full text was known until the fifth century AD, when St Augustine quoted from Cicero's work in his *On the City of God*, written AD 413–26. After that it was known only in fragments. The situation changed dramatically in 1822. Cardinal Angelo Mai, the Vatican librarian, discovered in 1819 and published in 1822 a palimpsest of 151 leaves – that is, a manuscript where the original fourth-century text (in this case, Cicero) has been rubbed out not very well and reused to provide a later text (a commentary of St Augustine on the Psalms). It contains about a third of the original work, most from the first two books. The most recent Latin text was published in 2006.

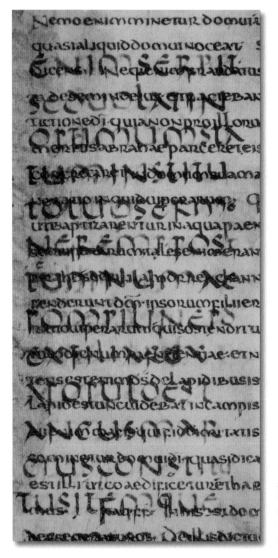

Part of a page from the Vatican palimpsest of Cicero, On the Republic. *The original large, bold script is of the late fourth or early fifth century AD, while the later, smaller script dates to the seventh century.*

Political paralysis, 54–53 BC

By the late 50s BC the political system of republican Rome was in serious disorder. The Roman people were no longer able to elect their magistrates without violence and disruption. Competition was extreme: too many candidates, unprecedented bribery, and the malign influence of Caesar and Pompeius in a city with a population approaching a million people without any organized police force. Two fortuitous events added to the uncertainty of the political situation: in the autumn of 54 Iulia, the wife of Pompeius and the daughter of Caesar, died in childbirth and then in June 53 Crassus was killed in the East. The Three had become two and although Caesar tried to arrange another marriage connection, Pompeius did not take up his offer. Cicero lamented the state of affairs in a letter to his brother.

I am grieved, my sweetest brother, I am grieved that there is no *respublica*, no courts, that in these years, when I ought to be flourishing with the *dignitas* of a senator, I am busy with work in the courts or kept going by literary studies at home; while what I had wanted to have from childhood – **'to be best by far and to be pre-eminent over others'** – has wholly collapsed. Some of my enemies I have 5 not attacked, some I have even defended; my mind is not free and I am not free to hate either.

Tusculum, October/November 54 BC

Cicero, *Quintus* 3.5.4 (*25*)

After a huge electoral scandal in 54 BC no magistrates, other than tribunes, were elected until July 53. That year too ended without elections. Rome seemed to be becoming ungovernable. In January 52 violence erupted on an unprecedented scale, obliging the *optimates* to turn to Pompeius for help.

The death of Clodius and the trial of Milo

A brawl occurred on the Appian Way and Clodius was killed by slaves of Milo. His body was brought back to Rome and on the following day was cremated in the senate house by an enraged mob. The senate house and some neighbouring buildings were burnt down. The *optimates* turned to Pompeius as the only person on hand capable of dealing with the situation. On the motion of Bibulus he was elected 'consul without a colleague' and immediately set about restoring order and arranging for the trial of Milo. Cicero spoke for the defence, basing his case on the themes: 'Which of the two plotted the ambush for the other?' and 'Whose was the advantage?' Cicero sets out the facts, but a careful reading will reveal much insinuation.

---

to be … others   a quotation in Greek from Homer's *Iliad*, 6.208, repeated at 11.784.

A reconstruction of the interior of the curia *(senate house), built after a fire in the third century AD on the site of the republican senate house.*

27   Clodius was aware … that Milo was required by religious ritual and by law to journey to Lanuvium on 18 January to elect a priest, for Milo was chief magistrate there; Clodius himself suddenly left Rome the day before to set an ambush for Milo in front of his estate. This is clear from what happened. Such was the manner of his leaving the city that he abandoned a disorderly public meeting held that   5 day. People missed his madness. He would never have abandoned it had he not wished to be on hand at the place and in time for his evil enterprise.

28   Milo, on the other hand, having been at a meeting of the senate that day until it was dismissed, came home, changed his shoes and his clothes, waited a short time while his wife got herself ready, as happens. He then left home at a time when   10 Clodius could have been back if he was intending to be in Rome that day. When he met Milo, Clodius was unencumbered, on horseback, with no carriage, with no baggage, without any Greek companions as was his custom, and without his wife, which almost never happened. Milo, this conspirator, who, so it is alleged, had organized his journey to commit murder, was riding in a carriage with his   15 wife, wearing a heavy cloak, with a company that was large, heavily laden, with women and a pretty troop of slave girls and boys.

29   He met Clodius in front of his estate about three in the afternoon or not much
      later. Several armed men at once launched an attack from higher ground, while
      others blocked his way and killed his coachman. Milo, having thrown aside his   20
      cloak, jumped down from the carriage and began to defend himself vigorously.
      Some of those who were with Clodius, having drawn their swords, ran back to
      the carriage to attack Milo from the rear, while others, because they thought that
      he was already dead, began to attack his slaves who brought up the rear. Some of
      these who were resolute and loyal to their master were killed, while others, who   25
      saw the fighting by the carriage, were prevented from coming to the help of their
      master. They heard from Clodius himself that Milo had been killed and thought
      that this was indeed the case. The slaves of Milo … without the order or the
      knowledge or the presence of their master, did what anyone would have wished
      his slaves to do in such circumstances.   30

                                                              Cicero, *Milo* 27–9

      We possess the commentary of the learned Asconius on Cicero's speech in
      defence of Milo. He describes the final day of the trial.

40/41 On the following day, 7 April, the last of the trial, shops had been closed throughout
      the city. Pompeius placed guards strategically in the forum and around all the
      approaches to the forum. He took up position in front of the treasury surrounded
      by a picked detachment of soldiers, as he had done the previous day. The selection
      of the jurors picked by lot on the first day was then made. The silence throughout   5
      the forum was as absolute as could be in any forum. Just after eight o'clock the
      prosecutors, the **elder Appius**, **M. Antonius** and **P. Valerius Nepos**, began to
      speak. They used the two hours allowed them by law. Cicero was the sole defence
      counsel. Some people thought the charge should be refuted on the grounds that
      killing Clodius had been in the interest of the *respublica* … However, Cicero did   10
      not agree that a person whose condemnation might be in the public good could
      therefore be killed without trial. The prosecutors had made the basis of their case
      that Milo had arranged an ambush for Clodius – this was false since the brawl had
      begun by chance – and Cicero seized hold of this point and argued on the contrary
      that Clodius had laid an ambush for Milo. His whole speech concentrated on this   15

---

elder Appius   he was the nephew of Clodius, the elder son of Clodius' brother, Gaius
Claudius Pulcher, who was in exile at this time.

M. Antonius   Marcus Antonius, friendly with Clodius in the early 50s but then estranged.
He joined Caesar in Gaul and stayed with him until 50, though he was in Rome from 53
to 52. He was quaestor in 51 and tribune in 49, when he fled from Rome to the camp of
Caesar. He played a major role in the history of Rome in the 40s and 30s. His prosecution
of Milo may have been a favour to Clodius' widow, Fulvia.

P. Valerius Nepos   'an obscure personage' – so E. S. Gruen, pp. 338–43, who provides a
detailed analysis of this trial and others in this chapter.

point. However, it was well known, as I have said, that the battle on that day actually happened by chance and not through the deliberate intent of either of them. An altercation had developed between slaves and had ended in the killing. It was also well known that each of them had often threatened the other with death. The fact that Milo had a larger escort of slaves than Clodius made him suspect, but the Clodians had been the readier and more prepared for battle than Milo's slaves. When Cicero began to speak he was greeted with a barrage of noise by the supporters of Clodius, who could not contain themselves despite their fear of the soldiers who were standing around them. Thus Cicero did not speak with his usual resolve.

42

20

25

Asconius, *Milo*, pp. 40–2 (Clark)

Notice how Asconius sets the record straight: the death of Clodius was not pre-arranged, the brawl began by chance. He gives the votes of the jurors: senators 12 for conviction, 6 acquittal; *equites* 13 : 4; treasury tribunes 13 : 3. He comments: 'The jurors seemed to have realized that Milo did not at first know that Clodius had been wounded but they found that when he had been wounded he was then killed on Milo's order' (Asconius, *Milo*, p. 53 (Clark)).

The imperial historian Cassius Dio, who was not sympathetic to Cicero, reported on his apparent nervousness.

That orator, seeing Pompeius and the soldiers in the court, contrary to custom, was panic struck and in great fear so that he spoke none of what he had prepared but, having with difficulty uttered some brief statement that died on his lips, was glad to get away.

Dio, *Roman History* 40.54.2

When Milo later received a copy of Cicero's intended speech, which the orator sent to him, Dio records his reply.

Milo wrote back saying that it was fortunate for him that such a speech had not been delivered in the court, for he would not be eating red mullet in Massilia in exile if such a defence had been delivered.

Dio, *Roman History* 40.54.3

10 Governing Cilicia

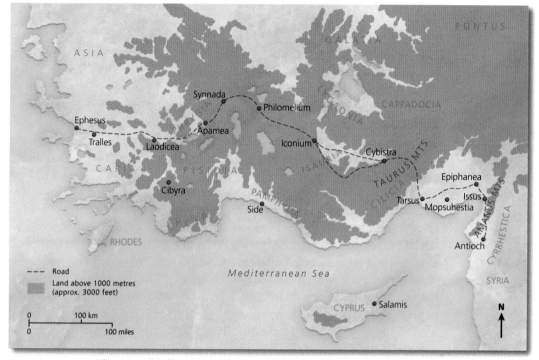

The eastern Mediterranean. The dotted line marks the road along much of which Cicero travelled during his governorship in 51–50 BC.

Pompeius passed a law in 52 BC that there should be a five-year interval between holding the office of praetor or consul in Rome and governing a province overseas. No magistrate of 52 was thus eligible for a governorship before 48 and for the interim period governors were selected from among those who had not previously held provincial appointments. A very reluctant Cicero found himself assigned to Cilicia with Cyprus in south-east Asia Minor. The province of Cilicia with Cyprus extended much further than the geographical area of Cilicia itself. It formed a buffer between the Roman province of Asia in the west and Syria in the east. Its coast had been a notorious base of pirates. Full details of his governorship and administration in Cilicia can be found in LACTOR 10, *Cicero's Cilician Letters*.

The governor's edict

An intending governor issued an edict declaring the laws and regulations he planned to follow during his period of office. He normally took over the edict of his predecessor so that form and content became traditional, though there could be changes, as Cicero records.

I have a similar but more cautious clause, taken from the edict for the province of Asia of **Q. Mucius**, son of Publius: 'A contract will be considered valid except where the business has been so transacted that it ought not in good faith to be continued.' I have followed many of Scaevola's provisions, among them the one where the Greeks reckon they have been given their liberty. **Greeks** are to conduct   5
their disputes among themselves according to their own laws. My edict is short because I have made a division. I thought the edict should be published in two parts. One deals with matters of the province and embraces the finances of the communities, debt, interest, bonds, and everything to do with the *publicani*. The other part contains such matters as cannot be dealt with satisfactorily without an   10
edict: possession of inheritances, possession of property, appointment of receivers, sale of property, matters which are usually both legally and otherwise dealt with in accordance with the edict. I have left the third part, containing everything else to do with the administration of justice, unwritten. I explained that for this part I would adapt my decisions to the edicts of the **urban and peregrine praetors**   15
and that is what I am doing, so far satisfying everybody. The Greeks are delighted because they have judges of their own choice. 'Mere fools,' you will say. But what does it matter? They think that they have gained autonomy.

Laodicea, 20 February 50 BC

Cicero, *Atticus* 6.1.15 (*115*)

The duties of the governor: dispensing justice and waging war

Cicero describes events during his governorship to Atticus.

1   … You know about my arrival at **Ephesus**, since you even congratulated me on the

---

Q. Mucius   Q. Mucius Scaevola, the pontiff, Cicero's old teacher, probably governor in 94. He was regarded as a model governor and was a leading lawyer. He considered the concept of 'good faith' to be of fundamental importance for Roman law, as the clause of his which Cicero took over shows.

Greeks   the population of Cilicia was mixed, the coastal area containing Greek cities founded in the third and second centuries BC while the native population occupied the wild, mountainous inland parts – the sort of peoples against whom Cicero campaigned.

urban and peregrine praetors   the praetor in Rome responsible for legal cases between Roman citizens (urban) and between Roman citizens and free foreigners (peregrine).

Ephesus   in the province of Asia, from where Cicero travelled overland to his province.

welcoming crowds I had that day. Nothing has ever given me greater delight. From there I was remarkably well received in such towns as there were and I reached Laodicea on 31 July. There I stayed for two days in great state and I removed all the **outrages of the previous four years** with courteous addresses. I did the same 5 at Apamea where I stayed five days, at Synnada for three days, at Philomelium for five days, and at Iconium for ten days. My administration of justice could not have been in any way more impartial, more gentle or responsible.

2   From there I reached camp on 24 August. I reviewed the army near Iconium on 28 August. Since serious reports were coming about the Parthians, I proceeded 10 from this camp to Cilicia through that part of Cappadocia which borders Cilicia with the intention that the Armenian king Artavasdes and the Parthians themselves should reckon they were barred from Cappadocia. When I had been in camp for five days at Cybistra in Cappadocia, I received information that the Parthians were a considerable distance from that gateway into Cappadocia and 15 were posing a greater threat to Cilicia. I therefore marched at once into Cilicia through the passes of Taurus.

3   I reached Tarsus on 5 October. From there I pressed on to the Amanus range, which divides Syria from Cilicia. This mountain range has always been full of

our enemies. Here on 13 October we killed a large 20 number of the enemy. We captured and burnt some well-fortified strongpoints, **Pomptinus** in a night attack and myself in the morning. I was given the title *imperator*. For a few days we encamped near **Issus, where Alexander**, a decidedly better general 25 than you or I, had pitched camp against **Darius**. We stayed there five days, plundering and laying waste the Amanus, and then we left …

Cicero, *Atticus* 5.20.1–3 (*113*)

Alexander the Great, at the battle of Issus, dashingly portrayed with his hair flying.

- What differing qualities does Cicero display as a judge and as a general?

outrages of the previous four years   a reference to the regime of his predecessor as governor, Appius Claudius.

Pomptinus   Gaius Pomptinus, praetor in 63, legate of Cicero in his governorship.

imperator   commander, general: a title of honour given to a victorious general.

Issus, where Alexander   Alexander the Great defeated the Persians under Darius III at the battle of Issus in south-east Cilicia in 333 BC.

Darius   the Persian king, Darius III, defeated by Alexander and murdered in a plot in 330.

I am at Pindenissum, a well-fortified town of the **Free Cilicians** which has been under arms as long as people remember. They are wild men and fierce fighters and prepared in every way to defend themselves. We surrounded them with a rampart and a ditch, a massive earthwork, protective coverings, a high tower, a good supply of siege artillery and a large number of archers. With a great deal of effort and 5 armaments we finished the business. We suffered many injured but no loss to the army as a whole. The **Saturnalia** was certainly a happy time for the soldiers. I gave them all the booty apart from the **captives**, who are being sold off today, 19 December. As I write this there are about 120,000 sesterces **on the platform**. I am handing over the army to my brother Quintus to take from here to winter 10 quarters in territory which is not fully subdued. I am returning to Laodicea.

Camp at Pindenissum, 19 December 51 BC

Cicero, Atticus 5.20.5 (113)

- How does modern warfare differ from the description Cicero gives here?

Cicero wrote regularly to Atticus from his province. He describes his model governorship and the reactions of the provincials. Even allowing for some exaggeration, his letter shows what the provincials normally experienced and why there was such fierce competition for provincial posts among the governing elite.

7   I myself left Tarsus for Asia on 5 January, and I can't say how marvellous the regards from the communities of Cilicia and particularly the people of Tarsus were. After I had crossed the Taurus mountains, I was eagerly awaited by the districts of Asia in my province, which in the six months of my governorship have received **not one letter from me, nor one compulsory guest**. Before my 5 governorship that time of the year had regularly involved profiteering of this sort.

Free Cilicians   the inhabitants of the Amanus range of mountains between Cilicia and Syria. The exact site of Pindenissum is unknown.

Saturnalia   the festival in honour of Saturn, 17–23 December.

captives   the usual Roman procedure was either to slaughter the captives, keep them for a triumph or to sell them on the spot, as here. Other loot was given to the soldiers – one of the attractions of military life to the rural poor who were the predominant source of recruitment to the Roman army.

on the platform   the auctioneer's platform, thus the takings so far.

not one … guest   governors regularly sent communities letters requisitioning goods and services and demanding they provide board and lodging for their officials and friends.

Wealthier communities gave large sums of money to avoid having troops quartered on them, the people of Cyprus **200 Attic talents**. While I am governor not one penny (I'm not exaggerating but speaking the plain truth) will be demanded from that island. In return for these benefits which quite dumbfound them, I allow no honours except verbal ones to be decreed me. I forbid statues, shrines, **chariots**. I cause no nuisance at all to the communities – but perhaps to you when I go on about myself in this way.

8   My journey through Asia was such that I even considered **famine** desirable, though it is the most dreadful of calamities. It was then affecting that part of Asia in my province, for the harvest had completely failed. Wherever I went, without using force, legal action or rough language but by my authority and encouragement, I made Greek and Roman citizens who had hoarded corn promise a large amount of it to the people.

9   On 13 February, the day of this letter, I have begun to hold court at Laodicea for the districts of Cibyra and Apamea. I shall try cases here from 15 March for the districts of Synnada, Pamphylia … Lycaonia and Isauria. After 15 May I shall go to Cilicia to spend June there, I hope without trouble from the Parthians. If things turn out as I wish, July will be taken up with my return journey through the province. I reached Laodicea and my province on 31 July in **the consulship of Sulpicius and Marcellus** and so I ought to leave it on 30 July.

Laodicea, 13 February 50 BC

Cicero, *Atticus* 5.21.7–9 (*114*)

Cicero completed his year's governorship by dispensing justice and making his homeward journey through his province.

---

200 Attic talents   4,800,000 sesterces, a fortune.

chariots   four horses with a chariot in which stood the figure of the governor.

famine   for the poor in antiquity famine was never far away, as is also the case in much of the Third World today. The people were no doubt grateful for the 'authority and encouragement' of the governor which made the rich hoarders disgorge. Although Cicero might consider famine desirable so that he could exercise a benevolent administration, the locals might have preferred there to be no famine at all.

the consulship of Sulpicius and Marcellus   Servius Sulpicius Rufus, M. Claudius Marcellus, consuls in 51.

Money-lending by Pompeius and Brutus

Roman nobles increased their wealth by lending money to provincial cities and individuals. Members of the senate were prohibited by law from engaging in business, but the law could be evaded. Some protection for provincials was attempted by the praetor's edict setting interest rates, but it was often ignored. Because the provincials were in desperate need for cash, they were forced to pay the exorbitant rates that the moneylenders set. In the business of money, things do not change.

When Cicero came to his province, two associates of M. Brutus approached him about some debts owed by the community of Salamis in Cyprus. Cicero's predecessor, Appius Claudius, had given one of these creditors, Scaptius, an official position together with a troop of cavalry, with which he was putting pressure on the Salaminians. Cicero stopped this at once and tried to settle the matter fairly, but, as he told Atticus, his patience was sorely tried.

Now I come to Brutus. I embraced his friendship very eagerly at your instigation and I had even begun to be fond of him, but I tell you I have had to restrain myself to avoid offending you. Now don't think I wished to do anything but fulfil his commissions or that I have worked harder on any other business. He gave me a notebook containing the commissions and you had discussed the same matters 5 with me. I have followed up everything with the greatest attention.

Cicero, *Atticus* 6.1.3 (*115*)

Cicero had to avoid becoming too friendly with Brutus and offending Atticus' strict moral standards.

3   … Firstly I pressed **Ariobarzanes** to give Brutus the [gap in the text] talents, which he was promising *me*. While the king was with me, the matter was going along smoothly but later he was pressurized by hordes of Pompeius' agents. Now Pompeius is more influential than anyone else, for which there are many reasons, but one particularly – it is thought he will be coming out for the war against the 5 Parthians. So this is how he is now being paid: **33 Attic talents** every 30 days, and

---

Ariobarzanes the Third, young king of Cappadocia titled 'the Pious' and 'Friend of Rome'. Cicero informed him the senate had recognized him as an ally of Rome. He had inherited from his father the debt to Pompeius, 'the literal owner of the East' (E. Badian, p. 84). Pompeius is quite happy to take regular payment of almost full interest and is not bothered about the principal. The sum of money involved is staggering, and Ariobarzanes was a petty king.

33 Attic talents   792,000 sesterces. 400,000 would qualify for the equestrian and senatorial orders, 900 was the annual pay for a legionary soldier – and that had only recently been doubled by Caesar.

that from special taxes, which does not even satisfy the monthly interest. But our Gnaeus takes it without complaining. He goes without the principal, is satisfied with the interest and even that not paid in full. Ariobarzanes does not pay anyone else because he cannot. There is no treasury and he has no regular revenue. He imposes taxes following the arrangement Appius made. These scarcely make up enough for the interest to Pompeius. Two or three friends of the king are very rich, but they keep hold of their money as carefully as you or I do. For my part, I continue to ask, badger and censure the king by letter.

5   Now learn something about the Salaminians that I see is as much of a surprise   15
to you too as it was to me. I never heard from Brutus that the money was his. Furthermore I have his notebook in which there is the entry: 'the Salaminians owe money to M. Scaptius and P. Matinius, my associates'. He recommends them to me and adds – to apply the spur, so to speak – that he has gone surety on their behalf for a large sum of money. I had arranged that they should pay with interest calculated   20
at 1 per cent per month for [gap] years with additional interest for individual years. But Scaptius was demanding 4 per cent. I was afraid you would cease to be my close friend if he got his way. I would have departed from my edict and would have utterly ruined a state which had been placed under **the protection of Cato and of Brutus himself** and which I had honoured with favours of my own.   25

6   Now at this point Scaptius thrust a letter from Brutus into my hand which informed me the business was his own liability, a fact which Brutus had never told me or you.

Cicero, Atticus 6.1.3, 5–6 (115)

All is revealed. It is Brutus himself, not his agent, who is the principal and making the extortionate demands.

He further requested that I should award Scaptius a **prefecture**. But I had already made a stipulation through you that I would not appoint businessmen and, if I had made an exception, it would certainly not be for him. He had been a **prefect** with Appius and had actually possessed a squadron of cavalry, with which he shut up the senate of Salamis in the senate house and laid siege to it, with the result that five   5
members of the senate died of starvation. The day I set foot in my province, envoys from Cyprus came to meet me at Ephesus. I sent a letter ordering the cavalry to leave the province at once. I suspect therefore Scaptius has written something unfavourable about me to Brutus.

Cicero, Atticus 6.1.6 (115)

---

the protection of Cato and of Brutus himself   Cato, with Brutus as his *legatus*, had been responsible for the annexation of Cyprus in 58–56 and both would therefore be regarded as protectors of the province.

prefecture, prefect   an office established, a person appointed officially, by a magistrate, usually a provincial governor.

Roman provincial administration is starkly revealed. There is a continuum of misgovernment from the 'honourable' Brutus to the criminal Verres. Cicero preserved decency.

However, my attitude is as follows: if Brutus thinks I ought to decree interest at 4 per cent, when I am adhering to 1 per cent throughout the province as I had decreed in my edict, which was even approved by the most harsh money-lenders; if he complains that I have refused a prefecture to a businessman, in the same way as I have refused our friend Torquatus in the case of your friend Laenius,   5 and Pompeius himself in the case of Sex. Statius, and with their approval; if he is annoyed that the cavalry have been withdrawn, then for my part I shall be sorry he is angry with me but much more sorry he is not the man I thought him to be.

Cicero, Atticus 6.1.6 (115)

Duty and responsibility before friendship commend Cicero, but even he slips slightly.

Scaptius will at least admit the fact that by my legal ruling I gave him the chance to take all the money my edict allowed. And I'll add the further point, which I fear you will not approve. According to my edict the interest ought to have stopped. The Salaminians wished to deposit the money but I prevailed upon them to say nothing. They granted me this favour but what will happen to them if **Paulus**   5 comes here? But I did this entirely as a favour to Brutus. He has written you the most good-natured letters about me. When he writes to me, even when he is making some request, his style is as a rule insolent, arrogant and tactless. I would like you to write to him about these matters, so that I may know how he takes them. Please let me know.   10

Laodicea, 20 February 50 BC

Cicero, Atticus 6.1.7 (115)

Cato and Cicero, 50 BC

Cicero wrote at length to Cato about his exploits because he was hoping that the senate would award him a triumph, which his campaign merited. He realized that Cato exercised a preponderant influence in the senate and that if his request were to succeed, he would have to convince that stern and inflexible man. Cato's principled reply was not to Cicero's liking.

Paulus   Lucius Aemilius Paulus, consul in 50. He was the son of M. Aemilius Lepidus, the rebel consul of 78, and brother of M. Aemilius Lepidus, the later triumvir. He was married to Iunia, the half-sister of M. Brutus.

M. CATO TO M. CICERO IMPERATOR, GREETINGS

1 I am glad to do what the *respublica* and our friendship encourage me to do: to rejoice that your ability, integrity and diligence, which have been recognized in

the most important matters of civil life here in Rome, are being applied and working with equal diligence in military life abroad. I have been able to act in accordance with my 5 judgement and to praise in my statement and by my vote your defence of your province through your integrity and strategy, your preserving the kingdom of Ariobarzanes and the king himself, and your recovering the hearts and minds of our allies to support our empire. 10

A bronze bust of M. Porcius Cato, inscribed 'CATO' on the breast, found in 1944 at Volubilis in Roman north Africa (modern Morocco).

2 Now concerning a **decree of thanksgiving**. In a case where it was not chance but your own excellent strategy and careful administration which made provision for the *respublica*, I am delighted if you would prefer us to give thanks for it to the immortal gods rather than have it put to your account. But if you think that a decree of thanksgiving is the preliminary to a triumph and for that reason prefer 15 chance to be praised rather than yourself, a triumph does not always follow a decree of thanksgiving. The judgement of the senate that a province has been held and kept safe more by the mild and upright conduct of the governor than by the force of arms and the benevolence of the gods is something much more distinguished than a triumph. That is what I proposed in my statement. 20

3 I have written about these matters to you at greater length than is my custom precisely so that you may realize, as I very much hope you will, that I am doing my utmost to convince you that I wanted what I thought was the most impressive for the dignity of your position. Secondly I rejoice that what you preferred has been done. 25

Goodbye and kind regards. Now you have established your course of action, hold to your strictness and diligence for the allies and *respublica*.

Rome, April 50 BC

M. Cato to Cicero, *Friends* 15.5 (*111*)

---

decree of thanksgiving   decrees such as those for Caesar's victories in Gaul show clearly that they brought honour to the person concerned, not as Cato suggests to the gods. He knew this full well. Cato's words are pious humbug.

A certain formality and stiffness can perhaps be perceived, even in translation, from this key figure of the time. The sentiments obviously did not satisfy Cicero.

But I explained to you in my previous letter the reason for my wish – for I shall not speak of 'desire'. Even if you did not consider it wholly justified, it does not, on the other hand, mean that the honour should be excessively coveted but that, should it be offered by the senate, it should not, in my view, by any means be turned down.

Tarsus, late July 50 BC

Cicero to M. Cato, *Friends* 15.6.2 (*112*)

Marcus was clearly struggling for words! In a letter to Atticus, he writes of Cato's disgraceful spite.

He gave me a testimonial for integrity, justice, clemency and honesty, which I did not ask for. What I requested he refused. That's why in a letter in which he congratulates me and promises me all, Caesar really jumps for joy at Cato's most ungrateful insult. And yet the same Cato votes a thanksgiving of 20 days to Bibulus! Pardon me – I cannot and will not put up with such things.

Brundisium, 25 November (?) 50 BC

Cicero, *Atticus* 7.2.7 (*125*)

This fascinating letter reveals Caesar, in his letter with congratulations and promises, as quick to seize an advantage at Cato's expense, and Cato as happy to favour his son-in-law, Bibulus, with a thanksgiving of equal duration to the two awarded to Caesar for his campaigns in Gaul. Although Cicero did not see it in this light it is possible that Cato and the senate thought Bibulus responsible for the withdrawal of the Parthians from Syria.

End-of-term report

I have completed the administration of justice, I have filled up the coffers of the cities with money and kept their remaining dues safe for the *publicani*, including what was owed from the previous five years, without any complaint from the provincials. I have made myself agreeable to private individuals from the highest to the lowest. I now have it in mind to set out for Cilicia on 5 May. As soon as I have 5 made brief contact with the start of the summer campaign and put the troops in position, **I will leave** the province in accordance with the senate's decree. I am keen

---

I will leave Cicero states his intention to leave his province at the first possible date in accordance with the senate's decree. He left without making proper interim arrangements before a successor arrived and acted quite irresponsibly.

to see you as aedile and I feel a remarkable yearning for Rome, for all my family and friends and you in particular.

Laodicea, May 50 BC

Cicero to Caelius, Friends 11.13.4 (93)

Caelius and Cicero correspond about the political situation in Rome

> While he was away from Rome Cicero arranged with his former pupil, M. Caelius, to keep him regularly informed about affairs in the city. It was a good choice, since Caelius not only was well informed but possessed acute political insight, as his letter to Cicero shows. He explains political developments in Rome in early 50 BC.

As far as the *respublica* is concerned, the whole struggle has become concentrated upon one issue: the provinces. On this issue Pompeius and the senate seem, as things stand so far, to incline to the view that Caesar should leave his provinces on 13 November. Curio has decided to allow anything rather than that. He has given up all his other proposals. Our friends, whom you know well, do not dare to 5
push the issue to a straight confrontation. The scenario of the whole issue is this: Pompeius pretends that he is not attacking Caesar but making a settlement which he thinks is fair to him [Caesar]; he says that Curio is looking for trouble. But Pompeius does not want Caesar becoming consul-designate before he has handed over his army and is obviously afraid of this happening. Pompeius is being quite 10
roughly handled by Curio and his whole third consulship is subject to hostile criticism. I tell you this: if they try every means to suppress Curio, Caesar will defend the veto of his tribune; if they shrink from that, as they seem likely to, Caesar will stay as long as he wants.

Rome, mid (?) April, 50 BC

Caelius to Cicero, Friends 8.11.3 (91)

> Caelius perceives the key issue. Caesar needed to retain a province and an army until elected and entering upon a second consulship. Were there to be any gap he would be liable to prosecution by his enemies and he could not let this happen. As often in history, while the politicians dealt with constitutional and legal points, the real issue was one of power politics.
>
> C. Scribonius Curio, tribune in 50, began the year as an ally of the *optimates*, switched allegiance to Caesar and proceeded to defend his interests against opposition. Curio either vetoed or threatened to veto a proposal that Caesar give up his command in November.

You will wish to know that our friend Curio's veto has had a splendid outcome. When the matter concerning the veto was referred to the senate, a referral made in accordance with a decree of the senate, the opinion of M. Marcellus, who proposed that **representation should be made to the tribunes**, was declared first. A **full senate voted it down unanimously**. **Pompeius Magnus' stomach** is now in such a poor state that he can hardly find anything to satisfy it. They have come to the view that one who does not hand over his army or his provinces should have official permission to stand as a candidate. How Pompeius will take that, I shall tell you when I learn. What will happen to the *respublica* if he does nothing or if he resists with arms, that's for you rich old men to worry about.

As I write this letter, Hortensius is near death.

Rome, early June 50 BC

Caelius to Cicero, *Friends* 8.13.2 (*94*)

> Cicero on his homeward journey begins contemplating the political situation in Rome. A key issue is the tension between loyalty to the *respublica* or to a person, Caesar or Pompeius.

The situation of the *respublica* concerns me greatly. I support Curio. I want Caesar to be treated with honour. I can die for Pompeius, but nothing is dearer to me than the *respublica* itself. You do not make much of your standpoint in it. I sense you are being pulled in different directions because you are a good citizen and a good friend.

Side, 3/4 August 50 BC

Cicero to Caelius, *Friends* 2.15.3 (*96*)

> The time was fast approaching when the Roman nobility would have to decide whom to support, and it was no easy decision. Response to a foreign invasion is generally clear-cut but in civil war people may face conflicting claims, as is shown here and in the histories of the English and American civil wars.

---

representation ... tribunes   this was a formal motion of the senate that pressure should be put upon a tribune to withdraw his veto, with threats that he would be removed from office if he did not yield.

full ... unanimously   the majority of the senate was for peace at almost any price.

Pompeius Magnus' stomach   Pompeius was seriously ill during the summer of 50 and the great concern shown by many Italian communities and their joy at his recovery encouraged in him and his supporters what, in the event, proved to be a false hope that they would support him when it came to armed conflict with Caesar.

In the following extract Caelius provides a typically acute analysis of the dispute between Caesar and Pompeius and the problem he and many others faced in deciding between principle and personalities.

2   On high matters of the *respublica* I have often written to you that I do not see peace lasting for a year. The closer the inevitable struggle approaches, the more obvious the danger appears. The issue on which they are going to join battle is this: Pompeius has decided not to allow Caesar to become consul unless he hands over his army and his provinces, while Caesar is convinced that he cannot be safe   5 if he leaves his army. He proposes that they both hand over their armies. In this way **their love affair and their odious partnership** has descended not to covert bickering but is erupting into full-scale war. I am not clear what course to take. I have no doubt that this thought is causing you trouble too. I have obligations and friendship **with these men** and, though I love the **other cause**, I hate **the men** …   10

3   I do not imagine it escapes your notice that, when there is a dispute within a state, men ought to follow the more respectable side so long as the struggle is waged by civil means and not by force of arms. However, when it comes to war and military action men should follow the stronger side and decide that the safer is the better. In this dispute I see that Cn. Pompeius will have the senate and **those who are**   15 **jurors** with him, while all who live in fear or have no good prospects will join Caesar, whose army is beyond compare. At least there is enough time to consider the resources of each and to choose one's side.

4   … To sum up, you ask what I think will happen. If neither of them goes to the war against the Parthians, I see the threat of a great quarrel which sword and force   20 will decide. Each side enjoys good morale and has forces at the ready. If it were possible without the risk of personal danger, Fortune is preparing a great and delicious spectacle for you.

Rome, about 8 August 50 BC

Caelius to Cicero, *Friends* 8.14.2–4 (*97*)

Caelius makes an interesting and realistic assessment of the strength and support likely for each side. He is quite cynical, and one might argue realistic, in what to do when it comes to war – or is he?

---

their … partnership   the so-called 'First Triumvirate'.

with these men   Caesar and his supporters.

other cause   the cause of the *respublica*.

the men   hatred certainly existed between Caelius and some of the leading republicans, perhaps even with Pompeius himself.

those who are jurors   those who served on the juries in the courts, members of the senate and the equestrian order, the rich and respectable.

11 Civil War and dictatorship

The background to the Civil War, 50 BC

Caesar wished to move directly from his provincial command to a second consulship, avoiding any interval as a private citizen when he could be prosecuted. His enemies, Cato and the *optimates*, were determined to prevent this. In early December 50 BC the tribune C. Curio proposed in the senate that both Caesar and Pompeius should give up their armies. When put to the vote, 370 were in favour, 22 against – there was an overwhelming desire for peace. The consul C. Marcellus, obstructed by tribunician veto from giving Pompeius command and forces to defend the *respublica* against Caesar, angrily declared he would not sit idly by while the *respublica* was threatened with invasion. He proceeded on his own authority, accompanied by his colleague and supporters, to Pompeius' Alban villa, where he handed him a sword, instructing him to defend the state against Caesar. 'I shall do so, if there is no better way,' Pompeius replied (Appian, *Civil Wars* 2.31).

In December 50 Cicero wrote to Atticus about the political situation. He perceived the motives behind the struggle and was critical of Pompeius and the *boni* for not having prevented the growth of Caesar's power.

It is for personal power that the two of them are struggling at this moment and endangering the *respublica*. If the *respublica* is now being defended, then why was it not defended when **Caesar himself was consul**? Why was I not defended **a year later**, when the safety of the *respublica* depended on my cause? Why was his **command extended**, and why in that way? Why was there such a fight for the tribunes to bring in the proposal about his **standing as a candidate in his absence**? It is because of these actions that he has gained such power that hope of resistance

---

Caesar himself was consul   Cicero is referring to 59 and the failure to prevent Caesar's land-law being enacted by violence.

a year later   he refers to 58 and the failure to defend himself from the attacks of Clodius, and his consequential exile.

command extended   Caesar's command in Gaul was extended in 55 by a law of the consuls Crassus and Pompeius, to enable him to continue and complete the conquest.

standing as a candidate in his absence   in 52 all ten tribunes passed a law to allow Caesar to be a candidate for the consulship in his absence while retaining his army in Gaul.

now depends on **one man**. **I would have preferred** that man not to have given Caesar such power, not that he should now resist him when he is so powerful.

Near Trebula, 9 December 50 BC

Cicero, *Atticus* 7.3.4 (*126*)

- What answers could Atticus have given to Cicero's questions?

Cicero meets Pompeius

Cicero had two meetings with Pompeius in December 50 BC. At the first he learned that Pompeius thought war inevitable and was convinced Caesar was alienated from him. Cicero reports on the second meeting to Atticus.

4   Pompeius overtook me near **Lavernium** on 25 December. We travelled together to **Formiae** and talked privately from two o'clock till evening. You asked if there is any hope of a peaceful settlement. As far as I could tell from my long and detailed conversation with him, there is not even a wish for it. He reckons if Caesar becomes consul, even after dismissing his army, it will be the ruin of the   5
respublica. Furthermore, he thinks when Caesar hears that detailed preparations are being made against him, he will not bother about the consulship **this year** and will prefer to retain his army and his province. If Caesar **takes leave of his senses**, Pompeius will be quite contemptuous of him, being confident in his own forces and those of the *respublica*. What more can I say? Although '**the god of war who**   10
takes no sides' often came to my mind, I was relieved of anxiety as I listened to a man, brave, experienced and of immense prestige, discussing like a statesman the dangers of a sham peace.

Formiae, 25/26 December 50 BC

Cicero, *Atticus* 7.8.4 (*131*)

In short, Cicero concluded that Pompeius, so far from seeking peace, even appeared to be afraid of it.

---

one man   Pompeius.

I would have preferred   Cicero thought that the alliance of Pompeius and Caesar had broken the power of the senate and that its break-up spelt civil war.

Lavernium   this place is unknown, but presumably it was somewhere in Latium.

Formiae   one of Cicero's estates in Latium.

this year   standing in 49 (this year) for election to the consulship of 48.

takes leave of his senses   starts a civil war.

'the god of war who takes no sides'   a quotation in Greek from Homer, *Iliad* 18.309, meaning that the outcome of war is never certain.

The beginning of war, 49 BC

In spite of attempts at compromise, the die-hard *optimates* were implacable and when the senate met on 7 January the 'final decree' was passed. Two Caesarian tribunes, Cassius and Antonius, were warned that their safety could not be guaranteed. They fled in disguise, with Curio and Caelius, to the camp of Caesar, where they appeared before troops whose loyalty was not in doubt. On 10 January or soon after Caesar invaded Italy. Civil war had begun.

Panic in Rome

Caesar's incredible speed – a rapidity of movement beyond belief (Cicero, *Atticus* 7.22.1 (*146*)) – caused panic and the evacuation of Rome. Pompeius withdrew to Campania and then made for Apulia. Cicero settled on his estate at Formiae. His letters reveal the general turmoil and perplexity at events. He failed to understand the actions of Pompeius and was openly critical.

1 'What is this, I ask you? What is happening? I am in darkness.' 'We hold **Cingulum**', he says; 'we have lost **Ancona**. **Labienus** has deserted Caesar.' Are we talking about a general of the Roman people or a **Hannibal**? What a mindless wretch! He has never seen even the shadow of what is honourable. And yet he says he is doing all these things for the sake of *dignitas*. Where is *dignitas* except where there is 5 honour? Is it honourable to have an army without authorization from the people, to seize cities of Roman citizens in order to gain easier access to the city of Rome, to plot cancellation of debts, return of exiles, and hundreds of other crimes to get hold of the greatest of gods – tyranny? …

3 How do you see Pompeius' strategy? My question – why has he abandoned Rome? 10 I am perplexed. Yet nothing seems more absurd. Would you abandon Rome?

Formiae (?), 21 January 49 BC

Cicero, *Atticus* 7.11.1, 3 (*134*)

1	Do you think Cicero's criticisms of Pompeius are justified?
2	Could Pompeius have offered a recent precedent to support his action?

Cingulum, Ancona   towns in northern Picenum, the subject of rumours from an unnamed source 'he'.

Labienus   Titus Labienus, Caesar's chief subordinate commander in the Gallic War.

Hannibal   the great Carthaginian commander and enemy of Rome in the Second Punic War, 218–201 BC.

This letter exemplifies the reaction in Rome: panic, turmoil, ignorance and horror at Caesar's actions. Cicero criticized Pompeius but the latter did not have troops to match Caesar's veterans and realized that Rome and Italy, if lost, could be recovered in the provinces. When Atticus asked Cicero about Pompeius' plan of action Cicero replied that he doubted whether Pompeius himself knew. Elsewhere Cicero wrote of bad generalship, lack of judgement, no courage, no plan, no forces, no energy. In no nation had any statesman or general ever done anything so disgraceful – abandoning the city and the country for which and in which it would have been glorious to die.

Cicero's concern for his family: evacuation from Rome?

Many heads of senatorial and equestrian families must have been anxious for their families and homes in the city. Cicero and his brother left Rome with their sons on 18 January while the women of the family remained in Rome. Cicero stayed on his estate at Formiae. Cicero combines a regard for the safety of his family with a concern for public opinion. The women should conform to the behaviour of their class.

FROM TULLIUS TO TERENTIA, FROM HER FATHER TO TULLIA, HIS TWO DEAREST HEARTS, AND FROM MARCUS TO HIS BEST OF MOTHERS AND DARLING SISTER – DEAREST GREETINGS.

If you are well, we are well.

The decision about what you should do is now yours and not mine alone. If **that man** comes to Rome and acts with due restraint, you will be all right at home for the present but if he takes leave of his senses and gives the city over to plunder, I fear that **Dolabella** himself may not be able to give us sufficient help. I am also afraid that we may get cut off so that you cannot leave when you wish. There is a further point, which you are best able to consider: are women such as yourselves remaining in Rome? If they are not, then you must consider whether it is honourable for you to be there. As things currently stand, you will able to live quite comfortably with me or on my estates, provided we can hold these districts. There is also some fear that there may shortly be a scarcity of food in the city. I would like you to consider these matters with Atticus, with **Camillus** and with

5

10

15

If you are well, we are well   a traditional opening formula to a Roman letter.

that man   Caesar.

Dolabella   Cornelius Dolabella, Cicero's son-in-law, who to Cicero's great embarrassment joined Caesar.

Camillus   an associate of Cicero, who looked after some of his affairs and was clearly from this letter a person to be trusted.

those you think appropriate and, quite simply, to be bold-hearted … Write to me, my dearest hearts, as often as possible about how you are doing and what is happening where you are. Quintus, father and son, send their regards. Farewell.

Minturnae, January 49 BC

Cicero to Terentia and Tullia, Friends 14.14.1 (145)

---

1 Evacuation from cities in times of war has happened throughout history, never more so than in the modern world – Warsaw, September 1939, Beirut, July 2006. What was Cicero afraid of?

2 What do the inhabitants of cities fear today?

The pros and cons of each side

Cicero's letters clearly reveal the dilemma which Roman citizens faced, acutely when they belonged to the senatorial and equestrian orders. He continuously seeks advice from Atticus about what to do.

1 I am troubled by grave and dreadful matters. Although there is no chance of our discussing them together, I still wish to make use of your advice. The issue for discussion is simply this: if Pompeius withdraws from Italy, which I suspect he will, what do you think I ought to do? I shall set out my thoughts briefly and it will then be easier for you to advise me.   5

2 It is not only Pompeius' conspicuous services for my restoration and the friendship I have with him but also the cause of the *respublica* itself which lead me to think that my actions should be joined with his and my fortunes with his. There is another point: if I remain here and desert the company of the best and most distinguished citizens, I shall be subject to the power of **one man**. Although he 10 makes it clear in many ways that he is friendly towards me – you yourself know how **I took precautions** that he should be, because I suspected this gathering storm – there are still two matters to consider. Firstly how much trust may I place in him? Suppose I can rely totally on his friendship, is it then appropriate for a brave man and a loyal citizen to remain in a city where he has held the highest 15 office and commands, has carried out the greatest deeds and holds a great priestly office, when he will not enjoy his previous standing and will have to face danger and some disgrace, if ever Pompeius should recover the *respublica*?

---

one man Caesar.

I took precautions Cicero made friends with Caesar in the later 50s, particularly through his brother Quintus' period of service with Caesar in Gaul. There may have been more to it than protection, but we can only guess. A letter to Atticus of July 54 (*Atticus* 4.16.8 (*89*)) reveals that Cicero was involved with Oppius in the purchase of land for Caesar's grandiose building plans for both the forum and the Campus Martius.

3   Now look at what the other side offers. Your Pompeius has not shown wisdom or courage. He has acted throughout contrary to my suggestions and advice. I pass over earlier actions … what more dreadful and disorganized than this departure from the city, or rather, this utterly disgraceful flight in which we are now engaged? Any terms should have been accepted rather than abandoning the city. They were bad terms, I agree, but could anything be worse than the present situation?

4   But he will recover the *respublica*, you say. When?

Cales, 18/19 February 49 BC

Cicero, *Atticus* 8.3.1–4 (*153*)

Cicero was in difficulty because he was friends with both leaders, but he never ceased to recall his gratitude to Pompeius for his restoration. He believed some sort of agreement could have been reached, but both leaders were out for personal power and both wanted to be kings and had no thought for the happiness and lives of the citizens. In the country he found people interested solely in their fields, farms and investments. They had once favoured Pompeius, now they adored Caesar. It was the supporters of the *respublica* who bore responsibility. Who could be happy when Pompeius abandoned his country, when Caesar overwhelmed it? An unjust peace was, in Cicero's view, better than the most just of wars against one's fellow countrymen.

Confrontation between Cicero and Caesar

On both points I acted in accord with your advice. What I said made him think well of me rather than thank me and I stuck to my position not to go to Rome. We made a mistake in thinking Caesar to be accommodating. I have never seen a person less so. He said he was being condemned by my decision and that if I did not come the rest would be more reluctant. I said their position was different from mine. After much talk he said 'Come and work for peace, then.' 'On my terms,' I replied. 'Is it for me to lay down terms for you?' he asked. 'Then I shall take the line that the senate does not approve **your going to the Spanish provinces**, or **transporting an army to Greece**, and,' I said, 'I shall speak at length lamenting the position of **Gnaeus**.' 'Those are certainly not the sort of things that I wish to be said,' was his reply. 'That's what I thought,' I replied, 'and that's why I am

On both points   Atticus had advised Cicero to maintain his dignity and resist going to Rome.

your going to the Spanish provinces   Caesar was planning to deal with the Pompeian forces in Spain.

transporting an army to Greece   in 48 Caesar transported his forces to Greece to confront Pompeius.

Gnaeus   Pompeius.

unwilling to go to Rome. I must either speak like this or not go. There are many issues I could not be silent about if I were there.' The upshot was that he asked me to think it over. It was as if he was looking for a way out. I could not refuse. So we departed. I believe he is not pleased with me but I was pleased with myself and   15
that has not happened in a long time.

Formiae, 28 March 49 BC

Cicero, Atticus 9.18.1 (187)

> This is a jolly conversation and we can surely admire Cicero for sticking to his guns. What Caesar's followers lacked was class. They were a dreary lot – 'Ye gods, what a crew!' was Cicero's comment in the same letter to Atticus – and they could not compare in quality with those around Pompeius; they were 'more like beasts than men' (*Atticus* 9.19.1 (*189*)).

Advice from all and sundry

> Cicero supported the *respublica* and Pompeius, for he could never join Caesar, but he continued to hesitate over what to do. Friends offered advice. When his intention to join Pompeius became public, his beloved daughter Tullia wrote frequently begging him to wait in Italy until the outcome of Caesar's operations against the republican forces in Spain was known, and added that Atticus agreed with her. At the beginning of May M. Antonius wrote begging Cicero not to compromise himself, 'not to trust a man who to do you a service first did you an injury' (*Atticus* 10.8A.2 (*199A*)), nor to run away from Caesar, who desired his well-being and dignity. Then Caesar himself wrote to Cicero.

I beg you in the name of our friendship **not to do this**. In the last resort, nothing is more fitting for a good and peaceful man and for a good citizen than to steer clear of quarrels between citizens. Though some approved such action, they have not been able to follow it through fear, but consider carefully the testimony of my life and the criterion of our friendship. You will not discover anything safer or more   5
honourable than keeping out of all conflict.

On the road to Massilia, 16 April 49 BC

Caesar to Cicero, in Cicero, Atticus 10.8B.2 (199B)

> Almost immediately Caelius, who was with Caesar, urged Cicero not to join Pompeius – 'the height of folly'. He warned that a victorious Caesar would not show clemency and was now talking of cruelty and savagery – he had been angered by the senate and irritated by vetoes.

---

not to do this   to leave Italy and join Pompeius.

Do think about this, Cicero, over and over again so that you don't completely ruin yourself and all your family and take yourself, consciously and with your eyes wide open, down a path where you see there is no way out. If words of the *optimates* worry you or you cannot tolerate the arrogance and boasting of some people, I recommend you choose some town away from war while these issues are 5 being decided. They will be completed quite soon. If you do this, I reckon you will have acted wisely and you will not offend Caesar.

Liguria, 16 April 49 BC

Caelius to Cicero, *Friends* 8.16.5 (*153*)

---

1 What is the tone of Caelius' advice?
2 Was neutrality a possible option for Cicero?

Cicero replies to Caelius.

You know how I was utterly opposed to abandoning the city when I heard about it. I told you quite firmly that I would put up with anything rather than leave Italy for civil war. What has happened to make me change my mind? All that has happened makes me more resolute in my standpoint. I would like you to believe me in this matter – and I think you realize it – that in this wretched situation I 5 want people just to realize I preferred peace at any price. When there was no hope of peace, then there was nothing I steered clear of more than civil war. I do not think I shall ever regret that decision.

Cicero to Caelius, *Friends* 2.16.3 (*154*)

Cicero is not frightened by Caelius' warnings – the dangers are common to all. Had he been able to rescue the *respublica*, even at the expense of personal misfortune, he would have been overjoyed.

6   I am not awaiting the outcome of the business in Spain – I am convinced it is as you say – and I do not have any clever schemes. If there is to be a community eventually, then there will surely be a place in it for me. However, if it is not to be, you will, I think, come to the same deserted regions where you hear I have settled. But I am perhaps playing the prophet and everything will turn out better. I recall 5 the despairing thoughts of those who were old when I was a young man. Perhaps I am now imitating them and indulging in the vice of old age. I wish it were so, but I fear otherwise.

7   … My final point is this: I shall do nothing wild or rash. I beg you, wherever I am, to protect me and my children as our friendship and your loyalty demand.   10

Cumae, 2/3 May 49 BC

Cicero to Caelius, *Friends* 2.16.6–7 (*154*)

More than a hundred letters to and from Cicero from January to May 49 BC bear testimony to his anxieties about the war and what he should do. In the end, impelled by sensitivity to criticism or by obligation or by fortune, he decided to join Pompeius. He sailed from Italy on 7 June and joined the republicans in Greece. He soon regretted his decision. The troops were inadequate and not fit for war, while the leaders were, with the exception of Pompeius and a few others, all deeply in debt, avid for plunder, and their talk so bloodthirsty that Cicero dreaded their victory. He despaired of victory and advised peace, but when Pompeius disagreed Cicero suggested delay. He wrote to a friend in April 46 recalling his experiences (Cicero, *Friends* 7.3.2(*183*)).

Cicero in the camp of Pompeius

He did not deny that he regretted he had come. He trashed Pompeius' preparations and made carping criticisms about his plans behind his back. He was all the time jeering and making witty remarks about the allies. He himself always went around the camp without a smile and with a sad look, while he made others laugh when they did not want to.   Plutarch, *Cicero* 38.2

While in the camp of Pompeius, Cicero received a remarkable letter from his son-in-law Dolabella, who was with Caesar. His previous advice – to join Caesar or to remain neutral – had not been given for party reasons and he was now advising Cicero solely as a loyal and devoted son-in-law. Pompeius' situation is clear: he lacks the protection of allies and an honourable retreat. His is a desperate and humiliating position.

2   Therefore consider, in virtue of your good sense, what Pompeius can hope for or what benefit you can be to him. In that way it will be easiest to resolve what is the more beneficial for yourself. If he escapes the present danger and takes refuge with his fleet, I beg you to take thought for your own best interests and at last to be a friend to yourself rather than anyone else. You have fully satisfied the claims 5 of duty and friendship; you have also satisfied your party and the particular
3   *respublica* of which you approved. It remains for us to be where the *respublica* is now rather than to pursue the old version and be in none at all.

Caesar's camp at Dyrrhachium, May (?) 48 BC

Dolabella to Cicero, *Friends* 9.9.2–3(*157*)

The final sentence of the extract is remarkable for the concept of *respublica* it propounds. Cicero is not to consider the *respublica* as something fixed and immutable. Dolabella concludes his letter by hoping that Cicero will move to Athens or some other neutral place if Pompeius is forced to withdraw.

The defeat of Pompeius, 48 BC

Pompeius might have accepted Cicero's advice to delay had not one military success at Dyrrhachium given him confidence in his troops. As a result an army of recruits fought against Caesar's veterans at Pharsalus on 9 August 48 and was defeated. The republican camp was captured and Pompeius fled to be slaughtered on the shore of Egypt, where he was seeking refuge at the Alexandrian court of the young Ptolemy XIII, son of Auletes.

Cicero writes to Atticus, giving his reaction to the news of Pompeius Magnus' death.

As for the end of Pompeius, I never had any doubt. For kings and peoples had become so completely convinced of the hopelessness of his situation that wherever he went I thought this would happen. I am unable not to grieve for his misfortune, for I knew him as a man of upright character, clean living and of serious disposition.

Brundisium, 27 November 48 BC

Cicero, *Atticus* 11.6.5 (*217*)

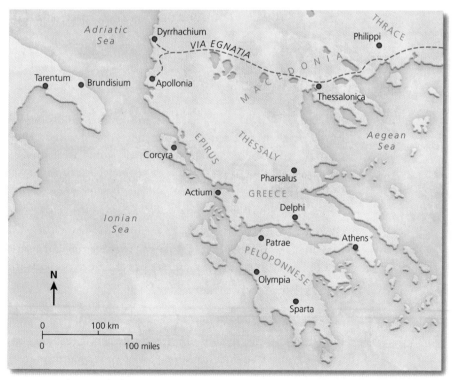

Greece, Macedonia and Thrace.

After the battle of Pharsalus many survivors gathered at Corcyra and Cato offered Cicero, the senior consular present, command of the republican forces. Cicero refused and Gnaeus, the elder son of Pompeius, had to be restrained from killing him on the spot (Plutarch, *Cicero* 39.1–2).

Cicero went to Patrae in the Peloponnese, where he met his brother. They had a serious quarrel, the exact nature of which defies discovery. Relations were never the same again and they were never reconciled (D. R. Shackleton Bailey, ch. 19).

Cicero returns to Rome, 48 BC

By October 48 BC Cicero was back in Italy at Brundisium where he spent a miserable time with domestic anxieties – he divorced Terentia during this period – and worries about how Caesar would treat him. It was not until September 47 that he met Caesar on his way back from the East and was able to return to his estates and Rome. But the changed circumstances did not please him – far from it.

Curius, a friend of Atticus, had a business in Patrae. Cicero had stayed with him on his way home from Cilicia in November 50 and again after Pharsalus before he returned to Italy. Cicero wrote to Curius lamenting the state of affairs in Rome.

I remember when I thought you crazy because you lived among **those people** rather than with us. A house in this city, when it really was a city, would have been much more suitable for a person of your charm and culture than all the

---

those people   the Greeks.

Peloponnese, let alone Patrae. But now, with the situation here pretty desperate, I think you showed considerable foresight when you took yourself off to Greece 5 and I consider you not only wise but lucky too in being away from here. But can anyone now be at all wise *and* fortunate?

Cicero to Manius Curius, *Friends* 7.28.1 (*200*)

> • Why was Cicero unlikely to follow the example of Manius Curius?

Cicero explains that he gains solace not from being abroad but from his books and his writings, of whose importance Manius will be the judge. The years 46 to 44 BC were for Cicero a remarkably productive period of writing – the consequence of a virtual withdrawal from politics.

I was **then** in mourning for the *respublica*, which was dearer to me than my life because of the benefits I had received from it and those which I had conferred on it. Now it is not only reason, which ought to be the greatest influence, that consoles me but the passing of time too, which as a rule brings comfort even to the stupid. I do however grieve that **something** we all share has disintegrated in 5 a way that there remains no hope of its being better in the future. This is not the fault of **the person who is now all powerful**, unless perhaps this situation ought never to have occurred. However, some things have happened by chance, some through our own fault, so we must not complain about what is past. I see no hope remaining. That's why I return to my beginning – you were wise to leave here if 10 that's what you chose; you were lucky if it was by chance.

Rome, August (?) 46 BC

Cicero to Manius Curius, *Friends* 7.28.3 (*200*)

The dictatorship of Caesar, 46–44 BC

Probably in late April 46, Caesar was named dictator for a period of ten years, with M. Aemilius Lepidus as his *magister equitum*. In April 45 he was named dictator for the fourth time and then some time between late January and mid-February 44 he was named dictator for life. Lepidus continued as *magister equitum*.

---

then   presumably after the civil war when he stayed with Curius.

something   the *respublica*.

the person who is now all powerful   Iulius Caesar, about whom Cicero is here quite restrained.

An appeal to Caesar to restore the *respublica*

Marcus Claudius Marcellus had been consul in 51 BC and was a die-hard opponent of Caesar. In September 46 Caesar agreed to pardon him and allow him to return to Rome. Cicero, who attended meetings of the senate but remained silent – he had not spoken in public for some six years – was now moved to speak out and to offer thanks to Caesar. At the same time he urged him to take steps to restore the *respublica*. However, Caesar, having been named dictator, celebrated an unprecedented quadruple triumph from 22 September until 1 October – not much sign of a restored *respublica*. Cicero addresses Caesar.

23   It is for you and you alone to revive all that you see lying in ruins inevitably shattered and overwhelmed by the violent shock of war. Lawcourts have to be reorganized, credit re-established, lust and passion checked, and the birth rate raised. Everything that is now in a state of disintegration and collapse needs to be
24   put back together by rigorous legislative measures … All these are the wounds of   5 war that you have to heal – and no one can heal them but yourself.

25   But, as things stand, the welfare of every Roman citizen and the whole state has become dependent on what you do. And so far from having completed your greatest achievements you have not even laid the foundations of all your plans …   10

27   This phase, then, still awaits you. This act of the drama has not yet been played. This is the programme to which you must devote all your energies: the re-establishment of the constitution, with yourself the first to reap its fruits in profound tranquillity and peace. And then, if this is your wish, when you have paid your country what you owe her, when you have fulfilled your debt to nature   15 itself, when you have really had your fill of life – then and only then may you talk of having lived long enough.

Selections from Cicero, Marcellus 23–4, 25, 27

Although this speech has the title 'On behalf of Marcellus', which gives the impression that it was a defence speech before a court, it was delivered before Caesar in person at a meeting of the senate and takes the form of a eulogy of the dictator. Notice in 23 what Cicero thinks needs to be done.

1   Is Cicero concerned with society as a whole?

2   What sorts of things do you imagine would have concerned the urban plebs?

3   How does this compare with modern repair and reconstruction in war-torn states?

Cicero entertains 'a grand and onerous visitor'

1   What a guest! It was an imposition on me but not one that I regretted. It was actually quite enjoyable. When he arrived at **Philippus'** on the evening of 18 December, the house was so filled with soldiers that there was hardly a vacant dining-room where Caesar himself could eat – all of a thousand men. I was really quite concerned what would happen the following day but **Barba Cassius** came 5 to my help and posted guards. Camp in the grounds; the house was defended. On 19 December Caesar was at Philippus' house until one o'clock and he admitted no one. He was, so I think, on accounts with **Balbus**. Then he went for a walk along the shore. He took a bath after two o'clock. Then he heard about **Mamurra** but his face did not change. **He was anointed** and he then took his place at table. As he was 10 taking **a course of emetics** he ate and drank heartily and agreeably from a lavish and well-prepared meal …

2   His entourage was entertained quite lavishly in **three dining-rooms**. The humbler freedmen and the slaves lacked nothing. For the better sort I offered choice entertainment. All in all we showed ourselves persons of taste. However, the guest 15 was not the sort of person to whom you would say: 'Do please come again when you are around this way.' Once is enough. There was nothing of substance in our conversation, much on literary topics. In sum, he was pleased and agreeably satisfied. He said he would be one day at Puteoli and another at Baiae.

There you have my entertainment, or quartering – an imposition, as I said, but 20 not vexatious. I shall be here for a short while, and then I shall go to Tusculum …

Puteoli (?), December 45 BC

Cicero, Atticus 13.52.1–2 (353)

This occasion was clearly more enjoyable than the confrontation in March 49.

Philippus'   Lucius Marcius Philippus, the next-door neighbour to Cicero at Puteoli.

Barba Cassius   an associate of Caesar.

Balbus   Lucius Cornelius Balbus, chief agent in Caesar's affairs.

Mamurra   chief of military engineers with Caesar in Spain 61–60. He gained great wealth there and a bad name – perhaps news was brought of his death.

He was anointed   oiling usually took place before one had a bath.

a course of emetics   doctors in the ancient world often recommended taking occasional emetics. Caesar had a reputation for being a light eater and drinker so was clearly enjoying himself at Cicero's.

three dining-rooms   first-, second- and third-class food and drink, 'just as undergraduates in the hall of an Oxford or a Cambridge College eat a less good dinner than the dons at High Table', as a distinguished Oxford scholar wrote of this passage in 1969 (J. P. V. D. Balsdon, pp. 42–3).

Stories abound of the prodigious eating and drinking at the court of Stalin, the red Tsar, while Hitler was distinctly dyspeptic; not that one would liken the motives of Caesar to those of two monstrous tyrants of the twentieth century. But 'Plutarch, on the basis of Caesar's figures, reports that a million Gauls were killed and another million enslaved. Requisitions of food and punitive devastations completed human, economic and ecological disaster probably unequalled until the conquest of the Americas.' So writes E. Badian in an article on Gaius Iulius Caesar (*Oxford Classical Dictionary*, p. 781). Caesar was a ruthless commander and brutality was a characteristic of the Roman world.

Painful events in Rome: the one-day consul

Cicero writes to his friend, Manius Curius.

1   You were not in the Campus at nine o'clock at the start of the elections for quaestors, when the seat of **Quintus Maximus**, who used to be called consul, had been put in its place. News came that he had died and the seat was removed. **Caesar had conducted the auspices** for the assembly of the tribes. He now held an assembly of the centuries and at one o'clock in the afternoon announced the 5 election of a consul who was to hold office till 1 January – the morning of the next day. Just think that no one had breakfast while **Caninius** was consul, that no crime was committed during his consulship since he was so wonderfully vigilant

2   in avoiding sleep throughout his period of office! You think this ridiculous but you are not here. If you were to witness it, you would not hold back from tears. 10 What if I write the rest? There are countless similar occurrences. Had I not taken refuge in philosophy and if I did not have my friend Atticus as the companion in my studies, I would be unable to tolerate the situation.

Rome, January 44 BC

Cicero to Manius Curius, Friends 7.30.1–2 (265)

Quintus Maximus   possibly Q. Fabius Maximus Sanga, elected consul, with Gaius Trebonius, at the beginning of October 45; he died suddenly on 31 December that year.

Caesar had conducted the auspices   the auspices were a precise religious ritual conducted before any formal state business. The auspices for a tribal assembly which elected quaestors were not the correct form for the assembly of the centuries which elected a consul. Hence Caesar was disregarding the correct procedure.

Caninius   Lucius Caninius Rebilus, long remembered because of Cicero's description here and other jokes he made about the one-day consul.

Cicero, in a letter to Atticus in March 49 (9.4.2 (*173*)) had put the following questions to himself:

- Should one be willing to live under a tyrant?

- Should one try to overthrow a tyrant, even if that endangers the state?

- Is it right to make war on one's country to rid it of tyranny?

- Is freedom worth every risk?

- If one does not approve of war, should one still oppose tyranny?

How would you respond to Cicero's questions?

It was Caesar's disregard for and impatience with the traditional procedures of the *respublica* that would stir up optimate animosity and hatred towards him. Furthermore, there were the ever increasing and more grandiose honours that a subservient senate proposed. Perhaps the final straw was the 'dictatorship for life', which made it quite clear that Caesar would not abdicate the office as Sulla had. In all his restless activity there was no clear constitutional programme such as Cicero had called for in his speech on behalf of Marcellus. Such general statements as 'bringing calm to Italy, peace to the provinces, and salvation to the empire' (Caesar, *Civil War* 3.5) hardly qualify. Rome had to await the emergence in 31 BC of a single ruler, the future emperor Augustus, for a solution to its constitutional and social problems. Caesar had decided on a military campaign to avenge the defeat of Crassus at Carrhae in 53 and intended to be away from Rome for some time. A plot was formed against him, in which 31 conspirators were involved, but Cicero was not included. On the Ides of March 44 the conspirators struck and Caesar was assassinated before the statue of Pompeius, as he was about to preside at a session of the senate in the meeting hall within the theatre of Pompeius. Liberty was the cry of the tyrannicides, and with it the name of Cicero.

After the Ides of March

Cicero left Rome on 7 April and stopped over at the house of Matius, a friend of Caesar. He reports their conversation to Atticus.

I have turned aside from my journey and put up at the house of **that person** whom we were talking about this morning. It's absolutely appalling! He says the

---

that person   Gaius Matius – a long-standing friend of Cicero and a link between him and Caesar, to whom he was closely attached, in the late 50s. At that time he was with Caesar in Gaul, though without official rank.

situation cannot be solved: 'if Caesar with all his talent could not find a solution, who will find one now?' Quite simply he said all was lost. I am inclined to agree, but he said it with delight. He declared that in less than twenty days there would be an uprising in Gaul: he had spoken only with Lepidus after the Ides of March. In sum he says these things cannot pass just like this. What a prudent man, Oppius! He too misses *him* but says nothing which may offend any loyal citizen. But enough of this.

Matius' house near Rome, 7 April 44 BC

Cicero, Atticus 14.1.1 (355)

'The Death of Caesar' by Jean Léon Gérome (1859).

if Caesar ... now? a view of Caesar's greatness and the enormity of Rome's problems. Cicero agrees with Matius' prophecy of doom but objects to his revelling in it.

these things cannot pass just like this there will be repercussions as a result of Caesar's murder.

Oppius with Balbus, chief agent of Caesar's business, who laments Caesar's fate but does not cause offence as Matius did.

him Caesar.

Civic duty or personal loyalty – the case of Iulius Caesar

The historian Sallust records (*Catilina* 53.6–54) that in his lifetime there had been two men of outstanding worth: Marcus Cato and Gaius Caesar. Cato committed suicide at Utica in North Africa in 46 BC rather than fall into the hands of the tyrant Caesar. Caesar was struck down by the hands of men who wished to restore freedom and the *respublica*. Both were at once the subject of discussion and the focus of moral conduct. Cicero shows and Matius provides a good and moving example.

A denarius of M. Brutus issued in 43/42, probably in Greece to pay troops. The obverse shows the head of Brutus – BRVT·IMP – hardly a republican symbol, and names the moneyer L. Plaetorius Cestianus – L·PLAET·CEST. The reverse has the slave's cap of freedom between two daggers and commemorates the murder of Caesar and restoration of liberty – EID·MAR – the Ides of March.

But you, Matius, as a learned man, will be well aware that, if Caesar was a tyrant – and that clearly seems to me to be the case – then your moral obligation may be argued in two ways. On the one hand – the argument I normally employ – your loyalty and goodwill ought to be praised since you revere a friend even though he is dead; on the other hand, as some people argue, the freedom of one's country 5 should be put before the life of a friend … There is nobody who more willingly and more often recalls the two acts which bring you the greatest credit: you were the most powerful advocate against embarking on civil war and in favour of acting with moderation when victorious. I have found no one to disagree with me on this point. 10

Tusculum, October 44 BC

Cicero to Matius, *Friends* 11.27.8 (*348*)

12 Antonius and Octavianus

The senate meets in the temple of Tellus

Following Caesar's assassination there was a political vacuum: the 'liberators' had no further plan – the tyrant was slain, therefore liberty was restored. The initiative was quickly seized by the consul M. Antonius, who secured Caesar's papers and his money. Lepidus, the *magister equitum*, occupied the forum with troops. Speaking in the senate on 2 September, Cicero recalls the meeting of 17 March.

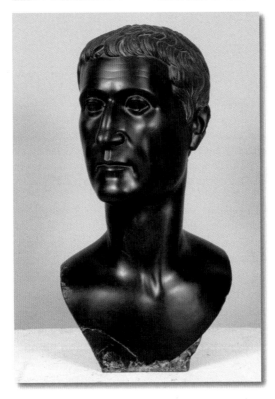

Marcus Antonius. This basalt head dates from 40–30 BC.

1 I hoped that the *respublica* had at last been restored to **your counsel and authority**, so I decided as an ex-consul and a member of the senate I ought to remain, as it

---

your counsel and authority   the senate's.

were, on guard. In fact **I never left Rome or took my eyes off affairs of state** from the day when we were summoned to the **temple of Tellus**. In that temple I laid the foundations of peace so far as I could. I revived the ancient precedent of 5 the Athenians and I even made use of **the Greek word** which that state used at the time in laying to rest their disagreements. I proposed all disputes should be forgotten and obliterated for all time.

2 The speech of M. Antonius on that occasion was excellent and his goodwill was outstanding too. Peace was finally established with **our most distinguished** 10 **citizens through him and his son**. And what followed was in accord with these beginnings.

Cicero, Philippic 1.1–2

Caesar's funeral

The following day, 18 March, Caesar was granted a public funeral and the contents of his will were made public. Cassius had – shrewdly – wanted to kill Antonius too and had opposed both the public reading of the will and the funeral, but Brutus overruled him. Popular reaction became apparent when the contents of Caesar's will – a grant of 75 denarii to every citizen and his gardens to the citizen body – were made known and when Antonius delivered the funeral oration. Cicero laments lost opportunities to Atticus.

Do you remember how I cried out **that very first day** on the Capitol that the senate ought to be summoned by the praetors? Heavens, what might not have *then* been achieved with rejoicing by all the *boni*, even by the moderately good,

---

I never left … state Cicero left Rome on 7 April and returned on 31 August. He set out on an intended visit to Athens on 17 July. He took no part in politics in Rome because he could see no useful role for himself. His statement is a somewhat economical use of the truth.

temple of Tellus the earth goddess, Tellus, had a temple on the Esquiline Hill.

the Greek word *amnestia* (amnesty) is probably the word Cicero means.

our … son Antonius arranged for the liberators, Brutus, Cassius and company, to come down and dine with himself and others, sending his son to the Capitol, where the liberators were sheltering, as a guarantee of his good faith.

Philippic(s) the 14 speeches of Cicero against Marcus Antonius, composed between 2 September 44 and 21 April 43. The name derives from the *Philippics* of the great fourth-century Athenian orator, Demosthenes, who was fighting for the freedom of Athens against king Philip of Macedon, father of Alexander the Great. A letter to Cicero from M. Brutus in April 43, *Brutus* 2.3.4 (*2*), is the first record of the name.

that very first day the Ides of March, when the conspirators gathered on the Capitol and Cicero urged that the praetors, Brutus and Cassius, summon the senate, the consul Antonius having taken refuge in his house in fear.

---

and with brigands crushed! You blame the **Liberalia**. What could have been done? By that time we had long been finished. Do you remember *you* cried out that the 5 cause was lost if he were given a public funeral? Well, he was actually cremated in the forum, given a **eulogy full of pathos**, while slaves and paupers were sent with firebrands to attack our homes.

Cumae, 19 April 44 BC

Cicero, Atticus 14.10.1(364)

Within a month the principal liberators were forced to withdraw from Rome for their own safety, and Antonius exempted Brutus and Cassius from their duties as praetors. He himself left Rome in late April to visit and settle veterans in Campania. When he returned, he found a new arrival on the scene.

The arrival of the heir

In his will Caesar adopted and named his great-nephew, Gaius Octavius, his principal heir. At the time of the assassination Octavius, who was 18, had been at Apollonia in Illyricum with the troops destined for Caesar's Parthian campaign. In spite of contrary advice Octavius accepted the inheritance and became Gaius Iulius Caesar Octavianus, though not formally before his legal adoption in August 43. He called himself 'Caesar' but it is modern practice to call him Octavian to distinguish him from Iulius Caesar. Octavius arrived on 18 April in Neapolis, where he met Balbus early on the following day. Balbus informed Cicero that Octavius was going to accept the inheritance but feared trouble with Antonius.

Octavius is with me here – very respectful and friendly. His followers call him **Caesar**, but **Philippus** does not, so I don't either. I say he cannot be a *good citizen*.

Liberalia   17 March, the feast of the god Bacchus (Liber), the day when the senate met in the temple of Tellus.

eulogy full of pathos   the funeral speech of Antonius, which may in fact have been quite a modest piece but which ignited the highly charged emotions of the crowd. Cicero later in 44 described it as a beautiful eulogy, with pathos, and incitement to action. Nothing survives and ancient sources disagree about whether it was short and simple or in the grand style. Shakespeare in *Julius Caesar* gave Mark Antony the grand style derived from Plutarch. Cicero clearly thought Antonius responsible for the violence.

Caesar   Octavius, but he at once styled himself 'Caesar' to exploit the magic of that name and to avoid revealing he was merely adopted, which would have been the case if he had used the name Octavianus. He was, as Antonius said (Cicero, *Philippic* 13.24), the boy who owed everything to his name: the son of C. Octavius and Atia, the daughter of Caesar's sister, Iulia. His father died in 58 and his mother remarried.

Philippus   L. Marcius Philippus, consul in 56, the second husband of Atia, stepfather of Octavius, immediate neighbour of Cicero at Puteoli.

*Gaius Iulius Caesar
Octavianus.*

There are so many around him who threaten **our friends** with death and say the **present state of affairs cannot be tolerated**. What do you think they will say when **the boy** comes to Rome, when our liberators cannot be safe there? They will always be famous and happy too – conscious of their deed. However, in our case we are heading for disaster unless I am mistaken … I don't like **these designates** either, who have forced me to give **lessons in oratory** so that I am not permitted to relax even **amid the waters**. 5

Puteoli, 22 April 44 BC

Cicero, *Atticus* 14.12.2 (*366*)

---

our friends   the liberators.

present … tolerated   supporters of Iulius Caesar and veterans who did not accept the compromise of 17 March – that no action be taken against the liberators, while Caesar's acts and laws would remain in force – and felt unhappy at the influence of the republicans. Cicero saw them as wanting war.

the boy   Octavius, born 23 September 63 and at this time 18 years old.

these designates   A. Hirtius and C. Vibius Pansa, moderate Caesarians, elected consuls for 43.

lessons in oratory   Cicero was giving lessons in public speaking, imitating the practice he himself had experienced in the 80s.

amid the waters   the area in the bay of Naples and particularly Baiae were favourite watering-places and resorts of the Roman elite.

Cicero later judged that Octavianus was not without intelligence or spirit. He appeared to have a satisfactory attitude towards the conspirators but Cicero was unsure how far to trust him, given his years, name, family and education. Nevertheless he was to be encouraged and kept apart from Antonius. He reached Rome in early May and formally declared that he accepted his adoption by Iulius Caesar. At the invitation of the tribune, L. Antonius, he addressed the Roman people in a speech which Cicero disliked.

Meetings of the senate on 1 June and of the assembly on 2 June

On his return to Rome, Antonius met Octavianus. Antonius refused to hand over Caesar's money and prevaricated over the adoption. He had decided that he needed to strengthen his position and proposed to exchange Macedonia, his proconsular province, for Cisalpine and Transalpine Gaul and to summon back to Italy four of the six legions in Macedonia, which had been intended for the Parthian campaign. His command would be for five years.

Lo and behold, on 1 June when **they** had summoned us to be present at a meeting, **everything was changed. Nothing was done through the senate** but many important matters were decided by an assembly of the people. However, **the people were not present** and were against the proposals. The **consuls-designate** said they did not dare to attend the senate. The liberators of their 5 country, who had removed the yoke of slavery from the city's neck, were kept away from that city, although the consuls themselves praised them in public speeches and in all their conversation.

Cicero, *Philippic* 1.6

---

they   the consuls Antonius and Dolabella, Cicero's former son-in-law, who assumed the consulship when Caesar was killed.

everything was changed   Cicero asserts that 1–2 June marked a significant change in Antonius' political action, but it was not so dramatic. Clearly Antonius felt the need to secure his position for the future.

Nothing was done through the senate   few members attended since they were afraid of Antonius' troops.

the people were not present   armed men and barricades apparently prevented opponents attending the assembly of the tribes, so that Cicero could allege proposals were passed without the support of the people.

consuls-designate   Hirtius and Pansa, moderate Caesarians, who were opposed to Antonius.

On 2 June the change of provinces was enacted in the popular assembly by force, without due notice and on a day when the assembly was not permitted to meet. On 5 June, at the instigation of Antonius, the senate decreed that Brutus and Cassius should be given a commission to superintend the supply of corn from Asia and Sicily. They could thus officially leave Rome, but Cicero considered it a calculated insult. Soon afterwards he attended a family conference where those present discussed how Brutus and Cassius should respond to the senatorial decree.

A family conference

I arrived at Antium before midday. Brutus was pleased that I had come. Then before a large audience, in the presence of **Servilia**, **Tertulla** and **Porcia**, he asked me what I thought he should do … I gave him the advice I had been contemplating on the way: to take up the superintendence of the Asiatic corn, for there was nothing else for us to do but to see he was safe. The defence of the *respublica* depended on it. 5
I had embarked upon my speech when Cassius arrived. I repeated the same points. At this point, Cassius declared with a brave face – you could say he was breathing Mars – he would not go to Sicily. 'Should I have accepted an insult as if it were a favour?' 'What are you going to do, then?' I asked. He said he would go to Greece. 'What about you, Brutus?' I asked. 'I'll go to Rome,' he replied, 'if you agree.' 10
'I certainly don't,' I replied. 'You will not be safe there.' 'But supposing I could be, would you agree?' 'Certainly I would and furthermore that you should not go to a province either now or after your praetorship. However, I'm not going to advise you to risk going to the city.' I stated the reasons – they'll surely occur to you – why he would not be safe in the city. 15

Cicero, *Atticus* 15.11.1 (*389*)

There followed a lengthy discussion with complaints, from Cassius especially, about lost opportunities and with harsh criticism of **Decimus Brutus**. Cicero agreed but advised there was no point in lamenting what was past. He was in full flow on what they should have done – remove Antonius, summon the senate, fire the people and take complete control of the *respublica* – when he was interrupted.

Servilia   formidable matriarch, half-sister of Cato, mother of Brutus, lover of Caesar.

Tertulla   daughter of Servilia, half-sister of Brutus and wife of Cassius.

Porcia   daughter of Cato, wife of Brutus.

Decimus Brutus   one of the liberators and now governor of Cisalpine Gaul.

Your friend exclaimed, 'Well indeed, I have never heard anyone speaking the like of it!' I restrained myself. However, I reckoned that Cassius would go – for Servilia promised to see that the superintendence of the corn was removed from the senate's decree – and our friend Brutus was quickly forced to retract his foolish talk about wishing to be in Rome. He therefore decided that the games should be 5 held in his name but in his absence. I had the impression he wanted to depart for Asia straight from Antium.

Antium (?), about 7 June 44 BC

Cicero, *Atticus* 15.11.2 *(389)*

---

1 Women played only a small role in Roman politics. Can you suggest why?

2 What factors have led to women playing an increasingly important role in modern politics?

Games in honour of Apollo were held annually in Rome from 6 to 13 July, shortly before the elections. The urban praetor was in charge and presided, but M. Brutus, urban praetor in 44 BC, was persuaded that it would be unsafe to be present in person. He made the detailed preparations and arranged that C. Antonius, brother of Marcus and a fellow praetor, should preside. He still hoped to derive political benefit from the games.

Octavianus put on games in honour of Iulius Caesar from 20 to 30 July. This gave him the opportunity to stress his membership of the Julian family and his piety towards Iulius Caesar and to make a greater impact than Brutus. Octavianus recorded that during the games a comet, normally regarded as a portent of disaster, appeared and was believed to signify Caesar's soul ascending to the heavens and to immortality.

Your friend   Servilia – could anyone else have put Cicero down in full flow? A wonderful moment!

myself   this word is *not* in the text but is inserted by modern editors, since without it the meaning would be that Cicero restrained Servilia – an unlikely act in the circumstances!

promised … decree   testimony to her formidable influence and revealing that some elite women could play a part in Roman politics. 'A woman possessed of all the rapacious ambition of the patrician Servilii and ruthless to recapture power for her house' (R. Syme, p. 23); 'But for a short time, at least, she was the most powerful woman of her generation' (E. Badian, *Oxford Classical Dictionary*, p. 1394).

On the very day of my games a comet was visible for seven days in the northern region of the sky. It used to rise about an hour before dark and was bright and visible from all lands. The general populace believed this signified Caesar's soul being received among the spirits of the immortal gods, and this gave rise to the addition of a star to the bust of Caesar that we dedicated soon after in the forum.

Pliny, Natural History 2.94

Antonius had dismissed the boy Octavianus at their first meeting, treating him as insignificant – a natural mistake, perhaps, in a society where political office and military command were associated with middle age. They were now deeply hostile to one another and by the end of the games there was a real danger of armed conflict. Their partisans now intervened and insisted that they be reconciled. Reconciliation took place publicly on the Capitol. This was an event of some significance in that the ordinary soldiers had asserted their interests.

Cicero and Antonius: a war of words

Cicero remained on his country estates and, after much hesitation, decided to travel to Athens to visit his son, who was a student there. Impeded by contrary winds he was forced to land in southern Italy and, while waiting, was encouraged by news from Rome. There was to be a full meeting of the senate on 1 August and there were high hopes that Antonius would accept the authority of the senate and a compromise would be reached, enabling Brutus and Cassius to return to Rome. Cicero had been missed in Rome and his absence criticized. He reached the city on 31 August. Antonius had summoned a meeting of the senate for 1 September to vote further honours to Caesar. Cicero, pleading exhaustion from his journey, did not attend and thereby avoided the embarrassment of opposing Antonius, who was most irritated by his absence. On 2 September, in the absence of Antonius, Cicero addressed the senate.

Before I begin to speak on public matters, I want to make a few complaints about the offensive behaviour of M. Antonius yesterday … I was aware of procedures and felt weak and was not at my best because of my journey. In view of my friendship with Antonius I sent someone to inform him of this. Antonius, as you heard, declared that he would come to my house with a gang of workmen. Those were 5 words of excessive anger and showed an utter lack of self-control. What is the offence that requires a punishment so harsh that he dared to say here in the senate that with workmen in the service of the state he would demolish a house **built at public expense by decree of the senate**?

Cicero, Philippic 1.12

---

built … senate   when Cicero returned from exile in 57, the senate decreed that his house on the Palatine should be rebuilt at public expense.

Cicero called on the senate to reassert itself. He complimented Antonius on his conduct of policy after the Ides but then accused him of betraying Caesar's laws and intentions from 1 June onwards. There were insinuations about financial corruption and intimidation and a warning to heed the fate of Caesar. It was quite mild invective but intolerable to Antonius.

Antonius prepared a reply 'in his den of drink and vice' and 'vomited it forth in his usual custom' (Cicero to Cassius, *Friends* 12.2.1 (*344*)) on 19 September. Cicero withdrew to Campania in fear for his life and wrote his response, the second Philippic. It purports to be an immediate answer to Antonius, but this 'monument of invective' (D. Stockton, p. 298) was never delivered. It was probably made public sometime during the winter 44–43 BC. The speech reveals some of the charges Antonius levelled against Cicero: violation of friendship, his consulship in 63, the death of Clodius in 52, detaching Pompeius from Caesar and thus causing the Civil War, instigating the killing of Caesar, his behaviour in the camp of Pompeius in Greece. Cicero dealt firstly with the charges and then went on the attack with a vehemence and vitriol that would incur prosecution in contemporary society, though it might attract the tabloid newspapers and paparazzi. It may be judged tasteless and offensive but this was an accepted feature of Roman political life. Here is a characteristic passage.

But let us leave aside these acts of thuggish wickedness; let us speak rather of the most depraved sort of frivolity. With that gullet of yours, those lungs, that robust body just like a gladiator's, you consumed so much wine at Hippia's wedding that the following day you found it necessary **to vomit in the sight of the Roman people.** An act disgusting to witness, even to hear of! If this had happened to you 5 at dinner in those same monstrous cups of yours, would anyone not reckon it shameful? But this was the *magister equitum*, conducting public business in an assembly of the Roman people. It would be disgraceful for him to belch, but he vomited and filled his lap and his whole magistrate's platform with chunks of food stinking of wine. He himself admits that this was among his sordid exploits, 10 so let us turn to his brilliant ones.

Cicero, *Philippic* 2.63

to vomit ... people   Cicero repeats this incident elsewhere and uses 'vomit' of Antonius' manner of speaking. The offence was not being drunk, but conducting public business when drunk. He might simply have been taken ill. A recent editor notes how this 'happened to the US President George Bush senior on a state visit to Japan in 1992' (J. T. Ramsey, p. 252).

However, Cicero ended on a note of nobility.

118   Look back finally, I ask you, M. Antonius, to the *respublica*, consider **your forebears, not those with whom you live**. Treat me as you will but return to favour with the *respublica*. However, you must look to your own position. For myself I shall make this declaration: I defended the *respublica* as a young man, I shall not desert it now I am old. I treated the swords of Catilina with contempt, I shall not be afraid of 5 yours. Moreover I should be glad to offer this body if the freedom of the *respublica* can be obtained immediately, so that the pangs of the Roman people may at last

119   give birth to what it has for so long been carrying in the womb. In **this very temple** almost twenty years ago I said death could not be untimely for one who had been consul. How much more truthfully shall I now say the same for one who is old? In 10 my case, members of the senate, death is now even desirable since I have completed the offices I obtained and the tasks I undertook. I have just two wishes: one, to die leaving the Roman people free – nothing greater can be granted by the immortal gods – and second that each be rewarded according to his service to the *respublica*.

Cicero, Philippic 2.118–19

Cicero had identified Antonius as the public enemy of the free *respublica* who had to be destroyed, as Catilina had been 20 years before. It was to be a fight to the death.

In autumn 44 BC Cicero, aged 62, was demonstrating an astonishing energy. He was active again in politics, and writing letters to provincial governors, to friends, and to Atticus. While he was working on the second Philippic, he was composing two philosophical works – three books *On Duties* for his son Marcus and a short essay *On Friendship* for Atticus, who had expressed his delight in an earlier essay, *On Old Age*. He sent the speech for criticism to Atticus at the end of October, wondering when it would be proper to publish it, adding a few days later, 'It won't come forth to the light of day unless the *respublica* is restored' (Cicero, *Atticus* 15.13a.3 (*417*)).

---

your forebears   for example, his grandfather, M. Antonius the orator.

not those with whom you live   his wife Fulvia, and his brother, Lucius Antonius, the tribune.

this very temple   the temple of Concord, on 5 December 63, in the debate on the Catilinarian conspirators; this sentence continues the fiction that the speech was actually delivered at the meeting of the senate on 19 September.

In October 44 BC things started to happen. There were rumours of an attempt on Antonius' life. He left Rome with Fulvia to meet the Macedonian legions. Cicero writes about events to Q. Cornificius, who was governing Africa.

2   The masses think Antonius has trumped up **the charge** in order to raid the young man's money but the intelligent and *good men* believe it happened and approve. What more? There are high hopes of **him**. He is thought to be willing to do anything for the sake of honour and glory.

Antonius, our friend, though he caught would-be assassins red-handed in his   5 house, realizes he is so hated that he does not dare to make the matter public. So on 9 October he set off for Brundisium to meet **the four Macedonian legions**. He intends to win them over with money, **lead them to Rome** and set them on our necks.

3   There you have an outline of the *respublica*, if the *respublica* can exist in an army   10 camp. I often grieve for your plight, because you have not been able, **owing to your age**, to experience any part of the *respublica* in a sound and healthy condition. In previous times it was at least possible to have hope, but now even that has been torn from us.

Rome, about 10 October 44 BC

Cicero to Cornificius, Friends 12.23.2–3 (347)

Octavianus sent agents to tamper with the loyalty of the Macedonian legions, offering huge bribes, and went himself to seek recruits from the Campanian veterans – both actions were successful and treasonable. Octavianus looked to Cicero for advice and support.

On the evening of 1 November a letter arrived for me from Octavianus. He has

---

the charge   it seems unlikely that Octavianus would attempt to kill Antonius, since his removal would put the young man at a disadvantage with the republicans, killers of his 'father', whom he wanted to deal with first.

him   Octavianus.

the four Macedonian legions   the legions which Caesar had sent ahead for his planned Parthian campaign and which Antonius took over for his command in Gaul following the assembly on 2 June.

lead them to Rome   they were intended for the occupation of Cisalpine Gaul, but one legion was with Antonius heading for Rome.

owing to your age   Cornificius was quaestor in 48 and thus likely to be in his early thirties. He was to be proscribed (see Glossary) by the Triumvirs and killed at Utica in Africa in 42.

great schemes afoot. He has brought the veterans at **Casilinum and Calatia** over to his views, not surprising since he's giving them each **500 denarii**. He intends to go round the other colonies. He is quite plainly looking to wage war against Antonius with himself as leader. Thus I can see in a few days' time we shall be at war. But who are we to follow? Consider his name, consider his age. 5

Cicero, Atticus 16.8.1 (418)

> Octavianus wanted a secret rendezvous with Cicero, who declined the proposal as 'childish'. He then sent a friend to tell Cicero about Antonius' advance on Rome and the truculent temper of the Macedonian legions.

He wanted my advice: should he proceed to Rome with 3,000 veterans or hold Capua and block Antonius' route or go and join the three Macedonian legions now marching along the Adriatic coast, which he hopes to have on his side? … In a word, he puts himself forward as our leader and thinks I ought to support him. For my part I have advised him to go to Rome. It seems to me that he will have the support of the city rabble, and the *boni* too if he convinces them of his sincerity. O Brutus, where are you? What a great opportunity you are losing! I could not foretell this, but I thought something like this would happen. 5

Puteoli, November 44 BC

Cicero, Atticus 16.8.2 (418)

> Octavianus continued to bombard Cicero with letters begging him to get down to business and save the *respublica* a second time. Cicero saw that Octavianus had plenty of energy and was remarkably popular in the *municipia* but he was still plainly a boy. He writes in reply to a previous letter from Atticus.

I return to the *respublica*. I have often received many sensible words from you on political matters, but nothing more sensible than this letter. Although this boy is for the present blunting the force of Antonius' attack beautifully, we must wait to see the outcome. But **what a speech**! It has been sent to me. He swears 'so may he be permitted to achieve the honours of his father', while at the same time he 5

Casilinum and Calatia veteran colonies of Caesar in Campania. Casilinum was subsequently settled by Antonius too.

500 denarii more than two years' pay for a legionary soldier.

what a speech on his arrival in Rome, in the second or third week of November, Octavianus addressed the Roman people at the invitation of a tribune recalling 'his father' – Iulius Caesar – and declaring his hostility to Antonius.

stretches out his right hand towards **the statue**. I'd rather not be saved by such as he! But, as you write, I see the acid test will be the tribunate of our friend **Casca**.

Arpinum, November 44 BC

Cicero, Atticus 16.15.3 (426)

It is fitting that Cicero should here, in the last surviving letter to Atticus, pay tribute to his friend's political acumen, and that the final point should be his decision to come to Rome to seek help from Atticus to avoid bankruptcy. There were undoubtedly further letters but, for whatever reason, none has survived.

Antonius returned from Brundisium to Rome, while Octavianus, with insufficient forces to oppose him, withdrew to Arretium in northern Etruria. Antonius summoned the senate to meet, intending to make provincial arrangements and to attack Octavianus, but the defection of two of the four legions forced his hand. On 28 November, at a meeting of the senate that was illegal because it was held in the evening, provincial appointments were decided and Antonius left immediately to take over his forces and proceed to Cisalpine Gaul. All now rested on Decimus Brutus, the governor of Cisalpine Gaul, and the commanders of the western provinces, Lepidus, Plancus and Pollio, who had the military forces to decide the outcome of the war.

Cicero returned to Rome on 9 December and wrote to the governors encouraging them to defend the *respublica*. To Decimus Brutus he wrote:

The key point I would like you to appreciate thoroughly and to remember is that, in preserving the freedom and safety of the Roman people, you should **not wait for authorization** from a senate which is **not yet free**. That would be to condemn **your deed** (for it was not by a public decision that you freed the *respublica* and that makes the act all the greater and more glorious) and to judge the young man, 5 or rather the boy, Caesar, to have acted without good reason in undertaking a great

---

the statue   Octavianus spoke before the temple of Castor and Pollux in the forum. Perhaps he stretched out his hand to the statue of Caesar on the rostra on which Antonius had had inscribed the words: 'To the father for his distinguished service'.

Casca   P. Servilius Casca, a conspirator, who was due to become tribune on 10 December. Octavianus did not obstruct him.

not wait for authorization   an invitation to take unauthorized action, a dangerous suggestion in any situation, which perhaps reveals how desperate Cicero, the defender of the *respublica*, considered the situation.

not yet free   the senate was still filled with supporters of Antonius.

your deed   the assassination of Iulius Caesar.

public cause on his **private initiative**; and lastly to judge the soldiers, country folk but the bravest of men and excellent citizens, to have been out of their minds ... for having **judged their consul a public enemy** and gone over to defend the safety of the *respublica*. The will of the senate ought to be taken as its authorization 10 when that authorization is impeded by fear.

Rome, mid-December 44 BC

Cicero to D. Brutus, Friends 11.7.2 (354)

Cicero makes very clear here his view that there are circumstances where preserving the state may require drastic, unconstitutional, even extra-legal action. It then depends who makes the decision. In late republican Rome it was the senate that passed the 'final decree'.

- In what modern circumstances might the action Cicero is suggesting be justified? Give some examples.

Meetings of the senate and the people, December 44–January 43 BC

Cicero describes his return to active politics in the city.

1 The tribunes of the plebs decreed that there should be a meeting of the senate on 20 December, intending to put before it the matter of protection for the consuls-designate. I had decided not to come to the senate **before 1 January**. However, since **your proclamation** had been made public that very day, I considered it quite unforgivable that a meeting of the senate should be held with **your** 5 **immortal services** to the *respublica* being passed over in silence, which would have happened had I not come, or that I should not be present if you were given honourable mention.

---

private initiative   in the official version of his achievements Octavianus, writing as the emperor Augustus, begins: 'At the age of 19 on my own initiative and at my own expense I raised an army ...' The precedent had been set by Pompeius and both were military adventurers.

judged their consul a public enemy   the phrase disguises treason, since the commander was the consul Antonius and the troops had been bribed by Octavianus.

before 1 January   Cicero intended only to take part in politics in 43 when he reckoned he was no longer at risk from the consul Antonius in Rome.

your proclamation   Brutus had declared on the authority of the senate that he would retain the province of Cisalpine Gaul against Antonius.

your immortal services   Brutus' retention of Cisalpine Gaul, of dubious legality.

2   I arrived early at the senate house. When this was noticed, members of the senate assembled in very large numbers. What **I did in the senate** concerning you, what 10 **I said in a very large meeting of the people**, I prefer you to learn from the letters of others.

Rome, 20 December 44 BC

Cicero to D. Brutus, *Friends* 11.6a.1–2 (*356*)

The senate rescinded the provincial appointments made on 28 November and instructed governors to remain in place until further notice. The edict of Brutus declaring his intention to remain in Cisalpine Gaul was approved and he retired to Mutina with four legions to prepare for a siege.

Antonius began the siege of Decimus Brutus in Mutina before the senate met on 1 January, while Octavianus was advancing to bring him relief. The senate was in session for four days, during which there was much debate over what should be done between the consuls, Hirtius and Pansa, who were moderates and followers of Caesar, the supporters of Antonius, some independent ex-consuls, and Cicero, who was for immediate, full-scale action against Antonius. Many wanted to avoid war and there was discussion about sending ambassadors to treat with Antonius. Cicero addressed the senate in the fifth Philippic.

31   I propose, members of the senate, that **no mention should be made of ambassadors**. I think the matter should be taken in hand without any delay and acted upon forthwith. I say a state of emergency ought to be declared, suspension of public business proclaimed, military cloaks put on, a levy conducted in the city and throughout Italy, apart from [Cisalpine] Gaul, with no one being given 5

I did in the senate   the third Philippic, in which Cicero praised D. Brutus and his decision to hold on to Cisalpine Gaul; acclaimed Octavianus, and the legions which had deserted; and proposed a decree which the senate passed. He wrote to Cornificius: 'On that day I first embarked on the hope of liberty and on that very 20 December I laid the foundations of the *respublica*' (Cicero, *Friends* 12.25.2 (*373*)).

I said … people   the fourth Philippic, delivered to the people in the forum immediately following the meeting of the senate. Cicero reported the proceedings of the senate and declared that in praising D. Brutus the senate was condemning Antonius as a public enemy. As they once broke Catilina, so they would soon break Antonius. The people enthused and hailed Cicero as saviour of Rome a second time.

no mention … ambassadors   the debate divided between the proposal of Cicero in the passage and that of Fufius Calenus, father-in-law of the consul Pansa, who proposed that a trio of senior consulars should go with proposals from the senate for Antonius to seek a compromise and avert civil war. On 4 January this was adopted and three ambassadors (see note on p. 170) set out shortly afterwards.

32   leave of absence. If these actions are taken, the mere report and news of our stern measures will overwhelm the lunacy of a **criminal gladiator**. He will appreciate that he has taken on war with the *respublica*. He will experience the sinews and strength of a united senate, for he keeps on talking now about disagreement among the parties.   10

Cicero, Philippic 5.31–2

> During the debate Cicero had spoken of honours for D. Brutus, Octavianus and their troops. He referred to Octavianus as 'this godlike young man'. He knew the young man so well he was prepared to pledge his word of honour on his behalf.

I am even prepared to pledge my word of honour, members of the senate, to you, to the Roman people and to the *respublica*. I can assure you I would not dare to do this, since no force compels me, and I would be afraid of being thought reckless in a most serious and dangerous matter. I promise, I guarantee, I pledge, members of the senate, that Gaius Caesar will always be the sort of citizen he is today and the 5 sort that we ought most to wish and desire him to be.

Cicero, Philippic 5.51

> Both Cicero and Octavianus were playing a dangerous game and each needed the other if Antonius were to be defeated. Cicero imagined he could use 'the boy' to defeat the enemy and then discard him – he referred to him with the famous and embarrassing remark 'that he was to be lauded, applauded and discarded' (Cicero, *Friends* 11.20.1 (*401*)). He was singularly unfortunate in coming up against the most formidable 19-year-old in history.

The return of the ambassadors

> Two ambassadors returned at the beginning of February, one of them, Sulpicius Rufus, having died on the journey to Antonius. Not only had they failed to persuade Antonius but he had issued counter-demands. Pansa summoned the senate, Hirtius having already left to help Octavianus, and the 'final decree' was probably passed. Cicero wrote to Cassius.

I wish you had invited me to the feast on the Ides of March; there would have been **no left-overs**. Now **what you left over** is keeping me busy, me more than all the

---

criminal gladiator   Antonius.

no left-overs   one may doubt whether Cicero would have the steel to be an assassin.

what you left over   M. Antonius.

rest. We have outstanding consuls, but the **consulars are absolutely pathetic**; the senate is resolute, but the most resolute are **members of the lowest rank**. Nothing is more resolute, nothing better than the people, than all Italy; but nothing is more disgusting, more scandalous than the **ambassadors Philippus and Piso**. They were sent by decree of the senate to declare **specific terms to Antonius**; when he did not agree to any of them, they took it upon themselves to bring back **intolerable demands** from him to us. As a consequence people flock to me and I have become a popular favourite on this issue of the safety of the state.

Rome, 2 or 3 February 43 BC

Cicero to C. Cassius, *Friends* 12.4.1 (*363*)

The siege of Mutina

Pansa was busily engaged in recruiting more forces. All now depended on whether Decimus Brutus could hold out. In the West the provincial commanders would wait upon events; in the East Marcus Brutus now held Macedonia, while Cassius prepared to challenge Dolabella in Syria. The siege of Mutina continued into March. Pansa left Rome on 20 March with four legions of recruits and proceeded northwards, reaching Bononia on 14 April.

Antonius tried to intercept him before he could join the forces of Hirtius and Octavianus, but Hirtius anticipated his move. Battle was joined at Forum Gallorum on 15 April. A hard-fought engagement resulted in victory for Antonius, but then his retiring army was intercepted and defeated by Hirtius. The news reached Rome on 20 April and Cicero delivered the fourteenth and last Philippic in the senate on 21 April, the day when there was a further battle between the remaining forces of Antonius and those of Hirtius and Octavianus outside Mutina. The republican forces were victorious and Antonius was forced to give up the siege and withdraw northwards towards the Alps.

consulars are absolutely pathetic a regular comment of Cicero at this time. Many consulars had been victims in the Civil War and the survivors in 43, some 18 in total, of whom five were provincial governors, are described thus: 'various in character, standing and allegiance, as a body they revealed a marked deficiency in vigour, decision and authority' (R. Syme, p. 164).

members of the lowest rank those who had held the quaestorship.

ambassadors Philippus and Piso the ambassadors had been L. Piso (consul in 58), L. Philippus (56) and Servius Sulpicius Rufus (51). Sulpicius had died on the embassy and Cicero was moved to pay an eloquent tribute to him in the senate – the ninth Philippic.

specific terms to Antonius not to use force against D. Brutus, not to besiege Mutina, not to ravage the province, not to levy troops but to obey the senate and the Roman people (*Philippic* 6.4).

intolerable demands he wanted five years in Transalpine Gaul, at the end of which Brutus and Cassius should no longer hold provinces; rewards for his soldiers equal to those awarded to the troops of Octavianus; and acceptance of his acts and laws.

The deaths of the consuls

The republican victories were overshadowed by the deaths of the two consuls, Hirtius in the second battle and Pansa the day afterwards as a result of a wound sustained in the first battle. Their deaths had momentous consequences.

We have lost two consuls, good men in my view but at any rate good consuls. Hirtius fell in the moment of victory having won a great victory a few days earlier. Pansa fled having received wounds he could not survive. Brutus and Octavianus are pursuing the enemy survivors. All who follow the party of M. Antonius have been decreed public enemies.

Rome, 27(?) April 43 BC

Cicero to Brutus, *Brutus* 1.3a (8)

Writing shortly afterwards to Cornificius, Cicero says the *respublica* is freed of the brigand Antonius but not completely clear of difficulty, and declares that he is worn out but will continue the fight. On 27 April a meeting of the senate decreed honours to Decimus Brutus but not to Octavianus, despite a plea from Cicero, and then decided that further operations should be conducted under the command of Brutus alone. Octavianus and his troops refused to serve under the command of one of the liberators. Decimus came in for much criticism in the aftermath of the battle but his troops were in poor shape after a long siege and in no fit state to pursue Antonius.

Antonius got away and at the end of May joined forces with Lepidus, while Brutus joined Plancus, the governor of Transalpine Gaul.

Cicero and Octavianus

Cicero wrote to Marcus Brutus in Greece praising Octavianus and expressing the hope that he could keep him loyal to the *respublica*.

The character and good qualities of the boy Caesar are remarkable. I just hope I may be able to control and hold him as he prospers with honours and favour as easily as I have till now. It will be more difficult for sure but I do not despair. For the young man is convinced, most of all by me, that it is through his efforts that we are safe. Certainly if he had not turned Antonius away from the city, all would 5 have been lost.

Rome, about 21 April 43 BC

Cicero to Brutus, *Brutus* 1.3.1 (7)

The stern Brutus, who ignored all Cicero's appeals to come over to Italy with his army to help the *respublica*, was not impressed. He wrote to Cicero:

2   The senate ought not to give anything to anyone that may be a precedent or a support to people with evil intentions. That is what I am afraid of about the consulship. Your Caesar may think he has climbed so high through your decrees
3   **that the ascent from that point, if he is elected consul, will be shorter** ... I wish you could see the fear about that young man in my mind.

Camp, 15 May 43 BC

Brutus to Cicero, Brutus 1.4a.2–3 (11)

By mid-June Cicero reported that, despite his warnings, the fine and resolute young man had been encouraged by deceitful and malicious letters to hope confidently for the consulship. 'We are the playthings, Brutus, of the whims of the soldiers and the arrogance of the commanders. Brute force is ruling the *respublica*' (*Brutus* 1.10.3 (*17*)). By the end of July Cicero was in deep distress.

I seem scarcely able to make good what I promised when I gave a guarantee to the *respublica* on behalf of a young man, indeed almost a boy ... How can you pay what you have pledged to the *respublica*, if the person for whom you have gone surety is quite happy to have you pay up? However, I hope I shall hold on to him in spite of considerable opposition. There seem to be good qualities in him but he is at an   5
impressionable age and there are plenty of people ready to lead him astray.

Rome, 27 July 43 BC

Cicero to Brutus, Brutus 1.18.3 (24)

Cicero could not hold Octavianus, who now demanded one of the consulships vacant through the death of Pansa and Hirtius. A delegation of his troops was unable to persuade the senate, so he marched with his army on Rome. The senate came out to greet him, Cicero among the last, as the young man noted. On 19 August he was elected consul together with Quintus Pedius, a nephew of Iulius Caesar. His adoption was formally ratified; the declarations against Antonius and Dolabella were repealed; and the liberators and Sextus Pompeius, the son of Magnus, were outlawed. The soldiers were paid their money.

---

that the ascent ... shorter   translated and explained by D. R. Shackleton Bailey: 'Octavian may be so puffed up by the advances he has already made as to reckon himself already more than half way up the ladder leading to the consulship'.

Not long afterwards Octavianus journeyed north to Bononia, where he met Antonius and Lepidus. They appointed themselves 'triumvirs for establishing a constitution' for a period of five years and divided the empire between them. Antonius and Octavianus were to campaign at once against Brutus and Cassius. As the triumvirs needed land and money, 300 members of the senate and 2,000 *equites* were proscribed, among them Marcus Cicero and his brother Quintus.

The death of Cicero

The historian Livy, who is quoted in a rhetorical exercise of Seneca the Elder (about 50 BC–AD 40), records the circumstances of Cicero's death.

M. Cicero had left the city on the approach of the **triumvirs**, realizing, as was the case, that he could no more escape from Antonius than Cassius and Brutus could from **Caesar**. He had first taken refuge on his estate at Tusculum, and then crossed to his villa at Formiae so as to embark at Caieta. Although he put to sea several times, adverse winds brought him back or he was unable to put up with 5 the tossing of the ship as the waves of the dark sea heaved and rolled. In the end he was overcome with weariness of both flight and life and returned to his villa further inland, which was a little more than a mile from the sea. 'I shall die,' he said, 'in the country I have so often saved.'

Seneca the Elder, *Suasoria* 6.17

His slaves were prepared to defend him, but Cicero ordered them to put down the litter in which he was travelling. He leaned out from where he was sitting and calmly offered his neck. The soldiers cut off his head and his hands too. Antonius ordered the head to be exhibited between the two hands on the rostra.

triumvirs   M. Antonius, M. Aemilius Lepidus and C. Octavianus.

Caesar   C. Octavianus. Following the formation of the Second Triumvirate on 27 November 43, Antonius and Octavianus crossed to Greece to confront the republican forces led by Brutus and Cassius. Two battles were fought at Philippi in October 42 and the republican forces were defeated. Cassius and Brutus committed suicide. The republican cause was dead.

Conclusion

At the beginning of April 43 Cicero had written a letter to Marcus Brutus, who was in Greece.

I have done for the *respublica*, my dear Brutus, everything which a man ought to have done when he has been placed in the position that I have by the decision of the senate and people. That is not only what may be reasonably demanded of the ordinary man – honesty, vigilance and patriotism. These are things which everyone must show. But the man who voices his opinion among the leaders of 5 the state on matters to do with the *respublica* ought, I think, to show wisdom. When I presumed to take upon myself the helm of the *respublica*, I should have considered myself as much to blame if the advice I had given the senate were inexpedient as I should have if it had been dishonest.

Rome, about 1 April 43 BC

Cicero to Brutus, *Brutus* 2.1.2 (*1*)

We may criticize Cicero for what he did, but we should allow that he acted from genuine motives.

---

1 Cicero fought and died to save the *respublica*. Can you suggest points in his favour and points against him in his fight for the *respublica*?

2 Was the *respublica* worth saving?

The tomb of Cicero, near Caieta (modern Gaeta), in southern Italy. Its authenticity is doubtful but it is in the right area.

Further reading and references

The contents of this book are fully dealt with in various chapters of the indispensable guide to all aspects of the Roman Republic: **N. Rosenstein and R. Morstein-Marx**, *A Companion to the Roman Republic* (Oxford and Malden, Mass., 2006).

Reference works

An essential general reference work is **S. Hornblower and A. Spawforth**, *Oxford Classical Dictionary* (3rd edition, Oxford, 1996). There is an abbreviated version: **J. Roberts** (ed.), *The Oxford Dictionary of the Classical World* (Oxford, 2007).

The following are useful guides to the city and the sites: **T. W. Potter**, *Roman Italy* (London, 1987), **A. Claridge**, *Rome: An Oxford Archaeological Guide* (Oxford, 1998) and **F. Coarelli**, *Rome and Environs: An Archaeological Guide* (Berkeley and Los Angeles, 2007).

Translations

The Penguin Classics series and Oxford World Classics provide translations of selected works of Cicero. The Oxford series has fuller comments and notes. Cicero, *Defence Speeches* (2000), and Cicero, *Political Speeches* (2006), both translated by **D. H. Berry**, are excellent.

R. G. Lewis (ed.), *Asconius, Commentaries on Speeches by Cicero* (Oxford, 2006) provides an excellent translation and commentary.

LACTOR 3, *A Short Guide to Electioneering* and **LACTOR 10**, *Cicero's Cilician Letters* provide translations relevant to Chapters 5 and 10. Details are available from the LACTOR (London Association of Classical Teachers Original Records) website: http://www.kcl.ac.uk/humanities/cch/lactor

Biographies of Cicero

D. R. Shackleton Bailey, *Cicero* (London, 1971).
A lively study derived mainly from the author's great commentaries on the letters of Cicero.

C. Habicht, *Cicero the Politician* (Baltimore, 1990).
An account of Roman politics and the career of Cicero.

T. N. Mitchell, *Cicero: The Ascending Years* (New Haven and London, 1979).

T. N. Mitchell, *Cicero: The Senior Statesman* (New Haven and London, 1991).
The most detailed modern account of Cicero's political career and thought.

E. Rawson, *Cicero: A Portrait* (London, 1975; 2nd edn, Bristol, 1994).
A well-written and sympathetic account of the whole man.

D. Stockton, *Cicero: A Political Biography* (Oxford, 1971).
An excellent account of Cicero's political career.

S. Treggiari, *Terentia, Tullia and Publilia* (Abingdon and New York, 2007).
A comprehensive and sympathetic account of the women in Cicero's life.

Roman Republic

Introductory studies

P. A. Brunt, *Social Conflicts in the Roman Republic* (London, 1971).
The best single volume on the period.

J. R. Patterson, *Political Life in the City of Rome* (London, 2000) and
T. E. J. Wiedemann, *Cicero and the End of the Roman Republic* (London, 1994).
Two good introductory works.

More advanced studies

E. Badian, *Roman Imperialism in the late Republic* (2nd edn, Oxford, 1968).
An acute study of Roman rule.

M. Beard and M. Crawford, *Rome in the late Republic: Problems and Interpretations* (2nd edn, London, 1999).
An excellent and thought-provoking work for those with some knowledge of the period.

P. A. Brunt, *The Fall of the Roman Republic and Related Essays* (Oxford, 1988).
Essential reading for anyone with a serious interest in the period.

F. Millar, *The Crowd in Rome in the late Republic* (Ann Arbor, 1998).
The climax in a series of controversial studies aiming to show that the Republic was democratic.

R. Syme, *The Roman Revolution* (Oxford, 1939).
The classic study of the transition from Republic to Empire.

Authors referred to in the text but not mentioned above

J. P. V. D. Balsdon, *Life and Leisure in Ancient Rome* (London, 1971).

M. Beard, J. North and S. Price, *Religions of Rome* (Cambridge, 1998).

E. Fantham, *The Roman World of Cicero's* De Oratore (Oxford, 2004).

M. Gelzer, *Caesar: Politician and Statesman*, trans. P. Needham (Oxford, 1968).

E. S. Gruen, *The Last Generation of the Roman Republic* (Berkeley, 1974).

R. A. Kaster (ed.), *Cicero*, Speech on Behalf of Publius Sestius (Oxford, 2006).

P. McGushin (ed.), *Sallust*, Bellum Catilinae (Bristol, 1980).

R. Morstein-Marx, *Mass Oratory and Political Power in the Late Roman Republic* (Cambridge, 2004).

J. T. Ramsey (ed.), *Cicero*, Philippics I–II (Cambridge, 2003).

T. Rice Holmes, *The Architect of the Roman Empire*, vol. i (Oxford, 1928).

T. P. Wiseman, *Catullus and His World* (Cambridge, 1985).

J. E. G. Zetzel, *Cicero,* On the Commonwealth *and* On the Laws (Cambridge, 1999).

Greek and Roman authors

Appian   Alexandrian Greek, end of the first century AD, author of a Roman history.

Asconius   Roman, first century AD, from Patavium (Padua), author of a commentary on Cicero's speeches. The Oxford Classical Text of A. C. Clark is the basis of the translation in this book.

Caesar   Iulius Caesar, 100–44 BC, wrote commentaries on the Gallic and Civil Wars.

Cassius Dio   Greek from Nicaea in Bithynia, third century AD, author of a history of Rome from the foundation until AD 229.

Pliny the Elder   Roman, first century AD, author of a *Natural History* in 37 books.

Plutarch   Greek from Boeotia, first to second century AD, author of a series of *Parallel Lives* of Greeks and Romans, including a *Life of Cicero*.

Sallust   Roman politician and historian, 86–35 BC, who wrote a *Conspiracy of Catilina* and a history of Rome; the latter survives only in fragments.

Seneca the Elder   Latin writer of declamation (exercises in training for public speaking), who was born in Corduba, Spain, about 50 BC and spent much of his life in Rome; he died about AD 40.

Suetonius   Latin biographer, first century AD, author of the *Lives of the Caesars*, beginning with a *Life of Iulius Caesar*.

Valerius Maximus   Latin writer, first century AD, author of a handbook illustrating famous deeds and sayings.

Glossary

aedile   a Roman magistrate, one of four, responsible for administration of the city of Rome and certain public games; also the title of the chief magistrates in some Italian municipalities.

ancestor mask   (*imago*; plural = *imagines*) wax masks/portraits of Romans who had held senior magistracies, displayed in the houses of Roman nobility and by actors wearing them in the funeral processions of such families.

assembly of the centuries   an assembly consisting of 193 centuries (voting units); it met in the Campus Martius and elected consuls and praetors, with birth and wealth having a predominant influence.

assembly of the tribes   an assembly consisting of 35 tribes (voting units) in mainly local divisions (31 rural, 4 urban); it elected magistrates below praetors and enacted most legislation.

augur   one of 15 members of a college of Roman diviners, whose function was to interpret signs before public business was conducted.

auspices   the divination or interpretation of signs, originally 'the watching of birds', before public business could be undertaken.

Bona Dea   Good Goddess, a goddess worshipped only by women, whose annual festival was held in the house of a consul or praetor and supervised by his wife.

boni   'good men', loyal citizens, a term used by Cicero to describe wealthy and respected men who supported the senate and the established order.

Campus Martius   the 'Field of Mars', north-west of the Roman Forum, beside the river Tiber, where the assembly of the centuries met.

censor   one of two senior magistrates, elected every five years, whose function was to carry out a census of Roman citizens and a review of the senatorial and equestrian orders.

collegium/collegia   a group / groups of men having a common locality, or trade, or craft, often organized for political purposes.

comitia   formal meeting of the Roman people for the purpose of electing magistrates or enacting laws.

Comitium   a circular area in the north-west of the Roman Forum, in front of the senate house, where meetings of Roman citizens took place.

concilium plebis   the assembly of the plebs, organized by tribes, which elected tribunes and plebeian aediles and enacted laws (plebiscites) which were binding on all citizens.

concordia ordinum 'concord (or harmony) of the orders', a political formula, the unity of the senatorial and equestrian orders, achieved by Cicero when consul in 63 BC, which he hoped to maintain as a permanent feature of the *respublica* – unsuccessfully.

consul one of the two chief annual magistrates of the Roman people.

consular a term to describe one who had held the consulship, an ex-consul.

contio a meeting of the Roman people summoned by a magistrate.

curia the senate house, a consecrated space, where the senate regularly met.

cursus honorum 'the ladder [literally 'race'] of political offices': quaestor, aedile, praetor and consul.

curule chair an ivory folding chair or stool which curule magistrates – consuls, praetors and curule aediles – were entitled to use.

dictator originally a magistrate with supreme authority, elected in a crisis, for a period of six months. The office was revived in the late Republic by Sulla and Caesar.

dignitas dignity, the standing and respect due to a person because of birth, wealth, high office and command in the service of the *respublica*.

eques/equites originally cavalry, the term signified wealthy, landed citizens outside the senate, who enjoyed certain privileges and responsibilities (e.g. jurors in the courts) and often carried out state contracts. They were members of the equestrian order.

extortion court a permanent court of the Roman people, where citizens could seek to obtain redress from the acts of corrupt magistrates and officials, particularly provincial governors. It would more accurately be called the 'recovery' court.

fasces bundles of rods carried by attendants (lictors) before a magistrate with *imperium*.

'final decree' a modern term to describe a decree of the senate giving (normally) the consuls power to take executive action when the interests of the *respublica* were under threat.

Forum (Roman) the central area of Rome and the heart of political activity.

imperator commander of a Roman army, and in the late Republic a title which troops gave to their general following a military victory, often the first step to a triumph.

imperium the authority a higher Roman magistrate or promagistrate possessed to issue commands that required absolute obedience; also a term for the Roman empire.

interrex, interregnum   the magistrate in charge / the period when there were no regular magistrates (consuls, praetors, etc.) in office.

legatus   an assistant to a provincial governor or military commander; also an ambassador.

lictor   an attendant upon a magistrate with *imperium.*

magister equitum   master of the horse, the subordinate and assistant of the dictator.

maiestas   'high treason', a somewhat flexible charge in the late Republic which was often used against political opponents; provincial governors who waged war or went outside their province without authority from the senate might be liable to be charged with this offence.

military tribune   one of six officers attached to a legion, the basic unit of the Roman army.

municipium   a community, in this period normally in Italy, whose citizens enjoyed the citizenship of Rome and their own community, with a limited degree of self-government.

nobilis/nobiles   noble/nobles, those who had consular ancestors.

nomenclator   a slave or assistant employed to tell his master the names of those he met.

novus homo   a 'new man', one who had no consular or even no senatorial ancestors.

optimates   'the best men', the defenders of the traditional order and supporters of the senate.

otium with *dignitas*   peace with dignity, a political formula (*otium cum dignitate*) devised by Cicero to signify domestic tranquillity within the state combined with the dignity owed to its leaders.

plebs/plebeians   the name given to the mass of Roman citizens who at this period were distinguished from the rich and landed elite who held political office.

pontifex   a pontiff/priest, one of a college of 15, whose president was the *pontifex maximus*, responsible for the proper performance of Roman state religion.

popularis   'popular', an individual member of the political elite who cultivated the people/plebs and used their power, often against the interests of the senate.

praetor   the next highest magistrate to the consul; eight were elected annually and were mainly involved with the law and the courts during their year of office.

prefect, prefecture   a person appointed / an office established by a magistrate, usually a provincial governor.

proconsul, propraetor   an ex-consul/ex-praetor whose office was extended to enable him to hold a provincial appointment.

promulgation   the publication of proposed legislation, which the law required to be done 'three market days' before voting.

proscription   the publication of lists of persons declared 'enemies of the state', whose lives and property were thereby forfeited, associated with Sulla in 83 BC and the Second Triumvirate in 43.

publicani   those, usually members of the equestrian order, who undertook state contracts such as collection of the taxes of Roman Asia and supplying the army.

quaestor   one of 20 magistrates who assisted at the treasury in Rome or a governor in his province. It was the first step in the *cursus honorum* and gave its holder membership of the senate for life.

respublica   literally 'the public thing', it generally means the state, the republic.

rostra   the platform at the west end of the forum from which magistrates addressed the people.

senate   the great council of the state, a body of 600 magistrates and ex-magistrates that governed the *respublica*.

supplicatio   a vote of thanksgiving by the senate to a magistrate, usually a military commander, for victory over the enemies of Rome.

temple   a rectangular area, *not* necessarily a building, consecrated by the augurs, where state functions had to take place (e.g. meetings of the senate).

tribune of the plebs   one of ten annually elected officers of the plebs, who had the authority to summon the senate and the plebs, initiate business and legislation, and veto any proposal that in their view was contrary to the interests of the plebs.

tribune of the treasury   a class with a census rating just below the *equites*, who after 70 BC formed one-third of the panel of jurors in the courts.

triumph   the ceremonial procession to the great temple of Jupiter on the Capitol awarded by the senate to a general who had won a major victory (at least 5,000 enemy must have been killed).